WHAT'S UP?

Gateway to Hopeful Living

TREVOR O. TURNER

Scripture quotations are taken from the King James Version of the Bible.

LifeRich Publishing is a registered trademark of The Reader's Digest Association, Inc.

LifeRich Publishing books may be ordered through booksellers or by contacting:

LifeRich Publishing
1663 Liberty Drive
Bloomington, IN 47403
www.liferichpublishing.com
1 (888) 238-8637

ISBN: 978-1-4897-1229-5 (sc)
ISBN: 978-1-4897-1230-1 (hc)
ISBN: 978-1-4897-1228-8 (e)

Library of Congress Control Number: 2017905765

Print information available on the last page.

LifeRich Publishing rev. date: 05/31/2017

Contents

Dedication

I gratefully dedicate this book to the glory of the Almighty God and pray that each reader will realize a brighter future as they turn the pages.

A heart felt gratitude also to my two daughters; Stephanie and Vanessa who helped me navigate the intricacies of the internet when I became helpless and also to my two grandsons, Justin and Stephen who helped with the manuscript.

For any other who aided in anyway and to my writing buddies at Juanita's, God bless.

Learning to Navigate Life Successfully

The ideas expressed in *What's Up?* are varied. The primary purpose of *What's Up?* is to bring us face to face with ourselves and with situations of life, and to reference solutions that will broaden our horizons and bring us peace and stability as we sojourn down here on earth. The chapters serve as cultural critiques, touching on how things are presently and where we are heading. A synopsis of the author's life is interspersed throughout the book to show how he has used the examples outlined to help him navigate his own life.

For example, one chapter touches on navigating life successfully; another on the infinite and the profundity of simplicity; and yet another on profiting from simplifying the activities in our lives.

Some sections might sound like a sermon being preached. If you are at that place in your life where you need a sermon, then, please read carefully.

chapter 1

A CLOSER LOOK AT THE PRESENT SITUATION

As was the case at other times in in our North American society there is now a situation that assails and perplexes us to the point of torment. We are greatly assailed by the prevailing conditions and at our wits' end in trying to find solutions to the myriad problems that settle in on us. As I write *"What's up?* "There are numerous pressing problems confronting us: the refugee crisis in Europe, the ISIS crisis, the unrest between Russia and the Ukraine, flash flooding, earthquakes, and so forth. And then each person can give an account of his or her own personal tsunami. We do live among problems every day; there is no escaping them. They stare us in the face, and we must act or react to them in one way or the other. They burden or suffocate us, or they refresh and enlighten us, depending on which side of the fence we are on.

The question is this: Can we effectively find solutions to these problems? Or to put it differently: Can we manage them successfully, or do we surmount or ignore them? The truth is that the greatest minds succumb to the magnitude, complexities and weight of these problems. We are unwittingly creating a myriad of other problems while trying to solve the problems that presently confront us. Simply put, our resolve, determination and abilities are no match for the enormity of the problems. Only supernatural intervention will bring about viable solutions.

Isaiah the prophet gives us a description of our present condition, which reads like today's news. "We grope for the wall like the blind and we grope

1

as if we had no eyes: we stumble at noonday as in the night; we are in desolate places as dead men" Isaiah 59:10

This indeed is our plight and position without the guidance of the Almighty God. We stubbornly resist Him, but in the end, we will submit to His authority because He is the Almighty. We will acknowledge Him and petition Him for help, albeit in vain, for His mercies will not always strive with us.

I am laying down some facts or truths, along with some underlying causes for our troubles. We are in trouble, and if we do not or cannot see that clearly, then the calamities will come upon us with such force none will be able to escape them. These problems will shake us with such intensity that no one will escape.

False Practitioners

We were cut loose from our anchor a long time ago by false practitioners of the Gospel, who assured us that we need not stay anchored to the Rock, Christ Jesus. Today, false practitioners say we can venture out on the high seas without Him. They are the spin doctors dispensing false information. We have been led to believe that they know of and have a better way of existence, but to our consternation, they are leading us astray. Now we are lost on the high seas and are experiencing multiple problems.

There are many of these spin doctors prescribing all manner of solutions for our problems, but they fall short of finding a real cure to the problems. There is no shortage of these people. They are coming at us from every side and have bombarded us with strange ideas. They pretend to have the cures for our troubles, but these alleged cures fall miserably short. These spin doctors are unable to find the answers because our problems are inherently spiritual problems. We cannot circumvent this fact; we have to face it. The cure for our basic problem is a return to the Almighty God, who will restore to us what we have lost in our wonderings away from Him.

Many of the world's concoctions might work as cures for a few of our problems, but if a person is to be made holistic, he or she has to be regenerated, or made anew. Making that new person is a common occurrence; every single day, this type of new birth is taking place in every part of the globe. Men, women, boys and girls are finding themselves again and are thereby removed from the wilderness of darkness to the realm of light, where their purposes are restored.

When we are again clothed in our right minds by the indwelling Holy Spirit, then and only then can we see things realistically. We see them as they are, and we see where they are taking us. Then we rest in the assurance of a holy God who is in control of all things. We have all gone astray seeking a plan and a purpose for our existence but seeking it in the wrong places. Our indulgences are purely in material things to the exclusion or to the neglect of the spiritual dimension. There has to be a connection of the material dimension and the spiritual dimension if one is to have a successful existence. We are trying to do things on our own strength alone, but in doing so we the neglect of the great God, who rules supreme. We cannot succeed in our own strength without the partnership of the Almighty. Failure is inevitable without His guidance.

We are, in a sense, struggling to put the equipment together, whether it is a barbecue, a lawnmower or what have you. After floundering and wasting precious time, we revert to reading the user's manual and realize that there was nothing to completing the job after all. There are too many who know what is needed for a just society but cannot bring it about. They cannot instigate the plan that will work, because there are too many antagonists fighting constantly against them. The beast in a person's heart is the warring factor. And by ourselves, we cannot bring about even the good we envision.

Recently I came across a book with the title *Healing Society.* The author, Dr. Seung Heun Lee, envisions a grand plan to create a new human society. In order to achieve this, she says, we need 100 million "new humans" in the next 10 years. (Her book was written in 2000.) She specifies the attributes of these new humans as follows:

1. A new human needs to be healthy, as a healthy person is truly the master of his or her own body.
2. A new human needs to be intelligent, using his or her intelligence the way he or she intends.

3. A new human needs to be emotionally rich, feeling the beauty of existence and harmony.
4. A new human needs to be honest and conscientious, asking the questions "Who am I?" and "What is the purpose of my life?" while listening to the voice of divinity within.
5. A new human is a divine person. Divinity is an expression of energy that connects us to the cosmic energy.

These thoughts expressed by Dr. Lee are idealistic but implausible. She dwells in the realm of delusion. Does she intend to manufacture these new humans in a factory? Perhaps she intends to do just that. That would be a surer way of producing them than any other way I can think of. The sombre realities of life have apparently so disillusioned Dr. Lee that she seeks refuge in taking mental voyages to an idealistic world of beautiful fantasies and impossible chimera. Dr. Lee and others like her are mere dreamers, dispensing placebos to solve the malady of our souls and therefore are innocuous. Without a proper foundation on which to build any structure or even an argument, these band aid solutions fall apart. Give us some realities here, Dr. Lee. What you have outlined amounts to mere words. There is no realism in your words and that is what that proposition is, merely words.

On one count, Dr. Lee claims that these humans need to be divine, but divinity can be attributed only to God, not to human beings. I wonder if Dr. Lee even knows that there is such a One. A Divine Being that is. Some people may think that they are divine, but if they have reached that stage in their thinking, they have actually assumed the position of gods and that without any basis.

Earth is not a likely place for the implementation of Dr. Lee's plan. Like many others before her, she has compiled some thoughts and printed them, but those thoughts do not lay out for us principles that we can realistically use. These are not practical ideas that can be translated or incorporated into a person's life to lighten a load or alleviate an anxiety. We need practical solutions to deal with our strained economies, our mounting debt and our unsettled state of mind, not to mention the refugee crises that face the world as I write.

Many like Dr. Lee seem oblivious to the things that are happening around us. It is a mad world in which we are fighting harder and harder against each other and will not give an inch to the other person. The world has adopted a protectionist policy in which each country wants to share less and less with others. Everyone wants to keep more and more for themselves. This world is taking a meaner posture day by day, which leaves some of us in utter desperation when seeking a way to cope.

The selfish nature in us grows larger and larger, stronger and stronger, and there is no sign that it will diminish soon. We have come to the realization that the beast in us need not be tamed any longer. Let it loose and allow it to be as greedy and voracious as it ought to be. Simply allow it to roam freely. Throw the political correctness out the window, and let us live for ourselves first and foremost. Simply put, let us make ourselves comfortable so that we can feel secure. This kind of thinking has become the philosophy of a lot of people.

We see such a philosophy playing out in the person of Mr. Donald J. Trump. He wants to make the United States great again by, among other propositions, building a wall between the United States and Mexico. He wants to build not only a physical wall at the U.S. border with Mexico border but also an invisible wall around the entire United States. This wall would serve both to keep people out and keep people in. It is intended to keep all the jobs at home in the United States, all monies and the military might on U.S. soil, all intruders out. Trump's is not a strange voice. His voice echoes the voices of many who are just afraid to speak out. Many other countries no doubt harbour this protectionist idea also.

These protectionists visions are the realities that are being played out in our world and not just some grandiose ideas thrown out that cannot be realized. We would all like to see and live in a peaceful world, but the reality is that our world is not peaceful. Dr. Lee's view is only an idealistic view of things. Some human beings are still straining to be despots. Every chance they get, these rulers will show their true selves in order to rule over and subjugate their fellow citizens and strain also to influence others around them. We live with these tyrants around us; and no period of history is exempted. People such as these have always been a part of the mix.

Men expressing their hostilities toward others are the stark realities of our world. We have to be constantly vigilant, or else we will be overrun by those who deem it their right to exist and exert authority over us and even prosper at the expense of the unsuspecting and helpless.

A Cultural Critique

The thrust of *What's Up* is in part, a critique of our present culture. Too often we hide our heads in the sand and pretend that things are what they are not. We need to wake up to the reality of the conditions in our world and face them squarely.

In her book, Dr. Seung Heun Lee quotes the prayer she read (going by the name Litchi Lee) at the United Nations Millennium World Peace Summit of Religious and Spiritual Leaders on August 28, 2000. I quote the opening 7 lines of his 92-line Prayer of Peace here:

I offer this prayer of peace
Not to any one god nor to many gods
Not to the Christian god
Not to the Jewish god
Not the Buddhist god
Not the Islamic god
And not even to the indigenous gods of the many nations

Now, I think that if Litchi Lee is praying, then he should be directing his prayer to someone, a specific deity. He offers a prayer of peace not to any one god, and not even to the many gods. It seems to me that he wasted not only the time of the attendees of the summit but also his own breath by reciting what he deemed to be a prayer.

One would think that Litchi Lee would have a god with whom he wishes to connect. His recitation is so vague that it is pathetic. Dr. Lee states that people have a need to be acknowledged or recognized, which is quite so—a truism, to be exact. However, recognition by our fellows is an important thing, but to be acknowledged and recognized by our Maker, the Lord Jesus Christ, is the most important thing and the recognition that matters most. Without His recognition or approbation, we are outcasts—nothing at all.

Here is what Jesus says to us: "Whosoever therefore shall confess me before men, him will I confess before my Father which is in heaven. But whosoever shall deny me before men, him will I also deny before my Father which is in heaven." Matthew 10:32–33. Jesus has made it quite clear what will be done when He comes again. We have our clear warning of what is expected of us. And as much as the temporal is needful and necessary, we must not neglect to seek the approbation of God Himself. Here is where our eternal security lies: only in the recognition of Him who died and gave Himself a ransom for us.

We Must Have a Target

I shall use an analogy of a boxer to illustrate the point about prayer. A boxer is a boxer not because he shadowboxes but because he trains by using objects and opponents. He must have direct contact with something or someone in order to develop into an effective boxer. Similarly, we cannot simply pray to the breeze, that is, vaguely throw a so-called prayer out there and hope that some god will pick it up and answer us. Prayer by definition is a petition, an earnest request, a supplication, an entreaty to a person. In Psalm 4, David prays thus: "Hear Me when I call, O God of my righteousness: thou hast enlarged me when I was in distress; have mercy upon me and hear my prayer." In Elijah's day, the ungodly had their god, Baal, to whom they prayed but their prayers were not heard nor answered. No one can make their own gods.

A prayer can only be heard if it is directed to the Almighty God. When we write a letter, we direct our thoughts and sentiments to the particular person we are communicating with. We start off with the salutation, such as "Dear John" or "Dear Mary." Then after we have expressed ourselves in the letter, we get an envelope and address it—that is, we put the person's name and address on the envelope, put a stamp on the envelope, and mail it. We cannot write the letter, put it in an envelope, drop it in a mailbox without an address, and expect it to reach its intended recipient.

Such practical steps as in the analogy are the very basic principles of life; things that keep us functional and sane—and yet we consider ourselves so advanced that we think we can drop these very rudimentary things that make us intelligent beings. There are many fundamental principles that we dare not circumvent in life without exposing our lack of insight into the real world, which is a world of reality, where people live and die, and where people are harassed and discriminated against at work and in the marketplace and experience hardships at every turn in the road of life. We can imagine and portray great and magnificent things, but what is imagined and what is lived out are separate things. One generally is pie-in-the-sky, while the other is the hard facts, the dog-eat-dog reality. Reality is, as we say, where the rubber meets the road.

Some People Are Not Well-Rounded Students

Who would dare despise learning? To be erudite is a commendable goal and should be the aspiration of every person. However, many people are so learned that their learning blocks their view of reality and eternity. This is a sad commentary on many learned people. For some, learning is one-dimensional. They focus on one discipline and neglect the others. For many, life is snuffed out at the point of a certain plateau of learning; this plateau is where many cease to live. They might be math geniuses and not know the capital of Poland. Certainly, they are not as well-rounded in their learning as they should be. They have wrenched themselves from the anchor that fastens us tightly to reality.

One of my sons told me that he visited one of his school buddies one day and saw him cutting his bicycle wheel with a hacksaw to get his tyre off so that he could fix a flat. As my son said, in a little while that boy could become a doctor or a lawyer but not know a simple thing such as how to fix a bicycle tyre.

R. L. Stevenson in *Virginibus Puerisque* states, "Books are good enough in their way, but they are a mighty bloodless substitute for life." Might we say the same about many things around us today? For example, money does not make a person wealthy. A person might be rich in this world's goods and yet lack the lustre that life itself demands and affords us. Many so-called rich men and women are relatively poor. We look at them and see that the life has gone out of them. They are still making the best of it, but their lives are now only pretences, and they do their best to keep up appearances. This is the case with many other things, such as some marriages that are only pretences. The couple, perhaps once in love and committed to one another, are now merely keeping up appearances.

Books are good enough in their way, says R. L. Stevenson, but they do not infuse a person with life. Life is quite another matter. One of my hobbies is to observe people and their behaviours. I like to watch the poor and the rich alike living their lives. Many times it is not the rich who enthuse and encourage me; it is the poor and hardy. It might be the person who is burdened with a load that is fit for a horse, but the person is not bothered by it because he or she has to get home to prepare a meal for a loved one. People such as this are the ones who impress me with their resolve and grit. I am much less impressed by the rich folks basking in luxury and ease. In *The Merchant of Venice*, William Shakespeare states, "They are as sick as surfeit with too much as those that starve with nothing." I deduce from these words that a good balance of a ration is the key to good living.

What comes to mind for me now is an image of a young man whom I saw helping my sister at her birthday party in Jamaica in June 2016. This youngman was working, carrying stuff such as chairs and cutting water coconut, but he did not appear to be working. He was literally bouncing as he performed his tasks. He was like a swimmer doing the butterfly stroke in the water. I could not take my eyes off him; he was a pleasure to watch. It was not hard to see that he possessed life and that he was enjoying life to its fullest. I did not have the opportunity to speak to him other than to ask him for a water coconut, so I do not know his status in life, but I guess he was a common labourer. Given that he had very little to live on, I wondered, *why can't the rest of us with our plenty be as hopeful and as buoyant as he is?* He exhibited a zest for life indeed.

Why do we allow ourselves to become burdened down with things to the extent that they rob us of life? We must weigh the things we do carefully and truthfully to see if many of those are unprofitable and are robbing us of life—a "bloodless substitute" for life, as R. L. Stevenson said. Nothing needs to rob us of life. A person's life needs to be rich, fulfilling and well-rounded, barring, of course, extenuating circumstances such as poor health and disability and yet we suffocate our lives at times with overindulgences.

Through much learning, oftentimes our conscience gets seared and we lose the ability to differentiate clearly between right and wrong, falsity and truth. As human beings, we need to be clear-headed and truthful, especially to ourselves. We need as drivers to be able to drive the highways and byways, the city streets and the country roads. To only be able to drive Johnny to his hockey game on Thursday night is not good enough.

I was in line at the Licensing Bureau's Office one day when I heard a driving school instructor telling his friend this joke. He said: ``One of his student said to him that she does not want to go through all the rigmarole of driving, she only wants to be able to drive Mikey to Hockey and to drive herself to Loblaw's.``

Many are selling themselves short

Men and women long for just administrators in thought and deed, men and women who are honest and frank, speaking the truth always and not being disingenuous in order to profit financially. Our world is full of those who will literally sell their souls for power and money. Then people lie and cheat to fight their way through life, forgetting that there is an easier way. In Exodus 14:14, we read these words of assurance: "The Lord shall fight for you, and ye shall hold your peace." A dependency upon God lightens our load and frightens our enemies. We can shift our fears and direct them to the One who cares.

History shows that when people have burdens, they pray to the one true God. Here is an example of one man of the Bible who poured out his burden, or his heart, to his God. This prayer is called Habakkuk's Prayer: "O Lord I have heard thy speech, and was afraid: O Lord revive thy work in the midst of the years, in the midst of the years make known; in wrath remember mercy." Habakkuk 3:2. This prophet directed his prayer to his God, the living God who hears and answers prayers.

Elijah the prophet prayed unto God and He sent fire to consume the sacrifice: "Hear me, O Lord, hear me that this people may know that thou art the Lord God, and that thou hast turned their heart back again. Then the fire of the Lord fell and consumed the burnt sacrifice...." 1 Kings 18: 37-38.

Every child of God knows also to direct his or her prayers to this God. We know that He is a prayer-answering God. When I pray, I direct my prayers to the Almighty God, our Father, and I do it in the name of our Lord and Saviour, Jesus Christ. The new humans that Dr. Lee envisions are already here: it is those who are born-again. We who are born again constitute the Kingdom of God. The perfection that Dr. Lee hopes for will come soon enough. God Himself has declared to humankind that He is the only true God and that He is coming to establish His Kingdom which will be a sinless one.

The Bible records a time when the Assyrian king Sennacherib had grown powerful, had conquered all the nations around him, and now sent word to Hezekiah, the king of Israel, to surrender to him, citing his conquest of areas around Israel. Sennacherib's attitude was that he was invincible and could not be stopped. He had, at that point, forgotten who Israel's God was.

Upon receiving this threat, King Hezekiah went to the Lord and prayed this prayer: "Now therefore, our Lord our God, save us from his hand that all the kingdoms of the earth may know that thou art the Lord, even thee only" (Isaiah 37:20). The Lord confirmed Hezekiah's prayer through the Prophet Isaiah, saying, "Whereas thou hast prayed to me against Sennacherib king of Assyria" (Isaiah 37:21). "Then the angel of the Lord went forth, and smote in the camp of the Assyrians a hundred and fourscore and five thousand: and when they arose early in the morning, behold, they were all dead corpses. So Sennacherib departed" Isaiah 37:36–37. These are but a few of the demonstrations of His power.

There Is Only One God

There is no other God like the Almighty God; He alone is omnipotent. You will either embrace Him or be left out of the Great Supper of the Lamb at the consummation of all things. Revelation 19:9. We can make our own gods and cry out to them, but our efforts will be in vain, my friend. We may be able to move about in the marketplace appearing to be wholesome and respectable humans, but we are nothing more than empty shells without the gift of the Holy Spirit. Without His Spirit, we are without hope and without everlasting life. Many in the West today who once knew their God have sidelined Him. Like the Israelites coming through the wilderness, they are constructing their own gods and bowing down before them.

Herbert Hoover saw decadence in the United States in the last century. He knew that if the principles of the Gospel were not practiced, the nation would fall into inward decay. He called it: "suicide by compliance with evil." Every Bible believer knows that everyone will pay for his or her sins, it is only a matter of time.

If Mr. Hoover observed such a shift in his day from truth to untruth and from old ways to new ways, then he likely would be sick to his stomach to witness what is happening today. He saw the shift then in the United States, but this shift which is taking place in a godly country is also a worldwide phenomenon today. Many today would not know the truth if you struck them with it. Hoover spoke of intellectual dishonesty in public office and we are experience it as a norm in today's societies. Many of the virtues that made the United States strong are slipping away, being replaced by new paradigms, one of which is most troublesome, namely, that of individual liberty. The freedom to worship the Christian God and to propagate the Gospel is one of the virtues that are under attack. A Christian's faith has become a burdensome thing in a country that was founded upon the principles of faith and trust in God.

Jeremiah warned, "Thus saith the Lord, Stand ye in the ways, and see, and ask for the old paths, where is the good way, and walk therein and ye shall find rest for your souls. But they said, we will not walk therein" (Jeremiah 6:16). Many are now doing what seems right in their own eyes, ignoring the established ways, but the end will be their demise. Consider the question: "How shall we escape if we neglect so great salvation." (Hebrews 2:3)

Britain Alexis de Tocqueville of France visited the United States over a hundred years ago and upon his return home, he wrote, "I sought for the greatness of America in her harbours and rivers and fertile fields, and her mines and commerce. It was not there. Not until I went into the churches and heard her pulpits flame with righteousness did I understand the greatness of her power. America is great because she is good; and if America ever ceases to be good, America will cease to be great."

Of course, de Tocqueville experienced a United States filled with people who lived on their knees. They petitioned the holy God then for protection and guidance. Today the Americans rely on guided missiles and their own ingenuity to solve their problems. We can assess how well they are doing without God. Likewise, we see in Great Britain's heyday, when it ruled the waves, that the British people lived with God in their midst.

Someone once asked Queen Victoria what was the secret of Britain's greatness. In response, she simply held up the Bible. Let the record speak for itself, my friend. When an individual or a nation lays hold of God, then great things can be expected. Follow the history of Britain, that once great nation and compare it to what it is like today as it struggles as a godless nation. "Ichabod" "The glory of the Lord has departed" is written across that nation today. The foundation of the nation has been eroded, and now the nation is falling as a consequence. It has lost its stability and is floundering as many other nations on earth are.

Collision instead of Collusion

There is now a collision instead of collusion; there is no collaboration between many entities of Governments in our world because most are in conflict with each other. There is no longer unity in the camp. This is the tragedy: while one set is busy building, the other set is busier destroying or tearing down. The nations have succeeded in removing the underpinnings that sustained them and enabled them to build high. Now they cry out for help, but there will be none.

Goldie Meir once told of a man who killed his parents and in court asked for mercy because he was an orphan. Like this man, many have destroyed their source of help and strength, nevertheless they cry out for help when there can now be none. They have simply cut off their source.

Many of the positions we find ourselves in are, like the one just described, laughable, because they are self-inflicted. We have inflicted our own wounds and we agonize needlessly, wondering from whence came the pain. We pray for showers of blessings and there will be none because we have disconnected ourselves from the source of power. God has warned the nations that there is a time when He would not hear their cry.

It is the law of sowing and reaping. "Be not deceived; God is not mocked: for whatsoever a man soweth, that shall he also reap" (Galatians 6:7).

Throughout history, God has laid down this law to His people: "You will prosper if you obey My laws, and you will suffer when you disobey them." It is a simple and straightforward principle, one that has not ceased to be true. We wonder about the way things are and where things are heading, but we fail to see the cause of our plight. Many nations are like a ship with a damaged rudder sailing the high seas. The ship cannot be directed. It will eventually flounder and ultimately be grounded.

We have become unjust as nations and as people that the truth frightens us now. The truth which is really our compass frightens us. The Bible is the only true compass and many would rather believe that it is false because if they believe it is true, then there are consequences for their behaviours. As such the truth is now relegated to absurdity.

We just do not want to know where we are heading. We would rather wander listlessly. We are witnessing the suicide that Mr. Hoover spoke of. It is all around us. We are complacent about evil. We tolerate evil, we encourage it and we dwell comfortably in it. May God help us to see where we are and what time it is?

chapter 2

A GUIDE TO NAVIGATE
LIFE SUCCESSFULLY

The principles in *What's Up?* are intended to help you navigate your life using the very minimum amount of energy. It will help you develop the PRIDE principle—personal responsibility in daily endeavours. We are all personally responsible for ourselves, particularly for finding our individual niche in life, that is, the actualization of what we desire most, what it is that will give us the most joy and fulfilment in life, if you will. Our direction comes from the things that delight us. Finding that driving force and never losing sight of it is of great importance to living a successful life. It is the essence of living. Your niche will be your guiding star to energize you even when you are down in the depths of despair and discouragement. That one single most pressing desire or aspiration can be the golden thread that will lead you onward and upward. Simply find it.

Timing Is of the Essence

The sooner we find our star, the easier it will be to navigate our way through this maze we call life. Many of us do not have a firm grip on our deepest desires, the thing that will keep us focused all throughout our lives and as such we have wasted a lot of time trying to find the niche where we fit. There has to be a starting point. Although we may change directions a dozen times, we will not be worse off, but will be better off, on account of those changes in direction. Some of the most successful people are those plagued by failure, but in the midst of failure they had the resolve to succeed and triumph. Mr. Goodyear whose name is on a certain brand of tyre was in debtors' jail when he conceived of the vulcanization process. He did not sit and languish while in jail; instead, he lived, breathed and engaged his mind.

You might experience a lot of changes and disappointments during the course of your lifetime, but do not be discouraged, because each disappointment brings with it an accumulation of experiences that will be to your credit. In the end, it is the last page of the book that counts. How does that last chapter read? Does it end on a high note or a sad one? Does it leave some hope for someone, or does it leave no hope at all? Does it leave a footprint that a lost and forlorn brother or sister may see and use to take heart and live again? I lay in bed after waking from my last dream and wondered what success really is. Just how can I measure it for myself? Will I be able to maintain an even keel amidst the confusion and disappointments? Will my life be the thermostat instead of the thermometer? If these questions can be answered in the affirmative, then I will write an exciting last chapter.

Let's Reconfigure regularly

We must keep our lives exciting and fresh, never allowing boredom to suppress and stifle it. Boredom can suck the very life out of us and leave us helpless and empty. If we keep our lives exciting as we traverse this earth, we will be rewarded richly. Yes, I can attest to the fact that keeping life exciting will pay big dividends. Each of us has surely seen what a rich life is. We have seen it expressed through other people's lives. They are upbeat and vibrant in all that they do. They do the simplest of chores with vigour and exuberance, showing always that their lives are pleasurable and not boring or dull. They live and enjoy their lives, pure and simple. Life to them is a delight, not a burden as some people make it to be.

Like a circus board, people who live a rich life sample the delightful treats and pass on the less enjoyable ones. They avoid overindulgence and keep the appetite exciting. We can all learn to indulge lightly and not become gluttons. We observe and see the results on people's visages as they abstain or indulge. We must glean from life what is fruitful and productive and satisfying.

We wonder about these splendid people and even envy them, wanting to emulate them. There seems to be an aroma that emanates from such personalities. We wonder if they are really one of us or if they are from another world. Perhaps they have found a secret that evades the rest of us. We will see if the things that they possess are exclusive to some or if they are part of the common domain.

I believe that we can possess those qualities also and profit from them. Every aspect of life is learned behaviour; nothing is thrust upon us at birth. We can sink or swim, as the saying goes, but a lot is riding on us. The existentialist principle is alive and well, where each person has a certain responsibility and a propensity to shape his or her own destiny. It is within our grasp to do good or evil, to triumph or to be subjugated. Our lives lie ahead of us as a sea of adventure for us to navigate and explore. Will we be up to the task?

A rich life is simply a happy and contented life. It is not necessarily one with an insatiable desire for possessions, or one full of possessions. On one hand, you might go into a humble home and see a child playing with a toy from which he is getting an enormous amount of pleasure, and on the other hand, you may enter a wealthy home and see a child in a room full of toys engaging in no activity. The box and the wrappers may be of more interest to the rich man's child than the toys themselves. The novelty wears off quickly and boredom sets in just as fast. As we pursue the endeavours of life, we find more pleasant paths to tread when we learn the true meaning of things or possessions. We should enjoy things with a certain amount of detachment and should not allow them to have dominion over us or burden us.

Another measure of success is when we immerse ourselves in what we do and do it wholeheartedly. Enjoy what you have and do; learn to live free. Start where you are now. It does not matter what age you are; you can always learn the secrets of living free. Living free must be the objective of everyone who wishes to triumph over the circumstances of this life. In Canada, it seems that we are furnished with almost all the necessary ingredients to live a wholesome and satisfying life. Do they add up to make us the happiest and most contented people? Our individual philosophies are the key to securing that happiness that we seek. The way we think is the key to happiness.

A wise person wrote the following:

> Take time to work—it is the price of success.
> Take time to think—it is the source of power.
> Take time to play—it is the secret of youth.
> Take time to read—it is the fountain of knowledge.

These habits, when formed, can bring a wealth of happiness and untold joy to a person's life. Working, thinking, playing and reading are some of the things life is made of. We might think it strange that some people never see things in this light while others possess those qualities or insight early in life. A contented heart or spirit has to be cultivated by a person. The process is an ongoing one. It is never finished, but there must be a start. As in any other venture, we have to make a deliberate effort to resist negativity and develop positive and refreshing attitudes toward certain aspects of our lives. We must, in any case, break free from any unwholesome thoughts and attitudes before we will be able to achieve any measure of success with regard to living a triumphant and satisfying life.

0.02% of Canadian children once polled showed a tendency toward suicide. Many of them have investigated ways of committing the act. It makes you wonder: With so much to live for, why would so many contemplate such a horrendous act? Perhaps we are no longer offering our children something to live for. Hope has been deliberately left out of the equation, and because of this everything falls apart. Hope is the factor, the one ingredient that is most essential for survival at all levels.

Take Stock Regularly

As we grow older, we need to take the time that is necessary for proper growth, good health and longevity. If we rush unduly and squander our time, then not much is going to take root and develop in our lives. Many of us can attest to that fact. If we could go back and start over, we would do things quite differently. We have rushed into life without much thought about time, and as a result we have squandered our most valuable asset. I do believe that every man and woman, every boy and every girl, desires to live above every debilitating circumstance. Although many are handicapped either physically or socially, we all have this aspiration. Come to think of it, we were all created to live above the debilitating circumstances—and many of us have that opportunity to do so. We only need to look at things in a way that is different from the way we are seeing things right now.

Consider for a moment where you are right now and where you would like to be tomorrow. Start to create for yourself a formula to pursue. Plant the first seed in your garden, and then watch it grow and as you mulch it and water it. When you see it grow, you will want to sow more and more seeds in that beautiful garden of yours, so much so that others will admire your garden and share in its splendour. Some lives are just that, beautiful gardens laden with aromatic flowers and refreshing fruits. Why can't it be your garden?

The people whose lives are like beautiful gardens are attractive people, we want to be with them. The late President, Lyndon Johnson of the United States once visited an elderly African American woman who was over 100 years old and asked her what was her secret for longevity. Her reply was: "Mr. President, when I walks [*sic*], I walks [*sic*] slowly, when I sits [*sic*], I sits [*sic*] loosely, and when I feel the troubles coming on, I go to bed." Each of us must find a formula that works for our lives. Find an escape route from the troubles of life. This must have been a remarkable woman for the President to have had a conversation with her about life. Her remarkable life demonstrated that she found a way to deal with the vicissitudes of life. She showed us that she learned to deal with her problems as they arose.

She used this principle to buttress her attitude against life's problems. We might say that she had a handle on life. Yes, my friend, we must get a good grip on life or else we will flounder and perish in the sea of despair and drudgery. We were made to be overcomers and rulers—masters, if you will—and not slaves. We must learn to win with whatever hand we were dealt. Kenny Rogers said in his song "The Gambler," "Every hand is a winner." Conversely, every hand is a loser also. It is all in the playing of the game.

Quite often we are tossed in a sea of multitudinous endeavours and we stress ourselves unnecessarily. The frustration translates into extra stress on the body, resulting in some health problems. We see the results of fast-paced living all around us. Quite often we see the penalty paid by those who think that they have to re-create the world. It is sometimes true that the endeavours of such people make a gigantic impact, but more often than not, these people are the hammer that is worn out by hitting the anvil of life. They succumb to their injuries from hammering too hard.

A Guide to Life in Its Fullness

It is a guarantee that if you embrace my suggestions and practice the wisdom of *What's Up?* fervently and frequently, you will reap astounding benefits. I can attest to this fact. By embracing some of the principles outlined herein, I have been able to surmount many of life's difficulties and problems. And I am finishing with a burst of energy.

If you are young, grown up, or even old, you will benefit greatly from the contents of *What's Up?* which is tailor-made for those who are still seeking for some stability, some comfort and a destination in life. If you feel that right now you are listless and floundering, then there is hope for you in these pages. E. M. Bounds wrote, "The soul cannot be listless when some great desire fixes and inflames it." If indeed you are restless, listless and floundering, then know that this is as normal as breathing to the man or woman who loves life and wants to launch out upon the sea of life's adventures.

What's Up? Will encourage you to use your energy to hone in on your niche. It might be some time before you find that niche, but find it you will. It will serve as the driving force or engine of your existence that will propel you to a level of happiness. Happiness has been people's desire throughout the ages. Without it, life becomes empty and dull, bringing before us a mountain of unattainable expectations and insurmountable burdens. We need a proper vehicle to take us above any and every circumstance that confronts us. Overcomers we must be, or else we will sink into the mire as would a lead ball. Whatever it is that assails us, we are able to overcome. There are remedies for everything. The challenge is to find that remedy.

What is life worth if we possess it for up to 80 or 90 years and we do not discover its secrets? There are secrets for a good life. We must find them before they confound and drown us. I am sharing these secrets with you because I have overcome many of life's difficulties. Life is not always a bed of roses. We all know that. But if we do not learn to manage life's difficulties when they arise, we will be confounded by them.

Our objective is to be overcomers and not to surrender as victims. Can we succeed at this? Yes. We must if we wish to survive. There are oppressing and depressing circumstances that we must live with, but we are not tied down like a tree. Instead, we are mobile—and we have an intellect. Let us get moving and place ourselves in the situation and environment we desire. Happiness is our right. We must pursue it.

In my own life, I have learned to be an overcomer. I have found my niche, so to speak. I have realized that if I do not attach myself to the Supreme Being, I would not be able to survive. I have been like a rolling stone in essence. I have moved from one thing to another, sometimes having three or more irons in the fire at the same time. I manage only because when I feel the burdens pressing, I get on my knees and lay my problems before my heavenly Father, who hears and answers my prayers.

As you travel along life's path using the guidelines from *What's Up?* you will be greatly heartened and in wonder at its easy-to-implement plausible suggestions. You might even ask yourself questions such as: "Why do I make things so difficult for myself at present, is there not an easier way out."` Keep an inquisitive mind and reconfigure regularly.

I would like you to look at the big screen of life right now and see what it is that is most attractive to you. Is it sports, pleasure or an array of other things? Just what it is, you alone know. Whatever it is that you spend time on or with; you, like countless other people, are losing valuable hours that could be better spent on reading and learning worthwhile things. It might be the pursuit of a career, the pursuit of wealth, or just killing time that eats up your twenty-four hours. Does the pursuit have its basis in eternal values, or is it just transitory and fanciful, having only a fleeting glory?

The aim of *What's Up?* is to get you to see the big picture of life and to expand your horizons, providing you with a loftier pursuit. There are many loftier mountains for us to climb than the one we are presently climbing. Even as we climb the present mountain, we must eventually set our sights on the Mount of God, the crowning glory. There is such a mountain and you will find it if you are curious enough.

We must constantly set goals and try and reach them, as goals are the things that make life interesting and worth living. Note, however, that in and of themselves, achievements cannot bring joy and happiness; they are only the means to further our journey and lead us to more meaningful endeavours. Happiness lies in the pursuit of meaningful endeavours and not in any one accomplishment. We have to keep on moving, or else we stagnate and lose our place in the scheme of things.

Commit yourself to constant improvement. Learn another language. Become more proficient in the language you already know. Be a polyglot. Why not? Start now on that path, and eventually you will see that continuing the learning process has become second nature. Think big thoughts, but relish small pleasures. Be the most enthusiastic person you know. Do not be hard on yourself. Forgive yourself and others often for your mistakes and blunders. This is what life is made of; a lot of ups and downs.

Avoid negative people as much as possible. Radiate confidence in your demeanour; it is contagious and you can be of great encouragement to others carrying burdens. You will not be the person someone crosses the road to avoid when you are coming; instead, others will cross over to greet you. Be the shining light in a dark world. Sing a happy song—be the aroma that is attractive to everyone—because there are too many sad songs already being sung.

Build on the Past

We need not burden ourselves with the pressures of life as some do. We should understand that our lives are only an extension of the past, on which we would do well to build on. My saying that our lives are connected to the past does not mean that I believe in reincarnation. I mean that we do not learn everything entirely new; there is a beginning that started in the past and extends to now.

Most traditional values are the bedrock of our society. To abandon them would be to simply weaken our society, not strengthen it. There is one who weakens the nations. Isaiah 14:12 reads: *"How art thou fallen from heaven, O Lucifer, son of the morning! How art thou cut down to the ground, which didst weaken the nations?"* Satan, the adversary of humankind, is busy weakening the nations. If we are not aware of him, we will fall prey to his devices.

As I write *What's Up?* I know that we are in a sour state as human beings. Perhaps you, like many others, feel that life has become cheap. I personally feel that life has become cheap for some, when a life is snuffed out by someone for little or no reason. Many are evildoers and have no real purpose for living.

There will be a consummation, a summing up, if you will—an accounting. That is to say, business will cease for stock-taking. There has been a sowing, and now is harvest time, a reaping, if you will. Those who have sided with Satan to weaken the nations—and there are many—will not fare well during the accounting process. Those who have laboured against the Lord, High and Mighty will reap a reward of unimaginable consequence. They have given up any chance for future happiness. They will suffer the wrath of God Himself, labouring only for the things that perish. They will lose their past and future simultaneously. They will not be able to salvage anything from their lives; it will be a total loss and a frightening disaster to many.

We Are Always Building Anew

Human beings seem to have an insatiable urge to tear down the old and to build new things in places of the old. Building anew is business' primary occupation today. We hear often of "new and improved," all in the same package. We are fed misinformation day in and day out, and we fall headlong for their devices and deceptions. Bombarded with the word *new*, we fall head over heels in search of things that are new when they do not necessarily produce the value we anticipated as we are led to make the purchase.

Many have become great builders as their basic occupation, because they no longer know how to stand still. Traverse the highways night or day and you'll know just what I mean. They are busier than any other people at any other time in human history, and they see not that the clouds are appearing, the clouds of doom. The clouds are hanging like a black night, ready for a prodigious downpour. We as a people are building without making progress because we have left out the Chief Architect from our projects.

They have cornered themselves, and there is now nowhere to hide. Having left God out of our lives, we invest time and energy in finding things to replace Him, but to no avail. We cannot leave God out of our lives except to our ruin. Not only have we left God out of our lives, but also we now have the audacity to confront Him in defiance, some with our fists in His face. Recently I witnessed a Comedian hopping like a grasshopper on TV poking fun at the Lord Jesus Christ. How pathetic a scene that was, to witness for the short time before I switched off the TV.

Men have become so vile and callous and know nothing of the eternal things that they spare nothing sacred to include in their program to make money. We as Christians shudder and wonder: Are men like these so daft that they have no fear of God?

For the sake of fame and financial gain, a person dares to mock God. How depraved can one get? The person who does this has not the slightest idea of his own delicate and precarious hold on life. The life one possesses is only a breath away from death and yet one would not humble himself, instead he sees himself as master of his own destiny but until he sees his own helplessness and impotence, he will not fall at the feet of Jesus. A wise person fears God, but the fool—well, the fool says that there is no God. And if a person believes there is no God, then of course he or she has no one to fear. Such a person moves along like the ass with its nose to the ground and without any clear objective.

Is it any wonder that the wisest man who ever lived said that the fear of God is the beginning of wisdom? That is the positive side of the coin. On the contrary, a person who does not fear God has no wisdom. Remove the fear of God and we are left with a rift between human beings and our Maker.

We try to find security in new things, whether a car or a home, but these things are all vanity. The novelty wears off in a short time and we are left standing with a bitter taste in our mouths. We know the realities that the realization do not match the anticipation but yet we are impotent to act otherwise. May God help us to see the truth.

We can own things and we all do, but we must do so with a great deal of detachment. I say "a great deal of detachment" because everything we own, owns us in some way. Our things own us to a certain degree. We would do well to answer the question "To what degree do my things own me?" If we can lose our possessions and start again: "And never breathe a word about our loss" then we are not possessed or owned by them.

Possessing things could cost you your life; it could cost you your eternal life, which otherwise is a gift that is available to you. In the Bible, Matthew recounts the story of a rich young ruler who could not part with his world's goods and, in so doing, forfeited eternal life. This young ruler, longing for the gift and assurance of eternal life, approached Jesus, whom he knew could give it. The young man asked Jesus what he may do to inherit eternal life. Jesus, the discerner of all thoughts and intents, saw the man's heart and said, "Go and sell that thou hast, and give to the poor, and thou shalt have treasure in heaven: and come and follow me" (Matthew 19:21). After hearing this, the young man went away sorrowful, for he had a great many possessions he was unwilling to part with.

Here are some questions we should ask ourselves: Can the rich person be covetous, or is it only the poor person? Can we covet the things that we possess, or can we covet only the things that we do not have? Is covetousness a longing for, or a desire to keep, that which we have at all costs? I believe covetousness dwells in both camps.

We see in Matthew 19, that the very thing the rich young man desired, he sought, but went home empty-handed after petitioning the Source, the fountain of life itself, the Lord Jesus Christ. This young man, being wealthy, could have sold some of his possessions, as Jesus told him to, and still had more than enough left over, but he was possessive and covetous, unable to bear the thought of sharing his wealth. Many of us Christians are like that, tenaciously hanging on to things—our things, we think. The foregoing Bible passage essentially says, "Go and sell what you have, and give the money away."

Please, friend, do not let greed deprive you of eternal life. Jesus said that in as much as you give a glass of water to the poor, you give it to Him. We must not neglect to do the things He has commanded.

Jesus' disciples forsook all and followed Him in exchange for the assurance of eternal life and in the end; with the exception of John they all gave their lives for the cause of Christ.

chapter 3

A DILEMMA

The world is in a fix, and the prognosis is not good. Most are unaware of the situation. These are busy people who do not have time to reflect on things of eternal values. Their myriad activities delude them with the gratifying feeling that they are making great strides toward reaching lofty goals, but as I assess the situation, I see that many are busy constructing highways and byways to nowhere.

Our world is in panic mode. Secretaries of states make their abode on airplanes, hopping from country to country, trying desperately to be peace brokers but having little success. Occasionally we see some evidence that they have cut a deal, declaring a lasting peace. Little do they know that the cards are stacked against them? No deal, my friend. No deal. It is said that when a person is lost, he runs faster and faster—and he runs faster because he panics. We in our present situation can be likened to that person. We are lost. We are adrift because our connection with the life line is severed. I reiterate as I must to keep us abreast of things, that the Life Line is the Almighty God. He alone can keep us buoyant and directional.

Rudyard Kipling wrote a poem that acts as a reminder, that holding fast to moral and Godly principles are essential for a well-balanced life. Following are a few lines:

> The tumult and the shouting dies,
> The captains and the kings depart:
> Still stands Thine ancient sacrifice,

> A humble and a contrite heart
> Lord God of host, be with us yet,
> Lest we forget. Lest we forget!

Since we are prone to wander and forget our heritage he has penned those verses as a reminder. We all would do well to remember the God of Host of whom he speaks. David trembled at the thought that the Lord had forgotten him. Psalm 42:9. Being forgotten by God when we have separated ourselves from Him is a fearful thing.

Were it not for the constant reminders from the pulpit and from books, tracts, literature and the Bible itself, we would forget that we bear a responsibility to the Creator. We dare not neglect so great a work as salvation, nor can we be silent about it as Christians; hence the reason for a book such as this. *What's Up?* is yet another reminder of this responsibility the reader has to God. "*Prone to wander, Lord, I feel it.*" Robert Robinson stated it succinctly and voiced the sentiments of the redeemed when he penned those words.

A person wants to have his or her own way at every turn most of the time; wants to be his own master and captain of his or her own ship, and wants to be in charge not some of the time but almost all of the time. That is the frame and the makeup of us human beings.

A person likes to be free and not be bound to anyone. A person would rather be enslaved to and bound by things than be bound by anyone, even to God Himself. A person like this has declared, "No God!"—not because he or she thinks there is no God, but because he or she does not want to be bound by His laws. Such is a human being—and that is why human beings need to be kept in check, something that can only be done by the Word of God. If a person does not have the Word, then he or she wanders off the path of life and onto the path of death.

Everlasting separation from God is not an easy idea to grasp. I am in awe at the many times in the Bible the Lord turns toward His people, seeking and pleading with them to return to Him. Even after God's children turned and worshipped other gods. God desires to have fellowship with those who are called by His name. God demonstrates that He loves us and desires that we return to our original position in relation to Him.

The position of this relationship is ours for the asking. He wants us to have fellowship with Him. He does not desire to cast us off forever. Because of this, He keeps on pleading with us. Isaiah 1:18–19 gives us a glimpse into God's heart: "Come now, and let us reason together, saith the Lord: though your sins be as scarlet, they shall be as white as snow; though they be red like crimson, they shall be as wool. If ye be willing and obedient, ye shall eat the good of the land." Has God been pleading to a wayward and backsliding generation? Yes, He has. He is still pleading with us; He has not given up on us and will not give up on us until we have decided assuredly that we do not want Him. After His many pleas for us to reinstate our relationship with Him, we have sternly turned Him away. If we do this with finality, then He will have no choice but to stop pleading. A relationship is riding on us, it is in our hands.

The things we desire, we will find easy to do, for where our treasures are there will our hearts be also. We know, and we instruct others to do, what is correct and guaranteed to bring good results, but we fail to do these things at times ourselves. Failure, however, is not total loss. It is a milepost signifying that we have not yet attained but that we still may arrive at a safe haven.

Careful consideration given to the most important and essential matter of one's existence, one's relationship with his or her Maker, comes into play here. Do you really want to remain outside the camp of God's Kingdom. Do you think it more popular and profitable to dwell in a comfortable place and ignore the warning of impending doom? Doom is coming, and it is not far off. You need not be afraid if you have come to God. "There is a place of quiet rest near to the heart of God." Written by Cleland B. Mc Afee.

The writer of this hymn speaks of a place, a certain place where things are quiet and serene and hopeful and that is *"Near to the heart of God"*. This is an abiding place for every believer who loves the name of Jesus.

Debt traps

In our affluent society where we witness conspicuous consumerism all around us, it becomes a difficult thing to resist falling into the unmanageable debt trap. The banks inundate homeowners with offers and inducements that are hard to resist; nevertheless, we must be prudent and do what we are expected to do as Christians. We must live modestly and soberly, putting off debt as much as we put off the old person. Will the world know us by our modest lifestyle? They certainly should. Are we indulging in the things of the world as wildly as the ungodly? We should or must as Christians show prudence and restraints. We are the salt of the earth, tempering things and keeping them solvent. We must show our selves different by our indulgences and lifestyles.

The director of Christian Transportation (a Christian Organization ministering to railroad personnel and the trucking industries): Louis Voyer, gave us the councillor members an account of one of his experiences when travelling in the United States in the summertime. Where he travelled, water conservation was in effect, which meant, among other things, that lawn watering was forbidden. Louis was looking for one of his brothers. When he enquired of a man who lived on the street where his brother lived, the man's response was "Drive down the street and you will see where your brother lives." Louis asked the man, "How will I know the house?" The response was the same: "Drive down the street." As Louis drove down the street, he came to a lawn with brown and withered grass, which was quite a contrast to all the other lawns. He turned in to the driveway. That indeed was his brother's house. This brother had obeyed the water-conservation rules and probably was the only one on that street who had done so.

In everything, not only debt restraints but in all aspects of our lives as Christians we must make a difference. We must live that THE WORLD MAY SEE THAT WE HAVE BEEN WITH Jesus.

May those of us who are called by His name endeavour to magnify His name by being obedient to His calling. May we be willing to deny ourselves and follow Him as the Disciples did in Jesus' day?

Are Christians Identifiable?

A certain atheist who had travelled in some parts of Africa said that there were places in Africa where he could not rest for the night because he feared that his vehicle would be stolen or vandalized. He went on to say that there were some places in Africa where Christians lived, which were the only safe places to rest after a day's travel. This answers the question that Christians are identifiable because the change is remarkable.

My friend, there is a change in a person's heart when Christ enters in and that change is worked out in that person's life. The drunkard is changed, he stops drinking, the thief is changed, and he stops stealing and so on. One drunkard testified that the Lord changed beer into a dining table and chairs at his house. He meant, of course, that whereas once he spent all his money on beer, he had now been converted and stopped drinking, and was able to buy a dining table and chairs for his dining room.

This song is apt; *"What a wonderful change in my life has been wrought since Jesus came into my heart."* Charles H. Gabriel. This song rings true to many of us who have received Christ as Saviour. There is no longer the desire for the old wonderings but all things have become new. Our desires and outlook are heavenward now as the redeemed of the Lord.

Such testimonies are common occurrences after people convert to Christianity. As promised, new lives are being given to those who ask. Will you, dear reader, join the procession now? All of the redeemed will have the same experience of that wonderful change.

On this subject, it seems that many have come full circle and are crying out to return to their roots, where life was simpler, more practical and plausible, where they could understand and navigate life as a simple adventure. More is not better, and all that glitters is not gold. Many of the dazzling attractions are venomous and deadly, sucking the very life out of those chasing them, yet they run after them as though they were tied to them. Most cannot detect the danger until they are headlong into calamity.

Some of us need to cut ourselves loose from much of the glitter and walk instead of running. Take a break from the excesses, whatever that excess is. I once heard a preacher liken some of us to an eagle that hung onto a carcass while riding the waves, unaware of the approaching falls. The eagle slipped over the falls and was washed away still hanging onto the corpse. Will we not see and understand that some things will pull us down, down, down to our destruction?

There is a lot of misinformation being directed at us through the media, making false claims that what we are sold will bring satisfaction and ultimate happiness but many are hard-pressed to distinguish between truth and falsehood. It is time we all smell the coffee and wake up to the realization that we are being pulled on - on to oblivion. There is the case with the ad about SUVs. The ad shows a woman leaving her boyfriend's car and hopping into another man's SUV. Was that add effective, yes it was. Those ads ran about five or six years ago and today every other car is a SUV. We are led to believe something and we fall for it. Are the SUVS owners happier than the car owners, you are the judge.

Of course, no one objects to a good life, a comfortable one but the excesses are not worth fighting for, since the period of enjoyment is always in doubt. Many times that period is cut shorter than one thinks or planned for.

A comfortable lifestyle is desirable and wonderful, but it is not the cure-all. It leaves much to be desired. It can leave us feeling well pleased with ourselves and, in the process, eradicate any room for gratitude to the Provider. We all are to give thanks with a grateful heart, acknowledging the Great Provider.

Wealth, prestige and fame do not give the peace that we are meant to have. In many cases, these things rob people of the serenity and peace that can be afforded them in a different sphere of life. Jesus warned that we should first seek the Kingdom of God then all other things shall be added. Mathew 6:33. This simple means that we will have a right way of thinking and living when we are guided by Godly principles.

One must be careful to walk in light of the brevity of life and not to consider security outside of Christ. Security is only found in Christ alone and not in things.

Many people are living only superficially with little or no thought for the deeper things that are of eternal consequences. These deeper things are the eternal dimensions of our existence. Mans end is not at the grave and: ``*Dust to dust and ashes was not spoken of the soul*` `Henry Wadsworth Longfellow, in his poem; The Psalm of Life. The soul is eternal; it lives on for all eternity. Let us bear that in mind, it is a weighty matter.

The load of business weighs heavily sometimes and can break the back or neck of the one bearing it. I was in property management for 25 years. Now that I am out of that field and am able to look back upon the hazards that I sometimes faced, I thank God that I am free from such involvement. One day, one of my tenants emptied the contents of a fire extinguisher into another tenant's face and struck him in the forehead with it. After that tenant left, I read where he had killed a landlord. When I saw the former tenant's name in the paper, I was shocked and had the thought that he could have murdered me. Another landlord was killed on the property opposite my rooming house. I have had many more unpleasant experiences that I won't mention here, but I will say that property management is a risky business. Just living is a risky business. We must gather our thoughts together and live soberly.

The last property I sold was a bed and breakfast. I am reminded sometimes that if I had kept this or that property, I would now be rich, but I am richer now than I ever was when I owned those properties. Who can put a price on freedom? Patrick Henry declared, "Give me liberty or give me death." A caged bird has one desire, to soar, because that is the thing that delights it most. Whenever the chance comes to soar, a caged bird will take it. Humans were also made free but unintentionally many have enslaved or shackled and burdened themselves with much of the possessions that they deem necessary.

It is easy to fall into a groove, allowing something to grow on us to the point where it controls our life, but we can drop it off whenever it reaches the point of threatening to take over our life. Do not be controlled by vices, unhealthy habits and desires. Many of these alluring things are traps that ensnare us. We do not recognize that they have trapped us until it is too late sometimes, at which point these things become our demise— our punishment and our reward at the same time.

Sometimes we have metaphorically built a wall and are standing on the inside with no way out. We have cornered ourselves by our devices and desires. Simultaneously we cry out for the values and customs of the past. Often we hear of people in North America crying out for the values of the past and decrying the values that are currently thrust upon them. They realize that not all the tinsel and glitter are substantive; they are illusionary at best, for the most part. People long to relax beside a quiet stream and feel the refreshing water wash over their feet without a harassing master looking over their shoulder and giving direction.

Many of us would like to see the earth remain undisturbed and unchanged. That way, we could enjoy it as it once was for the rest of our lives. Many others are thinking this same thought, dreaming of a life without the intrusions of the modern age. Having experienced the modern age, people are overwhelmed by it. Many are sick of it. It is leading us nowhere. We travel two hours to work and two hours back home only to plunk our exhausted bodies on a sofa to watch the news and fall asleep while we do so. The body cannot sustain such a routine. It was not made for such rigours and harassments.

It is noteworthy that work is man's great function and without meaningful work we would stagnate and remain unchallenged, however one can burden him or herself with work that overwhelms.

Technology was intended to serve our needs and supply our wants, but it has become our master. Now we are trotting to keep pace. How very sad that technology has become a burden to many. That which was intended to serve us is now controlling us. The irony is that we are not masters after all. We are little more than slaves. The many inventions leading to the products we now own are swirling our heads, giving us a giddy feeling and leaving us in a state of disequilibrium. We now think that we have arrived, but we do not know just where we are on the sea of life.

Many are losing their bearings gradually on the true issues of life and a lot of confusion seems to be the order of the day. There is much ado about nothing literally where some endeavour to subjugate and enslave their fellow men and there is not an abiding trust both of nations and individuals alike. Many countries are as apprehensive about their future as they were in the fifteenth centuries when colonialization was rampant.

In North America there is still an ongoing conflict between the

First Nations people and the Federal governments. The distrust and deceptions which started at the beginning of their encounters have prolonged without a conclusive solution to the present. Even among those who were entrusted to bear the Gospel to the natives were instruments of conniving and intrigue. Many dealt falsely with the very ones they came to enlighten.

The disruption of their lives brought on fear and sure enough, they were right to be fearful. The Natives were transformed into fearful, bewildered human beings, another one of humanity's ever growing list of sad songs.

In some parts of Africa, colonialism and Christianity arrived simultaneously. Because of this, a lot of blame was placed on the Christians for dirty deals. One of the favourite sayings of the African natives was "The Christians came and told us to look up. When we looked down again, the land was gone." Many wore the Christian's badge falsely and thereby deceived many. Not all European Christians had ulterior motives for colonizing Africa. Many men such as Charles William Pearson, pioneer of the Church of Uganda, Henry Townsend, missionary in West Africa and the renowned and immortal Dr. David Livingston of Scotland gave their all for the cause of the Gospel of Christ in earnest on the African Continent.

In essence, the Christians gave and are still giving, and are not takers as such.

A quote from Dr. Livingston showed that he was more than a missionary; he was an explorer at heart also. *"[I am] serving Christ when shooting a buffalo for my men or taking an observation [even if some] will consider it not sufficiently or even at all missionary."*

Dana L. Robert has pointed out the following: "While courageous individual missionaries mitigated the effects on indigenous people, by and large the missions benefited materially from European control." There is until this day a stigma associated with the Christians. Everywhere the Christians feel the effects at times, a backlash, if you will.

Here in Canada I personally bore some of it when I tried to witness to one First Nations man. These are the things that some of them remember and point to. Some First Nations people put all of us Christians in the same basket because many of their people were abused under the banner of Christianity and now find it hard to look beyond the experiences of neglect, deception and betrayal.

The Partnership

The connection with God has brought North America thus far, making it a prosperous and free continent. That connection has brought prosperity and a host of other blessings such as stability and rest to the Nations. Whether we realize it or not, whether we acknowledge the Creator as God or not, we do have that connection. It is under His Lordship that we prospered and we cannot break away from Him entirely. We are happiest when we find our way back to the Father although we may wonder away from Him.

After all, home is where the heart is. Each of us struggles to find a purpose for our lives, some with a great measure of success, others with little or none at all. Is it that some have learned to struggle with good guidance and a focused compass whiles the rest of us wander with no guidance or without a compass? We must have some sort of compass and guide if we are to gauge our progress in life. I believe that progress is not measured by the accumulation of wealth or accomplishments but in the level of comfort and serenity that we derive from our endeavours.

We must learn to travel through life as free men and women absolutely and unequivocally. We came in unburdened and unencumbered, and we should live and make our exit equally unburdened and unencumbered. The unsuspecting persons are easily drawn in by pitches of the manipulators; oftentimes the consumers cannot differentiate between the manufacturers greed and their needs.

This superfluous consumerism is likened to dining at a buffet. Unable to consume everything on offer, one tries nonetheless; in the end walking away overstuffed and sick. An hour or so later, one is disgusted with oneself for having eaten so much.

Personally I liken life to travelling through a jungle or going on a hike. How many things will we pack for such a trip? It should be the bare minimum, of course, because we do not want to be bogged down by trivial things. We are not going to carry a TV set, an ironing board and so on—absolutely not. We will travel as lighty as possible. If we would treat our lives likewise, we would be happier and healthier.

As we travel, we cannot tell what the next adventure or tragedy will be, but if we do not have any set expectations, only goals, then we will not suffer great disappointments. We cannot tell what the next turn will reveal to us or what danger awaits us around the next corner, but we know that these things are expected. As we travel, we will refresh ourselves at a stream, cool our heels in the cool water, climb the cliffs and enjoy the shade, but expecting and enjoying as we go. We will not be hindered by difficulties, those we already expect and anticipate. We are mentally prepared for anything, so nothing can come upon us unexpectedly. This principle of anticipating any and every difficulty should govern our outlook.

One man has said, *"The trouble is not that there are problems but that we believe that there should be no problem. That is the problem."* (Theodore Isaac Rubin.) Those who are unprepared to handle problems do not understand life in general, or this world that we live in.

There are unsettling things from day to day; the vicissitudes of life if you will that assails all of us in one form or another which at times rear its ugly head like a beast, we must learn to recognize it for what it is so that we can deal with it. The beast could be any form of oppression that we have to overcome. It may be a huge problem or a simple one but it sticks with us.

The sooner we understand the nature of that beast the better equipped we will be in dealing with him and handling his rage. When we can handle the beast, then we soon will be riding it instead of fighting it. When each day's endeavours has brought us some measure of peace, which we all seek eventually, then we can settle in after a day's work and relax and know that for another day we have beaten the odds or should I say the beast.

We must have a compass to navigate life and a yardstick with which to measure our progress. The absence of these two things spells disaster. Many of the younger generations tell themselves that they are hardy, self-sufficient and resourceful and that they need little guidance to be successful in life, but history has already proven them wrong. Without a conversation with the past, a person's life is a futile struggle. Everyone needs the guidance and wisdom of those who have travelled before us.

A certain man told his story of venturing out on Lake Michigan without a compass. He thought he could navigate it without a compass. He was heading to a certain town across the vast lake. After hours of sailing, he sighted the outlines of a city and was overjoyed. But as he came closer, he realized that the city he saw was the one he had left hours before. Wouldn't he have known, shouldn't he have known, that a destination would have been guaranteed if he had equipped himself according to the rules of navigation? No doubt, he took with him drinking water, signal devices, an extra can of gasoline and so on, but his confidence was strong enough that he crossed without a vital part of the navigational system: his compass.

How quickly we feel that we have become masters of our own destinies and that we are self-sufficient enough that we have the confidence to do things alone. That sailor's attitude is more common than not. For example, when we seek to assemble an item, consult the manual only when our efforts fail We struggle needlessly although we have guidance, a manual that we can consult-but our confidence gets in the way.

It is always a good thing to consult the manual from time to time and not to rely on our own inclinations. The things that are written to provide us with guidance and help are written by others who have experience with certain things and who wish to spare us the laborious process of encountering certain problems ourselves. We can be helped, but we also must be pliable and willing to submit. It is the attitude that counts largely, the willingness to submit. Yes, submit.

Have you ever noticed the 2-year-old child who thinks he can navigate the streets by himself and does not want to take his mother's hand? He feels quite capable of crossing the busy street, but he does not have the experience to judge the speed and distance of the oncoming traffic. It would be folly for him to cross the street without this knowledge—and the consequences will be dire. We all have an infancy stage and need the guidance of those wiser than us to lead us to maturity, but are we willing to be helped? That is the big question. Are we willing to be helped?

Time is of essence in the brief life that we are given. The faster we learn the paths and pitfalls, the sooner we are able to travel unhampered. It can be done, it must be done, learning and understanding what life really is all about. Life with all its problems, real and imagined is not a dream; it is real and it takes a determined effort and perseverance to navigate it successfully.

Are you making real headway in spite of its demands and still enjoying it in the relaxed atmosphere in which it was meant to be lived, or are you harried and frustrated by the many things life throws at you? Take stock now and learn to become a victor rather than a victim, which is made possible only by taking as your guide the One who can bring that to fruition. With God, we may still struggle, but with the assurance that we will come safely through the maze. Knowing this will inevitably take a load off your mind.

There is still time to turn the tide in your favour if you are not living it as you would like, whether you are 20 or 90. The dividends are enormous and enjoyable, to say the least, when you take from life only the amount you are allotted. I say "allotted" as though we have an allotment, which in essence we do. The Creator has promised to supply our needs, but we reach beyond, and in many cases far beyond, grasping more than that which could easily satisfy our needs. Conspicuous consumerism seems to be the norm for many people today. Many would strain to provide for themselves and their children far beyond that which is necessary to live happily.

The Western World has adopted this lifestyle as a norm almost totally with few exceptions that an abundance of goods are necessary. Our Western Democracies advocates and promotes consumerism to its max.

When Nikita Khrushchev visited the United States in the 1960s, he was dumbfounded to see people fighting for parking spaces. He could not imagine that there could be so many cars on the roads.

According to Karl Marx's writing in the 19th century, Western society is run by "irrational exuberance and mob psychology." What he saw then is nothing compared to what we see today. Today, many people feel that they must have it all. Feeling they must satisfy their rapacious nature, people show their neighbours that they have good taste in all things. People yield to the temptation of amassing unmanageable debt so as to be seen as being affluent. The very things that lure people to take the plunge becomes the millstone around their necks. Lust has pulled some of us down into the mire, never to resurface. Be warned that what is sold us as a product to enhance our lives is just a part of a fool's paradise. Such products are merely entrapments that can hold us hostage and make slaves of us.

chapter 4

OUTLANDISH APPETITES

To begin with, we work to improve ourselves, which is something we should do throughout our lives, yet I wonder at what point in life do we begin to work against ourselves. I know that people work against themselves because of what I see manifested in their lives. I watch their rapacious behaviours and see them exerting themselves on projects that overwhelms them totally. Some with limited resources embark on building projects for instance without counting the cost. They have laid plans and started building only to stall midway because of lack of funds. As a result they are left with unfinished projects and no prospect of ever completing the plans.

Jesus warned against such behaviour. He instructs us to count the cost before we embark on such a projects.

Oftentimes people self-destruct in the midst of these ventures. It is quite a misfortune when the things we sought after should cause our demise. In essence, we become the hunted instead of the hunter.

Oftentimes we see the wealthy person looking as shaky and miserable as the beggar. Dress them each in either rags or purple robes and you cannot tell the difference. Why is that? Has wealth made a healthier, happier, more caring person out of a person than poverty has made of the other person? The difference between the two is almost indistinguishable. One simply would not be able to tell the difference if the two were put together in the same surroundings and dressed alike.

Many of us have acquired a taste for bigger and better objects, be it a house, a car or even exotic foods and extravagant vacations, but when night comes and we draw near to our beds, we find that we can still be empty. All of the extraneous indulgences have not delivered on what they promised us. Emptiness resides still. Something, we find, is still lacking; there is a void still to be filled. Are we deceiving ourselves for settling for nothing when something tangible exists? Living on the froth when the real substance is attainable? It is time some of us wake up and smell the roses.

There is a treasure that we can find and that treasure rests in the heart of God's word the Bible but we need to search for it. As the miner searches diligently for a vein of gold amidst the mound of aggregate, so we must search life to find our treasure. That treasure is like a mountain stream gushing with cool and refreshing water, soothing the tired body and comforting the troubled soul. Upon finding your treasure you can experience a long and comfortable rest. You can bask in the light of truth and know the business of life truly when you revel in the light and knowledge of God's word. I urge you to start exploring the pages of the Bible today.

The Disturbing Truth

If the business of life has become burdensome for you, then you have to recalibrate and see where you went wrong. You did not start like this. Instead, you picked up some unwanted baggage while on life's journey. It is now time to drop that baggage. Let some of the stuff go. Do not clutter your life with it any longer. Let it go and get on with the business of living. Why am I telling you this? Because I have done it myself. I have lightened my own load here and there because my health and wellbeing is worth more than dependency upon things manufactured.

What people managed with 20 or 30 years ago is but chickenfeed compared to what we demand today. Our appetites have grown exponentially over this period of time. Given this, are we living truthfully, or are we living a lie? Are more things adding to our quality of life, or are they detracting from it? I remember when the Swedish auto maker Volvo did an analysis and concluded that the Canadian market was ready for a $10,000 Volvo. No, I am not 100 years old. It was not too long ago when a person could buy a Volvo for $10,000. Today I believe you need $50,000 to purchase a new Volvo. And our roads are full of these expensive cars anyway.

As my four year old daughter once said: `Daddy in Canada there is no money problem.`` It now seems that way.

The appetite for having bigger and better things than everyone else is nothing more than a sign of immaturity. The words spoken by Karl Marx were prophetic indeed; capitalism is based on "exuberant consumerism and mob psychology". The mentality of most consumers today is simply scandalous. What we see is a flagrant, outlandish display of greed. The display of greed is a far cry from any need. Enough is not enough; people want it all. Theirs is an appetite that cannot be quenched, because things cannot satisfy the deepest longings and needs. People will line up for hours, even days, to get a new gadget. Such behaviour to acquire things that are not food or clothing is beyond my comprehension.

If only our appetites were satisfied without looking at our neighbours, life would be simpler. We are ever dissatisfied with our lives, and we always stir up our greedy nature, which we should seek instead to quench and subdue. Too often we see the futility of excess. We overreach, and then come the failure in midstream. Moderation is the hallmark of success, as you have already gleaned from what I have said. Moderation will keep you on a path of humility and fulfilment. It is said that there was a farmer who didn't want much; all he wanted was his farm and any land that touched his farm. I think many of us are like that, in that we are never satisfied.

Palaces like the Taj Mahal will be built, but we cannot all build one. The Bible makes it clear: ``But Godliness with contentment is great gain.`` 1 Timothy 6:6. Have you ever gone to the Supermarket and seeing how some kids behave. One is there with his or her mother very contented and happy while another harasses his mother. Now which kid are you drawn to and given a smile.

Let us not deceive ourselves and overestimate our capabilities. Since all of us have limitations, we should discover them before they find us out.

Strive, yes, but do so within reason. Keeping our hopes and aspirations within certain boundaries is sensible and prudent. It is said that we should hope splendidly and never lose sight of our dreams but that we should not stretch too far to realize those dreams. Still, we should set our goals higher than we are able to reach and then reach them nevertheless.

In a moment, I will provide a few statistics to show you how destructive we are as humans. First, though, I would like to say that we pollute and degrade our planet, causing great damage on this earth, while thinking we are making great strides by producing goods and services at a great rate. We do so in the name of job creation or progress.

Every step we take, we are burning energy that needs to be produced and replaced simultaneously. Every house that is built is energy-intensive. For the cinder blocks, the foundation and the mortar, we need to produce cement. To produce cement, we need energy to burn the limestone. Most energy-intensive industries burn coal as the fuel to power their factories even today as governments are cutting back on carbon emissions. Burnt coal emits large quantities of carbon dioxide into the atmosphere, which is a toxin. It chokes the lungs and diminishes our quality of life considerably. Millions die each year around the world as a result of of coal burning emissions and in the United States the estimate is pegged at 10,000 deaths yearly.

These deaths and the sufferings leading up to them could be prevented if alternative sources can be utilized.

Now here are the stats: In the year 2000, 1.5 billion metric tons of carbon dioxide were emitted into our atmosphere. By 2012, a record 3.5 billion tons was released into the atmosphere. This rise came from the developing powerhouses such as China and India. We know that over this period, China came on stream as a big producer and exporter of goods to the West. We longed for and piled up China's cheap goods, whether we needed them or not. If the Western countries, particularly the United States, had not mitigated this condition by turning to natural gas as an alternative source of energy the suffering and death rate would be higher than it is at present

Just where are the concerned citizens of our planet who know when to say, "Enough is enough"? Each of us must make a stand against pollution or else we will pay with our lives. The bottled water we crave for is a great source of pollution. We haul the water to the factories, haul the processed water to the stores, and then haul the plastic bottles after they are used to be recycled and made into new bottles; again using more energy to process those bottles.. The cycle never ends. In places where the tap water is tested and proven to be as good as the bottled water the use of bottled water has not abated. It has become a habit in many households to buy bottled water nevertheless.

On the subject of bottled water, some people feel that they cannot live without it. But it is only a fad, like many other things. Where there is no recycling program in place for used plastic bottles the littering is woeful. In the countryside in Jamaica I witnessed this littering wherever I walked. It seems that there is not a proper recycling method to handle the used bottles and whenever a bottle is used it is thrown by the wayside.

Many things do not add to our quality of life, do they? Many things only appear to do so. As for me, I don't see why I should spend a dime for water that I can get from the tap for a fraction of the cost of bottled water. Besides the savings, I help protect the environment when I do not create an unnecessary waste. We keep piling up our troubles, but in the end we will be hit by them as if with a ton of bricks. We will wonder what hit us. Being bewildered and dazed, we will be powerless to respond.

The Search for the Elusive Happiness

Let's start with the question of happiness. "What about happiness?" you ask. Well, is it your goal to be happy? If not, why not? And just how far are you from attaining that goal? Are you happy? If so, is your happiness sustainable, substantive and real or transitory, elusive and fleeting? Can you truthfully say that you have attained happiness by doing the things you engage in, and solely on account of those things, that your happiness is generated and sustained? If that is the case then you are managing your life successfully.

If, on the other hand, you seek happiness but it eludes you, then I have some suggestions of things that you might implement. First, get connected to the source of wisdom. Get plugged into that source of power. I can authoritatively recommend this source because I have been connected to it for over fifty years now. The source of which I speak is the Bible. If you are already connected to it, then you have this matter settled.

Do not be like William Wordsworth's cloud, "wondering lonely o'er vale and hills". Your failure to connect to the Bible can cost you. I do not know where in life you are at this moment, but I do know that the need for action is urgent. We do have access to happiness. We can find the road to it. That access was restored to us through the cross of Calvary. Christ suffered and died on the cross to redeem us, make possible our personal relationship with God our Maker and restore our fellowship with Him. The reason we do not seek God is that we are not burdened by sin. As a whole, sin does not disturb us much anymore, as our consciences are seared and numb. We go about our businesses as though it is business as usual but the truth is that the scales are being tipped against those who are not mindful of their eternal future.

Outside of the fold of Christianity, the soul is not only hungry; it is famished and dehydrated to the point of exhaustion—although it does not realize being in that state. That famished soul does not know just what a fulfilling life would be in Christ. In Luke 12:16–21, Jesus gives us the parable of the rich fool to show us the brevity of life and the folly of adding tomorrow to the equation.

The ground of a certain rich man brought forth plentifully: And he thought within himself, saying, what shall I do, because I have no room where to bestow my fruits? And he said, this will I do: I will pull down my barns and build greater; and there will I stow all my fruits and my goods. And I will say to my soul, Soul thou hast much goods laid up for many years; take thine ease, eat, drink and be merry. But God said unto him, Thou fool, this night thy soul shall be required of thee, then whose shall these things be, which thou hast provided?

This story speaks of a common occurrence throughout history and one that is present even in our day. People are laying up treasures for themselves, but they are not rich toward God. They cannot truthfully answer the question "Where is your brother?" We are so enamoured with ourselves and our immediate families that we often neglect others. Too much of what we are blessed with stays at home and does not cross the street. That is regrettable, because soon everything vanishes or we will be separated from it. Too many of us will hear the pronouncement, "Thou fool." There is another part of that sentence which keeps coming back to me; `Then whose shall these things be.`` Many of us have not given this question a thought.

Nothing has changed since Christ told that parable. As a matter fact, in May 2016, a remarkable story turned up. Here in Toronto, Canada, this week, a professional athlete—a celebrity—bought a very expensive house in a prestigious Toronto neighbourhood (the Bridle Path) for $5 million. It is a bungalow, but apparently that is not good enough for this athlete, who is going to have it torn it down and is planning to build a two-storey house in its place. Of course, such madness is a common occurrence in today's society. There is so much wealth floating around that people do not know what to do with their cash.

You be the judge and assess the times we are living. We are either witnessing pride multiplied or stupidity personified. Do people know the value of money, or are they only dreamers, pretending to be living in the real world? We have seen where people pay millions of dollars for a single painting only to learn that the painting is a fake. Some people spend money on things that avail little or nothing. What good is it to anyone to have treasures locked away, neither fattening the eyes of the owner nor adding to his or her daily existence? It is all vanity. If your wealth is not helping you navigate life with greater ease, then it is worthless. That is the way I see it, anyway.

We plunder the earth to extract precious metals at great cost to our environment, refine those metals, and then hide them away again in secure places such as great vaults where few eyes ever see them again. We are human beings indeed. When an animal hides something, it does so in order to return to that place and retrieve the thing in time of need. A squirrel hides nuts and a dog a bone for lean times, but people, we buy expensive treasures only to hide them out of sight, not so we can one day retrieve them and use them to nourish ourselves.

A child cries himself or herself to sleep from hunger and we care not that such is the case. Many must have their heart's desire and lose sleep just planning their investments. In essence, we are faltering because our priorities are unbalanced. A change in attitude toward others could solve a lot of the world's problems if we would be our brother's keepers.

chapter 5

WILL YOU MAKE A DIFFERENCE?

While millions of people around the world are starving, some people cannot find uses for their money except to splurge on vain projects. Jesus asks the question "In the end, whose shall these things be?" Who shall inherit our possessions after we are gone? That is the million-dollar question we must answer. We cannot truthfully dismiss this question, can we? We must face up to it. We all are stewards of the things entrusted to us. Ownership cannot and should not be attached to the things placed in our care, since in the broad sense we are only transitory agents. We can have and use things, but at one point we must leave them and move on.

A sister and I mulled over this question of moving on at church. We talked about the surprise in store for some wealthy folks who live in mansions and depend upon their maids to do all their chores, and do not believe in God, the Resurrection and the Second Coming of Christ when they wake up to an empty house. The phones will begin to ring. "Ruth! Is Pam with you?" "No, Mary. I was just about to call you to find out if Kathy is with you." "Hold on, hold on, there is something going on. There is a newscast saying a large number of maids, train engineers and bus drivers, and other people from all walks of life, are missing. Oh no! I can't take it. What's happening?" Planes are crashing everywhere the news caster is saying. I must go.``

Something took place which is called the `Rapture`` Gods children have been taken home.

The wealthy will understand what is happening by and by. Those who are left behind will get it immediately. They will know that what the Christians talked about when they discussed the Rapture—being snatched away by Jesus—was true. The big puzzle will be what comes next. What is next is beyond the scope of *What's Up?*. The purpose of *What's Up?* is to prepare you to meet your God at His Second Coming, which is anytime now. It is the opportune time to connect with God as you are reading *What's Up?* There is still time for you, dear sir or madam.

The import or thrust being stressed are certainties that are inescapable, so we better acquaint ourselves with them. These are circumstances or facts that we will face or are facing us. Stark facts they are that are confronting us, and yet we fail to grasp the gravity of them. We speak of ourselves as prudent and wise, coming on stream with such force and brilliance, but in the final analysis we are missing the mark. We fail miserably when we do not add God, the main ingredient to our lives.

The main ingredient is the foundational principle of a life aligned to God through His word the Bible. When last have you looked into God's word and find out what He wants or is saying to you. He wants you to find rest in your soul but would you know when you have not searched?

It Is Better to Give than to Receive

A great deal of happiness is found in sharing. I experience this happiness every day. I am willing to share, and I do share liberally. It is little wonder that Jesus said, "It is better to give than to receive." Those who share with others are happier people; our enjoyment of even the little that is left over is heightened. We simply enjoy life more when we know that others are living, on account of what we have shared with them. In essence, we live with little so that others might also have a little. We enjoy life much more than the miser with his accumulated millions.

Anyone who has ever read or watched the Christmas story of Scrooge after his encounter with his partner who died and then came back to haunt him knows the transformation that overtakes Scrooge when he loosens his purse strings. He becomes giddy-headed and as light as a feather. The degree of his happiness grows exponentially with the degree to which he gives. He finally finds the secret of joy, which is in the blessedness of giving. Being able to share is a gift that not all are given. The natural propensity of humankind is to hoard. Being able to share is indeed a blessing that blesses the sharer.

It seems to me that you can spot the difference between a giver and a hoarder from a mile away. There is a sweet aroma about the kind person to which one is automatically drawn. The person who gives has the attractiveness of a sweet-smelling flower.

How much does a person need to live comfortably? Does a person need two bedrooms, three bedrooms, four bedrooms, six bedrooms or ten bedrooms for a family of four? There should be a law against extravagance, especially when such a large proportion of people have so little. On the other hand, there would need not be such a law if our consciences were functioning correctly, because there would be a brotherly love compelling us to share.

A person such as an athlete who earns a disproportionate amount of money may use his or her money foolishly and at times gives away a little pittance. Many times when these celebrities die, we hear much talk about their having been fine Christians. Yes, they might have given to charity and made it public, or backed some humane organization by holding a placard while protesting in front of a news camera, but that is as far as they went in terms of helping other people. The people making the assessment that such individuals were good Christians are not speaking the truth.

There is a joke about a rich man who made his way to heaven's gate. St. Peter asked him what good he had done while he was on earth. The man replied that he had given five dollars to charity. Peter handed him back his five dollars and said, "Go to Hell." Many are of the opinion that giving a little from their abundance will make a difference come Judgement Day. It is really giving from the abundance of the heart that counts; it is not giving in a miserly way from an abundance of money and possessions.

Serving God is not a part-time occupation, nor is it based on the amount we give, be it great or small. Our giving matters on two counts: one, when we first give our hearts, and two, when our heart gives cheerfully. Total commitment and devotion is the standard. The person who has a greater foothold in the world than in the Kingdom of God and who calls himself a Christian is only fooling himself. In all practicality,

I could not be a member of a certain political party but then go out to canvass and plant signs for the opposing party. Surely, that would be counterproductive. I would have to take a clear position to be an effective member of the party I support.

We expend our energies on the things we believe in and back the sides we are devoted to. May God help us to draw the line so clear that we cannot be separated from our works? The things we do are intrinsically intertwined with our voice and our speech. We have to walk the walk and talk the talk, or else we become a sounding brass and nothing else.

We can sing loud songs about how much we love and praise God but then go out and neglect the things we are commanded to do. We care nothing of our neighbour's plight or for the poor beggar who needs a helping hand. We are like the priest and the Levite who saw a certain man robbed and wounded on the road and who passed on the other side, having no compassion for the injured man. How dare they say they have any connection with our God, who is a God of compassion and love?

Our actions clearly demonstrate our faith. Our actions and our faith are not separate; they are blended and become as one. They are intrinsically linked to each other. Like mixing the aggregate with water to form concrete, Christ in us becomes a formidable force. That new life cannot be lived in the fleshly indulgences any longer and the analogy here is that the alignment with God builds a life which is now a force for good.

A person may praise God for His many blessings upon his life. He lauds Him for his successes and wealth but denies a brother a simple request. "Wherefore by their fruits ye shall know them." Matthew 7:20. A good tree bears good fruits, pure and simple. Let us be up and doing, my dear brothers and sisters. A changed person demonstrates that that change has taken place. The old self has died and a new one emerges. The old heart of stone is removed and replaced with a heart of flesh.

Be Resolute in Your Perseverance

When the Israelites were taken away as captives to Babylon, there were four young Hebrew men, including Daniel, who would not bow to an image, who would not bow to King Nebuchadnezzar, and who would not eat the meat offered to idols. The Bible says that Daniel purposed in his heart that he would not defile himself by doing so.

When the three young Hebrew men Shadrach, Meshach and Abednego refused to bow to Nebuchadnezzar and he prepared a burning fiery furnace to put them in, he asked them, in defiance of their God, "... And who is that God that is able to deliver you out of my hands?" They answered, "... our God whom we serve is able... we will not bow to you." Daniel 3: 15-16.

Why aren't we Christians be as confident in the protecting hand of God as these three young Hebrew men were? Why don't we do the same today—make the determination to follow Jesus and not count the cost? Why don't we give the Lord a free hand to do as He pleases in our lives?

There is a determination in all of us, whether we are Christians or nonbelievers, to aspire to something and a desire to develop our full potential. Nothing is spared in most cases to achieve that goal; every stone is turned to make it possible. No one is singing, "Take me to the slum; take me to the pigpen." Do we see anyone sleeping in the pigpen? No! There are things that we rise above because we are humans and not animals. God desires to lift us up from the dunghill and set our feet on solid rock. In Psalm 113:7–8, we read, "He raiseth up the poor out of the dust, and lifteth the needy out of the dunghill; That He may set him with princes, even with the princes of His people."

Does this God sound like a God who does not love us? In Jeremiah 29:11, the Lord declared His love yet again to his people. After the Israelites' 70 years of captivity in Babylon, He said to them, "For I know the thoughts that I think toward you, saith the Lord, thoughts of peace and not evil, to give you an expected end." God is never finished with us no matter how far we wander. He will punish us for our waywardness, but He will not abandon us totally.

When God puts His hand on us and raises us up from the dust and dunghill, He sets us among princes and princesses. We are dressed in royal apparel, acting as children of the court. No longer are we beggars and castaways roaming aimlessly and without hope. Let us now know as children of the King, our station in life. We must cut free from the old life and embrace the new. It is this new life that is worth living; it is the new life that has purpose. Let us pursue it with all our heart, strength, soul and mind. Let us exert every effort to run the race and to obtain the crown.

William J. Gaither wrote the lyrics, "It will be worth it all when we see Jesus." I have no doubt whatsoever that it will be worth it. All the heartaches and despondencies that we suffer will not weigh against the magnificence that we will experience when we see Jesus. Just one glimpse of His dear face and all our worries will disappear. Ten thousand years will not be enough time to sing His praises, the one who took our place in death.

The three Hebrew boys taken into captivity were young men of integrity who honoured the Word of God. They would not sell their God short. We know how these young men fared amidst bitter opposition. We all as Christians must dare to be a Daniel. A fighter is taught never to let down his guard, as it is then that the opponent gets in his best shot, which can be deadly. We as Christians must be on our guard, shunning the immoral and foul things of life and purposing in our hearts not to do certain things that would pollute our conscience and dampen our testimony. We must purpose to grow into fine Christians, showing forth His righteousness.

Let us endeavour to honour our Lord and Saviour with all that is in us. Until we are willing to put Christ first in our lives, we have nothing going for us by claiming the Christian faith. We must be willing to suffer and not allow the cause of Christ to suffer. Paul admonishes us in 1 Corinthians 15:58 thus: "Therefore, my beloved brethren, be ye steadfast, unmovable, always abounding in the work of the Lord, for as much as ye know that your labour is not in vain in the Lord." Do not slacken off. Paul is encouraging us to be vigilant, because our reward is sure.

Be the best Christian you possibly can be. Do not give in to false doctrines. Study the Word so that you know what it says, and therefore, no one will be able to deceive you.

When a Christian flounders and becomes confused, turning to other religions, it is because he or she is not sufficiently grounded in the Word. He needs to keep digging for the nugget which is there in the Word.

One man told me that he was a Christian but he was making enquiries into a certain other religion. By so doing, he was only a seeker and not yet a possessor of the Christian faith. I say "not yet a possessor" because if he were filled with the Holy Spirit, then he would experience total satisfaction. Paul wants us to be anchored and grounded in the truth of God's Word so that we will not be swayed by any other argument. There is a lot of falsity out there which can easily be found.

Walter E. Isenhour wrote these words:

> There is a treasure that you can own
> That's greater than a crown or throne:
> This treasure is a conscience clear
> That brings the sweetest peace and cheer.

If we can but get a handle on the treasure of a clear conscience, then we shall be on our way to a great life. It is worth seeking after. Its value is far greater than any other treasure there is. In fact, this is the only real treasure there is. Get a hold on this treasure now, my friend. The treasure that you can own that brings the sweetest peace and cheer is the Lord Jesus Christ. No other person or thing can match the peace He gives. We lay up treasures here on earth and are rich in these things, but we are destitute and poor towards God. We will not spare a cup of water for the poor in His name, which shows how self-centred we are. We all should know that possessions and positions are empty without God which can set us free from a guilty conscience.. If our lives are to be rich and meaningful, then we must put our faith in God.

It is said that Abraham lifted up his eyes, saw the stars and became the friend of God by faith. Lot lifted up his eyes, saw Sodom and became a friend of the world. The outcome of each man's life was determined by the choice each made. The eyes see what the heart loves. There is no doubt about that. Have we as Christians subdued the rapacious heart

Ethel Percy Andrus wrote, "What I kept I lost, what I spent I had, but what I gave I have."

Is it any wonder that Christ said, "It is better to give than to receive"? I have experienced that good feeling in my life. To be charitable is the best feeling ever. To live miserly is to live a defeated and shackled life. What havoc is being wrought on the land because of material possessions!

Siblings live in distrust of each other and are divided over what they will inherit from their parents. Parents are in fear of losing their own lives because some of their kids seem unable to wait for their death to get their inheritance.

Jesus had much to say about riches and rich people. Let's look again at "The Rich Young Ruler" in Luke 18:18–23, a most disturbing story. Here, a rich prestigious young man came to Jesus seeking eternal life, but because he was unwilling to part with his riches, he went away sorrowful and unfulfilled. His riches stood in the way. His riches were worth more to him than the eternal life he sought. By keeping his possessions, he made a poor choice. Some of us might not see it that way now, but in eternity we will discover that they who failed to make the trade will regret it as their biggest mistake.

Here is the story as told by Dr. Luke: "And a certain ruler asked Him, saying, Good Master, what shall I do to inherit eternal life?"

Jesus referred the ruler to the 10 Commandments, and he affirmed that he had kept them from the time of his youth up to the present day. In this, he passed the first test but then came something harder. "Now when Jesus heard these things, He said unto him, 'Yet lackest thou one thing: sell all that thou hast, and distribute unto the poor, and thou shalt have treasure in heaven: and come follow me.' And when he heard this, he was very sorrowful: for he was very rich." Luke 18: 18-23.

We have all heard how people catch monkeys in certain parts of Africa. They scoop out a gourd, leaving a hole just big enough for a monkey's hand to go through, and then put some cooked rice inside. The monkey pushes in its hand to get a handful of rice. And although someone is near, the monkey will not let go of the rice. By hanging onto the hand full of rice, the monkey cannot extricate its hand from the gourd. The hunter then overtakes the monkey. The monkey does not realize it, but for a handful of rice it loses its life. Many of us are giving our lives away for a few trifles. We are tight-fisted with regard to our possessions and will not share with others. Consequently, we are dragged literally down into Hell. Need I say more? Consider your priorities.

If as we live and earn we share, then we are doing the right thing. Christ approves of that kind of living. What is important is where our hearts are. Do not set your hearts on things; that is to say, do not let things possess you.

Your Treasure is Where the Heart Is

There is the story told of two rich men, one a Christian and the other a nonbeliever. On a Sunday, the Christian was getting ready for church when he heard that one of his buildings was on fire. On his way to church, he and his wife went to the scene, where they saw a sad state of affairs. The building was beyond saving, fully engulfed in flames. After watching for a while, the man said to his wife, "Honey, there is nothing we can do. Let's go to church." At the same time, the other man came upon the similar situation and fainted. These were both rich men. This demonstrates clearly that each man had his heart in different places.

When Jesus calls us, He calls us to a life of commitment and surrender. We become soldiers of the cross, and as such we might be asked to give everything including our lives. What's that to the soldier when he has signed up for duty? As soldiers of Christ, we carry no white flag in our kits. Surrender is not an option; we are committed to the very end come hell or high water.

Jesus said, "No man that puts his hand to the plow and looks back is fit for the kingdom." These are harsh words, it seems, but they show that God demands total commitment. If there is a goal, then there must be the sacrifice also. We know that the prize is awaiting us, and because of this we strive to reach that goal of the high calling of God in Christ Jesus. There is no higher calling than to be in the King's army.

Paul says in Philippians 3:14, "I press toward the mark for the prize of the high calling of God in Christ Jesus." Paul counted himself a prisoner of Christ and in spite of all the hardships encountered in his ministry found it a privilege to press on for the prize which is in Christ Jesus. That prize will far outweigh the sufferings encountered when he beholds his Saviours face in eternity.

The song writer Esther Kerr Rusthoi states it this way: "It will be worth it all when we see Jesus." That meeting will be one that will overwhelm every believer. It will take forever to get over such an encounter and every sorrow borne down here on earth will count for nought in comparison.

Can We Enjoy the Good?

What is there that resides in the human heart that keeps people restless, unable to relax and enjoy the good? St. Augustine has said, "Thou hast made us for thyself and our hearts are restless until they rest in Thee." There is no doubt about the veracity of this statement. We cannot find rest and peace outside of Christ. Until we enter into fellowship with Him, we will forever be restless and haunted. God has made us that way so that we will have fellowship with Him.

In the natural realm where an athlete presses toward that mark in his effort to finish his triathlon, he does it by exerting every bit of energy. It requires everything of a man to get to the final lap of such a gruelling race. Triathletes give all that they have to achieve their goal. Nothing is held back to finish such a feat. Every physical effort is exerted and every mental capacity is brought to bear in order to attain the mark. After 10 rounds of a 15-round fight against Joe Frazier, Muhammad Ali wanted to give up, it was so gruelling. And that was after one hour.

In spite of the strength of the body and mind that it takes to complete a triathlon, triathletes fail to avoid simple temptations. They often fall victim to disastrous vices and eventually ruin their lives. We look and say, "How very sad. They did not learn to master their desires as well as they did their bodies." Proverbs 16:32 tells us, "He that is slow to anger is better than the mighty; and he that ruleth his spirit than he that taketh a city." In all of life, the emphasis is on the control of self. Self-discipline has a tremendous force or might. After you have learned to control yourself, you will be on your way to conquering life and life's problems, however great they might be.

When Paul said, "I press toward that mark," he meant that he exerted every bit of strength within him to finish the race. He had to fight all manner of obstacles in order to triumph. No one has suffered more than Paul for the cause of Christ, and yet because of the prize on which his eyes were set, he endured. At the end of it all, when we look back from the heavenly vantage point, we will wonder if we would not have been willing to give up a dozen lives for so great a prize.

"Discipline" Is the Operative Word Here

There was a battle brewing between two armies. The general of the larger army sent an envoy to the general of the smaller army. The former entreated the latter to give in now, for his army was sure to be defeated. There was a well nearby where the general got the word. He ordered one of his soldiers to jump into the well. Without hesitation, the soldier jumped in. The general said to the envoy, "Go and tell your general that my men are well disciplined and that tomorrow this time, we will slaughter you like dogs." Sure enough, the outcome of the battle was as the general had predicted. He and his smaller army won the victory over the larger army. Discipline won the day.

It takes discipline to measure up to anything worthwhile. We can learn to be just what we want to be if we try hard enough. About 50 years ago, I and a church brother of mine in Jamaica did some extracurricular studies together. When I went back to Jamaica five years ago, this brother told me that he had one more year to finish his bar exams. Well, I thought that I had courage and an insatiable appetite for learning, but this man taught me a lesson. Frankly, he inspired me beyond words. That is tenacity personified. Why not, he would be the same age today but without the fulfilment of a noble desire.

God needs a fierce army like the one we just heard of. He needs people who will take orders and not question Him. God gives us commandments, but human beings everywhere question Him. "Does He really mean what he says?" The following quotation shows that He means every word.

Acts 17:30 tells us, "And the times of this ignorance God winked at; but now God commandeth all men everywhere to repent." Most of us know of the Ten Commandments. If we do not know all of them, we know at least some of them. We do our best to obey those commandments, and we repent when we fail to keep them. In the past, when God spoke to us through the prophets, he winked at our ignorance, but today He speaks to us through His Son. This, therefore, is serious business. We are now cornered with no place to hide. We must obey or pay.

Authority speaks

We respond according to the degree of authority and whereas we can scoff at some authority others we tremble at. If a police officer comes and we jeered him and the duke came regarding the same matter and we poked fun at him; but when the king sent his viceroy then we would know it was a serious matter. And the king will act if we neglect the summons or the subpoena brought by the viceroy.

God has sent His prophets to minister to us and winked at our ignorance but when He sent His son, He expects complete obedience and compliance or He will act with a firm hand. Jesus is the light which is shining in this dark world and those who cannot or will not see it will perish in that state. We will not escape God's wrath if we neglect so great a salvation.

God is patient and long-suffering, not willing that any should perish (go to Hell). Because of this, He is making all manner of connections with us so we might see the Way or the Light. The Light is here. After His Son's appearing, He is now commanding us to repent. For every broken command there comes a penalty, and the penalty here if we refuse to repent is eternal separation from Him. God is not asking us to repent; He is commanding us to. Bow the knee or pay the price.

There are some who think that Christ's coming and dying is a simple matter. It is the weightiest of all matters; it is the central theme of all ages: His coming into the world to give His life shows His love for us. Our only connection to the Father is through the Son.

There is no other way to get to God but through the Son. We cannot get in to see certain dignitaries unless we are allowed in by the secretary. We cannot ignore her and simply enter the office of a manager, let alone the President. This is an example of the rigidity of the structure of Christianity. The rules cannot be ignored either. If you dare to enter the kingdom, you must come through the door, which is Jesus Christ. This is an explicit command.

chapter 6

WORRISOME TIMES AHEAD

The date 9/11 is one that stays with us. That date, because of the horrific scene of the planes crashing into the world centers undoubtedly marks a moment in time when our world was changed forever. The attack on the Twin Towers in New York City was such a calculated, cold-blooded crime that it sets the stage for a great upheaval and gave us of the free world an unsettled feeling from then on. That event has divided the world, many living in fear of such disruption ever since. The horror was heightened because it was peace time, no one was expecting an attack in such a manner.

The events of 9/11 lead us to ask the question "How could the perpetrators have given up their lives for the destruction of people they hated, the Americans?" This act of killing yourself in order to kill someone you hate must be the darkest of all crimes. This type of act defies any rational thinking. I could see a person giving his or her life to save someone else, but not to kill someone else. The latter is the most unnatural of all behaviours. Yet it has been done. And since 9/11, we have seen many such irrational acts. It seems to have become routine, men and women blowing themselves up in order to inflict death on others. The insanity of it is staggering.

The sanctity of life has gone out the window. Certainly, a person kills because he hates, but he wants to save his own skin nevertheless. It is nearly unheard of for a person to commit a murder and then turn himself in. The usual course of events is that law enforcement officers have to catch him first. Next he is tried in a court of law. And if he is found guilty, then he usually appeals the verdict, never wanting the death sentence.

Even if we find others unworthy of living, we cherish our lives and do not want to give our life in exchange for theirs. No one in his right mind would freely give himself up after committing murder unless he was sure he had a good defence. I have heard the bereaved of a murder victim pleading to the killer to give himself up. "Do the right thing and give yourself up." Well, that is naïve, I think, to say the least. If a man was foolish enough to give himself up, why wouldn't he have stayed at the murder scene until the police arrived? It is only a fool who would kill someone and give himself up. Wicked people are not necessarily foolish people.

When the smoke settled over what was then the World Trade Center's in New York, a stark reminder remained—to the delight of some and to the consternation of others. There in the basement of that once majestic edifice stood a cross, an iron cross. A portion of the steel post and beams was not destroyed. Those remains stood unmistakably as an iron cross.

Everything fell away, leaving distinctly and unmistakably an iron cross. That a cross should remain is a miracle. That cross to a believer represents hope and triumph. It is reaching out to all who will believe that there is hope of a better time ahead despite the destruction at hand. Like the rainbow in the sky, the cross stands as a reminder that human beings will return to our rightful place with our Maker.

A Guide to Having a Full Life

We must get connected to the Source of power, which is God Himself. Humankind's aspiration is an upward climb; it is not a downward descent. Humanity's climb is always a satisfying one, as it fulfills the desire to explore and discover the next horizon. We may flounder in that pursuit, yes, but we never relinquish the dream. We seek to satisfy that insatiable urge to fulfill our dearest and most pressing dreams. Until those dreams are realized, we remain unfulfilled and dissatisfied.

"Though made weak by time and fate yet strong in will to seek to find and not to yield," Lord Tennyson wrote. Humanity is always aspiring to higher heights. Human beings are never satisfied to settle on their present accomplishments. We have an insatiable urge to propel ourselves further and further. Only when we reach the stars will we be fulfilled and satisfied.

What the poet is telling us, is not to relinquish our dreams, we must understand that to mean that we should keep them burning. Although we grow old and physically weary, our inner person can still seek and find. We seek to find a path that will lead us safely home, upward and onward to the shining light that is still glowing. Although age takes its toll, keep growing as a green pine tree. Keep yourself interesting and relevant; do not become passé. We must refuse to yield to the pressures of life that drag us down; we must keep on striving for the good. Society has a way of limiting our actions. It tells us when we must run and when to stop running. It will not dictate to me. When I hopped over a fence and burst the skin on my hand between my thumb and forefinger, my doctor said to me, "You are an old man now. How is it you have done this to yourself?" That doctor did not know that I was only a 45-year-old teenager then. When I twisted my foot skating, the guard who assisted me asked, "What were you doing skating at your age?" I was only about 60 then. When I bought my first pair of rollerblades, a man asked me what I was going to do with those. He did not know that I was only about 67 then. A friend who was about my age and was learning to skate said to me, "You can fall on the ice and break a limb, so why not break one having fun?"

Is there an age at which we cannot do certain things? I have not yet seen it written as a commandment. Since I do not know that we stop certain activities at a certain age I keep on doing many things. I have a criterion by which I measure my activities, and that criterion is my strength. Whenever I feel that it is risky to continue doing certain activities, I stop doing them, but until that time comes, I keep on keeping on. No person will choose my mountain or tell me when to climb. I will, in my own time and at my own pace.

Here you are, my friend. You are only old when you regret not doing this or that. If you feel like doing something legitimate, then go and do it. Go break a leg, my friend. It is better than sitting down watching TV. We should be involved with something legitimate and kill the boredom forever. There is no time to stand and stare. We are all active participants in the scheme of things. There is basically no place for pleasure-seekers unless we are the faint of heart. We must be involved and be so fully, not half-heartedly.

We are all on a journey. The more involved we are with our trip, the easier things become for us. The time passes quickly and more pleasantly when you are fully involved in your life. With the many outlets and chances for self-improvement, I wonder how many people can afford to flit their time away unproductively. We should invest our time wisely and not just spend it.

I personally cannot understand how anybody can survive and not have a plan for his life. Having something substantial to do is a must for a healthy and sober person. Someone has said that when you are fully occupied, you will have no time to be bored. Even if it is birdwatching, get out and do something. And unless you get out regularly, you will miss a lot of birds.

There is no time to lose in achieving our goals because time flies by very quickly and soon we regret not having done what we intended to do. There is urgency because we do not have all the time in the world. Depending on your age, you might see time as fleeting without getting to do some or most of the things you would like to do. What exactly are we seeking here on earth anyway? Is it wealth, happiness, success? Either way, the most important thing of all things eludes us, which is making the transition from earth to our other existence. That top-of-the-list accomplishment is fundamentally the *peace of God*. Peace is the thing that is promised. If attained, it allows us to acquire every other wholesome thing we seek after. The peace of God will infuse us with enjoyment, and then our happiness will be complete. Then we will have the complete package. What we want will be within our grasp.

Jesus is the Christian's peace. John 14:27 tells us, "Peace I leave with you, my peace I give unto you: not as the world giveth, give I unto you. Let not your heart be troubled, neither let it be afraid." How sweet is that, my friend? When we latch onto God and His Word, we basically have it made. We can serve Him without reservation because we have found the pearl of great prize. There is no need to keep on searching, because we have found that unique prize. Receiving Jesus Christ is getting to the end of the line. Period. The search has stopped.

I recently spoke to a young man at a gathering who was raised in another religion. Many of his family members held permanent positions in that religion. He said that when he broke from that religion and received Christ, nothing could compare. For the first time in his life, he knew that he was liberated and had something real to look forward to. I asked him whether he would ever again worship with those members of his former religion. He dismissed that thought unequivocally.

A little boy was eating some honey from a jar. A man asked him what he was eating, and he replied, "Honey." "What does it taste like?" the man asked. "It is very sweet. It tastes like honey," the boy replied. Then he added, "Here, taste it." Ah, my friend, if the man had never tasted honey, he would not know what the boy was talking about. Likewise, if you have never trusted Christ, you will not experience His peace. You can only watch others live and enjoy that peace. You cannot know what it is like personally. You really have to taste and see, my friend. I invite you now to taste and experience Christ.

If after we have come to Christ the world had anything to offer us that compared to Him, we might consider going back to those things but it has nothing to compare. But think of it: when men and women are willing to lay down their lives for Christ, then His peace must be something that really passes all understanding. It is an extraordinary thing that we experience. We wonder how we ever managed without His peace. We would not trade it for all the tea in China, not for all the gold in Fort Knox. What is that rich young ruler thinking now? How often do we hear people complain, "I have everything—a new car and a large house—but I am not happy"?

A person seeks happiness but in the wrong places. Human beings cannot find happiness in earthly trinkets. Happiness starts with connection to the Almighty, our Creator. Knowing God is as basic to our happiness as an engine is to a car. Without God, we are practically immobile and shackled as a bird with a wing broken, and yet as soon as we get connected to God, we can take flight again. We can soar as the eagle above all circumstances, cares and debilitating conditions when we get connected to God.

Adopting godly principles is more than a suggestion. It is an imperative, a must, if you will. Without God, life is flat and insipid. The wisest man who ever lived, King Solomon, found this out. He had everything that a person could dream of. After he had relished it all, he came to the conclusion that it was all vanity and vexation of spirit. None of what he had satisfied him, and he had it all.

In our day, we find the same thing to be true. Celebrities, for example, did everything they could to make it to the top, but once there they have found out that they were happier when they were like ordinary people. They long to return to an ordinary life. Many have ended their lives by overdosing on drugs or shooting themselves in the head. Some who still live have sold out themselves to their fans and are no longer free and independent. They are now slaves to their fans. Even if they have to be propped up on stage, they must perform. They still try to give what little they have left but to their detriment.

Celebrities' fans promote them to the status of godhood, and they fall for it and fight to maintain that status. Some of them would rather die than relinquish that status. They live a lie. This is the norm when living in the flesh. The change comes when, with the Holy Spirit's indwelling, we take a hold of ourselves and come clean. This is when the new birth takes effect in a person's life. The individual becomes a new person. The old person has died; the new person takes his or her place.

The author of our salvation invites us to a place in His kingdom and says that finding His kingdom is a priority. His words are, "But seek ye first the Kingdom of God and His righteousness and all these things shall be added unto you" (Matthew 6:33). This imperative puts things in the proper perspective. It sets things right when we do as instructed here. We are not without guidance in living our lives here on earth for the time allotted to us. We can enjoy our lives and live in harmony with our fellows and with God. Simply put, we prioritize when we seek first, God's kingdom. This is the position God's Kingdom must occupy in our lives.

Jesus points out that there are choices. We can live in a cave or in a mansion. We have choices. We are all responsible people here on earth. We are careful to observe the rules and regulations made by our governments, but we basically ignore and spurn those given by the Creator. If you are driving on a street with an especially heavy vehicle, anything from a 40-footer to an 80-footer, you are careful to obey all the signs indicating where not to turn, where not to enter here and so on, especially the sign that reads, "Road closed."

You do not want to find yourself in a tight spot with a big vehicle, believe me. I have been in such a plight. Of course, no matter how bad it gets, you will get out of it. But eternity? Well, a wrong turn and you are in it forever and ever. Do not make that wrong turn. If you do, then all will be lost. It was just a little too much for my liking, that idea of being in Hell forever, so I settled the matter at the foot of the cross over 50 years ago. I am rejoicing today that I humbled myself when the Holy Spirit knocked then.

On the Old West wagon trail in the USA, there was a sign to warn of a rut ahead: "If you get stuck here, you could be in it for the next twelve miles." This is a hilarious way of saying, "You are done for. You are finished here. When you get stuck, your journey ends here." While you are here on earth, please avoid this rut. Instead, get on the Godway of life, where you will be safe.

Do you roll out of bed each morning with no clear vision as to where you shall be for the day? Are you listless and worn and have no anchor for your soul, unsure how you are going to make it through the day? Be assured that if you look well to yourself and examine your position, you can be made right with your Redeemer. There is still time, ample time, if you see the need. He has made us promises that we cannot exhaust, one of which is "If you seek me with all your heart you will find me" (Deuteronomy 4:29). God Himself has given us the desire to seek Him. He is waiting for us as we reach out to Him. His objective is that we be fully reconciled to Him. He anxiously awaits our return. I urge you, if you have not yet done so, please return to God now. If you neglect so great a salvation, then what will you have at the end of life's road, and what shall you have for your reward? You will have banishment forever from Him who pleads now.

It is coming. For some of us it is coming very fast. Before we know it, it will overtake us. Our resources and our health and ultimately our lives will be submerged by the overwhelming deluge. We will be suffused and buried under forever and ever. Will we have time to say, "Lord, have mercy"? Today is the day of salvation, if today you will hear His voice harden not your heart. Yield to Him while there is still time.

Put yourself in a position where you will have something to bring to Jesus's feet and worship Him. Do not be an outcast. For a long time He has been extending His arms, beckoning to you, *"Come."* You still have time as long as you are reading these pages. Fall now on your knees and say, "Lord, be merciful unto me, a sinner." He will honour His Word and save you. You will henceforth and forever be saved from His wrath and be given a home in His kingdom.

If this position is not one of security and happiness, then there is nothing more to be added to a person's life. We can quit living. This indeed is the ultimate, the highest, enjoyment that can be attained, and it is without cost, free. Accepting Christ as your Saviour amounts to the high soul taking the high road and finding peace and enjoyment there, in spite of the miseries and uncertainties around us. The vicissitudes of life are forever seen differently when one is with Christ. The madness is in the ways of the world, but when we are transformed and accepted into His kingdom, we become only observers; we cease to be participants in the present madness. Literally, we are dancing to a different drummer now. I say, that is a good beat to dance to, a better beat in fact. Find rest for your weary soul, dear reader. Seek Him while He may be found.

Where does the person who has Christ stand in all of this? He or she stands assured that his or her life is directed and driven by a higher Hand, the Hand that directs all things. He directs the events of this world. Things are certainly not out of control as some might imagine. This is indeed our Father's world. It will continue until the day of consummation, when He will bring it to a halt. He alone declares when it is enough. There will be a finality to it all; know it. Whatsoever He has promised will be accomplished. The order will be delivered and the angels dispatched. Then will come the consummation of the ages. Time will be no more. We are close enough to hearing that trumpet call now.

Isaiah 13:9 reads, "Behold, the day of the Lord cometh, cruel both with wrath and fierce anger, to lay the land desolate: and He shall destroy the sinners thereof out of it." This is where justice will prevail, when every person will get his or her reward according to the seeds he or she has sown. God is impartial and will not let anyone off the hook. Know that as a fact. Today, you and I have the privilege and the option of doing one thing or another, taking the high road or the low, but when eternity rolls, it will be fixed; that is, wherever you find yourself then, is where you will be forever and ever.

A Frightful Situation

There are four tons of explosives here on earth for every man, woman and child. All of these explosives are man-made and together are capable of blowing up the earth and creating a dust vortex to replace everything that is in existence here. That will not happen and cannot happen unless God allows it. Humankind will not destroy this earth; God will in His own time. Like Edward Snowden, I too am a whistleblower; I have inside information, I wish to share publicly. "Behold the day of the Lord cometh to lay the land desolate." Desolation is the future of this sin-cursed earth. The future is bleak for the person who dwells outside the camp, but the situation is not hopeless, because you are reading this line right now. You can turn your life around if you are heading in the wrong direction. The operative word is *repent*. "Believe on the Lord Jesus Christ and you will be saved" (Acts 16:31).

This is a gift ready to be picked up.

chapter 7

WHAT IS YOUR LIFE WORTH TO YOU?

In the *Toronto Star* on April 16, 2016, there was a headline reading, "Loving Life and Planning for Death." What could be more relevant and sensible than a statement such as this, which expresses the idea of loving life and making the most of it and yet having in mind the reality of death. This is a sensible and prudent outlook for each of us to have, it would seem. Here is a tandem reality that we must live with, whether we like it or not. Life and death are married together; we cannot separate one from the other. There is no divorce here. One is intrinsically connected to the other. "And it is appointed unto men once to die, but after this *the judgement*" (Hebrews 9:27, emphasis added). This is a truth we dare not deny.

Death is more than departing from this life it is a gateway into eternity or the other life which is eternal.

Here is the test of person's real worth, the way to determine what an individual is made of, if you will. Is he or she the person he or she should be, or is he or she only a paper tiger, crying and murmuring at every stage of his or her life, "I am unfulfilled"?

Surely you have observed a tree growing out of a rock and flourishing. Just how did that seed get started, and just how it survived, it is a miracle to me. We have to work hard at watering and feeding our plants for them to thrive, but then here is a tree doing just fine—from what sustenance I cannot tell. I have seen a beautiful flower shooting out of a cement wall. A mushroom bursting forth from under four inches of asphalt is a stunning sight to behold. It shows the power of life. That is what you have now, life, and you can have it more abundantly once you meet Christ.

As humans, we are mobile, yet some of us seem unable to thrive. We have been given two hands and two feet and are not chained to a post, but we complain and complain. I once worked with a Polish engineer who, like me, worked as an assembler here in Brampton, Ontario, Canada. All I heard from him were complaints. He was the most miserable man I had ever worked alongside. He thought that the world owed him a living, and his idea of a living was being an engineer only.

When I started in this factory, I had just finished my Commercial Accounting course at George Brown College I had a family then and I refused a job as manager of a small office because the pay was too low. I took this job as an assembler, which paid me a little more. With this job and a part-time job on the weekend, I could manage. This co-worker thought life had dealt him a dirty blow and that he was working beneath his rank. As a result, he did not put in a good day's work and proceeded to make others miserable. I left him there once I went on to another job after a year on that job. There were many interesting things that happened to me on this job, but I will mention only one of them. This is to show how the Lord looks after His own children.

After I had been at this job for about six months, there was a layoff. Being among those with the least seniority, I got a pink slip. On the day of the layoff, a man came up to me and said, "I know you have a family to support, Trevor, so I will go in your place." When there was a second layoff, I got another pink slip. One man who was apparently unhappy about being demoted left the company in anger, so I stayed in his place. I stayed until I left for a better job somewhere else. There are other times when the Lord intervened miraculously in my working life.

Our attitudes as human are callous. We are not nearly as grateful for and appreciative of our lot as we should be. We will cry and hound after the whole loaf that we are accustomed to having and not be grateful for the half loaf that we now have. Such attitudes breed unhappiness and unrest. We are always grasping for more and more, which is all right, but to be contented with little is a great achievement.

Getting back to the article "Loving Life and Planning for Death." Is this where we are now in our civilization? Each moment of our lives is centred on happiness and pleasure. We feel that life owes us these two things. And if we cannot have them, we make our exit. Will not we get whatever we want eventually if only we are patient? The politicians we have voted for who are playing god will get us whatever we desire. They will make the laws to fit our needs and deeds. After all, without God, all things are permissible.

If we experience life and death, then the certainty of Heaven and a Hell, which the Bible speaks of, must be considered also. Whether or not we believe this declaration, it remains a reality still. This is the declaration we get from the highest authority. When a decree is ruled by a court, the highest authority in the land, we must obey its tenets whether we like it or not. We obey or pay the consequences, whatever the penalty is. God says, "The soul that sinneth will die." That is our status; we are all dead people until we come to Christ. We all have become sinners as a result of our federal head: Adam. That is our inheritance just as we inherit our DNA from our parents.

This article "Loving Life and Planning for Death" is centred on a particular woman who thought that the bill passed by the Liberal government on assisted suicide was too narrow to include her. This woman has multiple sclerosis. She is disappointed that Bill C-14 is not broad enough to include her. "There were tighter-than-expected restrictions on who would be able to access physician-assisted dying," she said. Here we have a person who is lucid and is far from the point where her life consists of the two d's, dirigibility and dependence. Nevertheless, she is vigorously considering death and would have embraced the opportunity had the bill included provision for her illness. How very sad that is, that all this entire present world holds for her is *death*, no hope of a life beyond this one. Such people see no light because they are blinded.

Without God in the equation, soon such people will be subjected to everlasting torment. How sad to know that they are fooled by the Father of Lies, the Devil. The headline would be better stated: "Hating Life and Planning for Death." A person who cannot wait for the normal course of events to transpire, for the ultimate end of his or her life, and who thinks that the moment the drug takes effect life or existence will be forever extinguished, is in for a rude awakening. Once we have entered this world, we are in it forever, my friend. We are in it for the long haul, through Heaven or through Hell. Let me remind you that the body is temporal but the soul is eternal. The only thing that hits the ground is the body.

The soul cannot be extinguished. When the body dies, the soul will only be resting until the resurrection. We will all be raised again, the good and the bad, with the only difference being our eternal destinations. There will be a separation; both sides will run off to their rewards. Imagine the Lord saying, "Charlie, you may go now. Jane, you can go too." You will know as sure as I write these words just where you belong. You are not going to enter the wrong place. Do not be fooled: we cannot dictate to God. He is a just God and must give us what we deserve. If you have chosen death, then that is your portion. "Run along now, Charlie." Charlie will instinctively know his gate.

When those who cried for Christ to be crucified instead of Barabbas said: "Let His blood be upon our heads," they were implicitly saying, "We will bear the blame and the punishment, whatever that is." Of course, they knew not the judgement of God. Otherwise, they would have repented.

My discussion of "Loving Life and Planning for Death" continues here after another detour. The article does not mention whether this woman has given any thought to the afterlife. She was a French teacher for 30 years. Oh my! Living in a so-called Christian nation, she has not a single testimony of God in her life. How very sad indeed. (Here I pray a prayer that God will touch her heart.) Does she not know or has she not heard that we are accountable for the things we do while in the body? Her pupils were accountable to her when she taught, and she is accountable to God her Creator.

Again I must raise the refrain. How very sad that so many have no concept of what is coming; they live like dumb animals without the concept of accountability. They think that a person's existence ends at death, and as such that "there is always an easy solution to every human problem—neat, plausible and wrong," as the great American critic H. L. Mencken wrote over 100 years ago.

"What You Don't Know Will Not Hurt You"

There are many who think that since they do not believe something, that thing is not true. The person who believes in life after death needs no explanation, but for the person who does not believe, it is not possible to persuade him. There is a darkness that pervades the heart of humankind, and it is only the Lord Himself who can lift that veil. Until then, the person lives in constant night. We have heard the saying, "Ready or not, here I come." This is a refrain from a child's game, but it expresses a bigger event.

The appearing of the Lord Jesus Christ or the Grim Reaper, either, is something that will overtake us. God knows where we are, but do we know where we are? That is the question. There is no escaping one or the other. The Bible states, "Every knee shall bow and every tongue confess that He [the Lord Jesus Christ] is Lord" (Romans 14:11). The big question is, how shall we escape if we neglect so great a salvation, the salvation that was purchased on Calvary's cross? We cannot escape it, my friend. We will pay. We will give our pound of flesh as is required of us, no less. Are we just a careless and irrational bunch? We take everything else seriously, but when it comes to eternity, we think, *well, that is for the birds.* Some of us are not even curious about the afterlife. My friend, there is nothing surer than eternity, and nothing should get our attention more earnestly than that subject. If you had the slightest inkling of its gravity, you would flee from whatever you are doing right now, fall on your knees and cry out to God for mercy.

Am I writing *What's Up?* to make money? I hope to God that I make some, at least enough to cover my cost. I am driving an 18-year-old Jetta now and would love to have a used Mercedes-Benz or a Jeep. (During the course of writing, I had to have the Jetta towed to a mechanic's shop to have a new clutch installed.) Perhaps you will buy an extra copy or two of *What's Up?* for your friends. If only one person bow the knee because of reading *What's Up?*, God knows, I would be happy to give away all the books free of cost. It would make me a happy man to know that. The purpose is not to make money but to use the book as a vehicle to awaken sleeping souls, souls that otherwise might not be sensitive to their eternal needs.

Presuming upon God's Mercy

Proverbs 29:1 states, "He that being often reproved hardeneth his neck, shall suddenly be destroyed, and that without remedy." There is a school of thought proposing that God is too merciful to send anyone to Hell. Surely He is merciful, but do not forget another of His attributes, namely that He is just. Being just, He will not overlook sin. The only sins He overlooks and forgets are those that have been repented of. All other sin, He cannot forget.

God's justice would not see us go free with our sins, so He sent His only Son to die in our place. There you have it. Justice has been satisfied at Calvary, sin has been paid for. It is a gift now to us. You cannot have things any other way. You cannot attempt to pay for your sin in any way. If you are aware of the fact that sin has to be dealt with, then you must submit to the only forgiver of sins, the Lord Jesus Christ.

Christianity differs from all other religions in that its adherents do not work for their salvation. Rather, salvation is paid for by the atoning blood of our Lord and Saviour Jesus Christ. That's the Gospel in a nutshell. He gave Himself as our atoning sacrifice, and as such He dictates the terms by which we can approach the Father. In John 14:6, He states, "I am the way, the truth, and the life; no man cometh to the Father but by me." This statement of Jesus puts things into a very narrow perspective. This statement makes Christianity a very restrictive path to follow. It certainly is not a broad road that accommodates all. Let us not allow someone to tell us otherwise and contradict the Words of God Himself.

Many preachers are popular because they deceive their congregation. I challenge you to try their sermons against the Written Word. Search the Scriptures yourself; the gravity of the situation is too weighty to leave it up to someone else. Jesus Christ, in His life, death, burial and resurrection, has fulfilled to the T numerous prophesies that the experts claim that it would be impossible to fulfill. He is God. If we fail to believe this claim, then we are left in the cold and the dark.

The Derided Followers of Christ

We must remember that the word *Christian* was once a derogatory term applied to the followers of Jesus Christ. In the times following Christ's death on the cross, those who believed that He was God adhered so fervently and closely to His teachings that other people began to mock them. These followers took His teachings too seriously, other people thought. His teachings must be taken seriously, my friend. He is God and nothing else. And because He is God, every word that He utters counts. Each word is weightier than all the worlds put together. If that has not registered on our radar, then you are adrift hopelessly. None of the words that Christ spoke must or can be neglected nor discounted. You may reject the Gospels altogether, but if you are a believer, do not try to lessen their value. The Bible is as stated. You take it all or leave it all, no sampling allowed.

It is not unfortunate if we neglect so great a salvation? It is a sin, a damnable sin. There is enough evidence of God in the Bible that if we reject it, we will be sent to Hell and suffer eternal punishment. How many scoff at the idea of Hell? Yet when a terrible tragedy occurs, we hear journalists describe it as "a living hell." Think about that. Often we hear when we witness to people, "Hell is not a big deal. I will face it when the time comes." Of course you will face it when the time comes. What else are you going to do? You must face it then. There will be no escape. As the writer to the Hebrews says, "Knowing the terror of God we persuade men everywhere to repent." Persuading people to repent becomes a burden for us who believe, because we know the punishment is an eternal one. Because of this, we do not take lightly our task of witnessing. We must do it whether we are received or rebuffed.

To the unbeliever, this talk about repentance and living and dying without Christ is fodder for the fire. Certainly it is kindle for the fire, but whose fire? It will be used to light the fire for the rejecter's eternal torment. Well, those who think that God cannot be equated with terror are dead wrong. The terror of God cannot be contended with. There is no way we can cope with His terror except to escape it by repenting. To put it plainly, we better be on His good side. Need I say more here?

We simply must not rebel against God. When the time comes for Him to put all things to an end, there will be no power on earth that will be able to counter His. He is coming to inflict judgement on the ungodly. He will sweep over the Enemy as a tidal wave sweeps over the ocean. There will be no stopping Him. God has spoken it. It is not so much that we want men and women to have a good and secure future, a place to dwell in eternal bliss, as much as we would not like to see the vilest person go to Hell. Hell by all accounts is a place the vilest person would not want to be in. Hell is torment that never ceases; it goes on forever. Please, if you are reading this sentence, stop now and ask God for help.

It is a certainty that there are only two options: acceptance or rejection of God. There is no neutral ground. There is no weighing in the balance, and if the good outweighs the bad, then we are in, as some so readily think. Our salvation is not of works but of faith, believing in the words of He who came to die for us. In John 5:24, Jesus said, "Verily, verily, I say unto you, He that heareth my word, and believeth on Him that sent me hath everlasting life, and shall not come into condemnation, but is passed from death unto life."

If you do not think that Jesus is God, you better think again. He is God. From the beginning, He has been with the Father. Also, He is the Creator. Some say that Jesus only came into existence as a baby in Bethlehem 2,017 years ago. These people have been blinded. They refuse to see the truth. There is disinformation given by the Devil—and why did he give it? Because he has his axe to grind. He is vying for your soul, dear sir or madam. He will tell you there is no God and that Jesus is not God, but he confronted Jesus many times and recognized him as God. The Devil knows Jesus and His power. He even knows that his own time is short. He is a liar but not a fool.

There is overwhelming evidence to support the existence of God. Because of this, no one should be a skeptic. The evidence for God is here, but the hardness of our hearts leads us to say, "We will not believe. We will and are prepared to pay the price." If that is the decision you have made, then you have cast your vote. But know that after the closing of your eyes in death, the matter is forever settled. At that point, it will be too late. With mercy gone, judgement comes. That will be your state.

False Prophets Are Coming Our Way

The 21st-century Christian in name only falls for many things and stands for nothing. This person is a friend of the world. The world loves him because he is neither condemning nor judgemental. He is very accepting and supporting. He will support you in all that you do, because he is not a Bible believer. He worships at the altar of Baal just like many others. His life is no different from the lives of non-Christians; it is only the way he is labelled that is different. He goes by the name "Christian." Such a person assures the ungodly, "After all, God loves everyone. Why should God send anyone to Hell? Christ died for all." This is the argument.

Yes Christ died for all that is why the Bible say whosoever will may come, that is come to Jesus.

This is a spurious gospel the Christian in name only teaches, designed to soothe your conscience, not to trouble it. This gospel comforts your heart and settles you into a comfortable dwelling place. What could be better than to listen to such a compassionate preacher, one who is even more compassionate then God Himself? Such a person is God's competition, having a greater following than God Himself. This type of person is the new prophet, but he is not from God. God has already warned us about him.

Some of these preachers are lauded by some people as some of the most compassionate Christians there are. A lot of good they are doing to the work of God. They are busy gathering followers, but not for the Kingdom of God. They are leading them in the opposite direction. Beware of false teachers and their eloquence, they are venomous wolves attacking and scattering the sheep. They have a spurious gospel that resembles the truth, but it is counterfeit. It will not get you into Heaven on Judgement Day. The craft will land, so to speak, and your ticket, being invalid, will not get you on board. You will be denied access as the doors are shut and the craft takes off without you. You will be left behind. Now is your chance to make sure you have a valid ticket and not a fake one.

These latest prophets have been sent our way to smooth things over here on earth, but they have not been sent by God. They are philosophers promoting their own ends. They want to make a good and smooth transition for those leaving this earth. They are spin doctors, and they claim they can do anything. They will certainly turn things around for those who are struggling with certain sin. They have the inside tract to God and they have found out that God is changing, especially as He gets older. He now has a grandfatherly nature. He is certainly not as harsh as He was when he was the Father. These latter-day prophets are spinning a yarn of a more humane God, saying that more people will be accommodated in the kingdom. It is not Hell that has enlarged its mouth; it is Heaven that has, according to these false prophets.

Those who are among this new breed of fisherman are not as selective as the old guard. Instead of fishing with a line and bait, they use nets. They intend to bring in all kinds of fish with their catch. Some are regular fish, but others of a different quality. Even some sea monsters will be in the catch. These fishermen will not throw back anything. The object is to have a big catch. Here, *big* is the operative word. They do not want to leave anybody behind, dear friend. They claim that heaven is now a more accommodating and larger place. There is a building boom in Heaven just as there is one here on earth, they say. Business is getting better all the time. Of course, the way of Christ is still narrow, never mind those who are widening it for you. Any claim of a broad road is misleading. As a matter fact, it is leading you down into Hell. Beware of those broad roads.

Warren W. Wiersbe wrote, "It is unfortunate when our churches create appetite for lesser things, for religious entertainment instead of spiritual food, for multiplied activities instead of spiritual ministries, for sentimental music instead of the spiritual songs of Zion. Having once created the appetite they must satisfy it." As for me, I say, "Here is my heart. Take it and seal it. Seal it for Thy courts above."1

This kind of setting where God is a changing and more benevolent God has put a lot of people at ease. Some will tell you, "I believe in God, but not as you believe." Now we do not have uniformity in our Christian beliefs and doctrines. There are too many cooks in the kitchen now, each doing his or her own thing, and the butler has no time to see what is cooking. It is with some degree of honesty when someone says, "I do not believe as you do, but if you do not believe as I do, you are not in. You are out." I simply believe the Bible and what is written as God's Word. If we believe, we have to believe totally. This is the message I am trying to get across. If we sign up as a soldier, then we must give up our rights totally and serve even unto death. We cannot remain of two opinions. We are obliged to do what we like and do not like. We must get moving when we are told to do so.

One aspect of the Bible the contemporary person finds hard to believe is God's wrath. His goodness and mercies are things that people can relate to, but His anger and wrath? No! "No way will He do the things He has promised," some people say. Have we no earthly comparison here with children and parents? I am sure we can find examples of a father or a mother (or both) simply discarding and abandoning their sons and daughters forever. If God spared not even the angels who rebelled, how much more will he punish the unbeliever? It is only fanciful thinking when one believes that what is written will not come to pass.

You, dear brother or sister, might feel lonely and alone, but do not be disheartened. Join in, and stand firm and fast. Elijah thought he was standing alone, but God assured him that there were many more like him who had not bowed the knee to Baal. We are not Baal worshippers; we are followers of the Lord God Almighty, who has the whole world in His hand. We will not be partakers in the ungodly deeds of others. How dare some of them call themselves Christians?

Many who show their faces should be ashamed to do so. They speak as though they are representing others of the faith. It is my hope that God will touch their hearts, and that they will repent and not meet the punishment of the ungodly. If they don't repent, it will be worse for them. Their Hell will be hotter, as we say. Certainly, their punishment will be worse, as more is expected of them because more has been given to them. God help the smart aleck who thinks he can tamper with God's Word.

It is beyond me, the fact that people gamble their lives away in this fashion. They are literally selling their souls in exchange for popularity. Fools, they are. Who would be so careless with the Word of God? Say you possess a valuable diamond and are crossing the ocean on a ship. Do you go up on deck, stand at the edge, and toss that diamond up into the air as high as you can? Would you do this as frivolously as you would a marble? Of course not. Instead, you would be hugging the diamond close to your breast the whole time you were standing at the edge of that deck. It is a precious item you have, and you must guard it. Christian, guard your most valuable possession, your soul. Let no one rob you of it.

Sons and Daughters of God Now

We are assured in 1 John 3:2, "Beloved, now are we the sons of God, and it doth not yet appear what we shall be; but we know that when He shall appear, we shall be like Him for we shall see him as He is." How marvellous and glorious is this realization. It is not that we will become the sons and daughters of God someday; it is that we are the sons and daughters now, today and forever. We will not be in the kingdom someday; we are in the kingdom now.

This blessed assurance makes me sing and dance all day long. Having difficulties like everyone else, I must triumph over them because I am the child of God. Like Job, I can say, "He knows the way that I take, when he has tested me I will come forth as Gold" (Job 23:10). Job had that confidence looking forward to the cross, so why shouldn't I upon looking back at the finished work? We are marching unto Zion, my Christian friend. The dogs may bark, but the caravan moves steadily and surely on. We are on a march; no human interference can disrupt or stop that march.

People are planning and are building without any knowledge of God. He has been dismissed from the projects as Chief Architect. As these people progress, they make more and more plans, not knowing that the time will come when they will be made impotent. They will be scattered abroad as the wind blows away the chaff. Why will this happen? Because it is written. God has declared it. That is why.

God's Word has said it, and it will be so. In Isaiah 24:1–3, we read, "Behold the Lord maketh the earth empty, and maketh it waste, and turneth it upside down, and scattereth abroad the inhabitants thereof. The land shall be utterly emptied, and utterly spoiled: for the Lord hath spoken this word." This proclamation is made because the people have forgotten their Maker. They have turned their backs on the Holy One of Israel. Shall God be pleased with and bless such a people? Of course not.

He has a plan for them, but it is not a good one like the He has for His children. Here is the plan that God has for His children: "For I know the thoughts that I think toward you, saith the Lord, thoughts of peace, and not of evil, to give you an expected end" (Jeremiah 29:11). So who can have God thinking of them? Anyone who submits to Him can be in His thoughts. God is impartial. If you repent of your sins and accept Christ, God will include you in His thoughts, no matter how vile a sinner you are.

Wicked people have been trying from the beginning to stop the Word of God from reaching its intended targets, but they are impotent to do so. God will raise up faithful men and women to carry His message. His army marches on and will continue until the final consummation, when he will put every enemy of the cross under His feet. And as Paul writes in 1 Corinthians 15:26, "The last enemy that shall be destroyed is death." Everything will happen as it is written. It is God's Word, all of it; none of it must be discounted or ignored. If we do discount or ignore any of it, we do so at our own peril. There is enough warning here. We must not swallow the Devil's lies or humankind's placebos.

chapter 8

BEARING HIS IMAGE

The image of Christ is unmistakably the one that every Christian must bear. Whether or not we bear it now is another matter; we should all aspire to bearing it ultimately. We should possess that radiance that says we are different, that we are not carrying the burden of this world on our shoulders as Charles Atlas did. This radiance shows naturally on our countenance if we are possessors of Christ. There must be that visible difference in us.

When I lived in Jamaica, a friend borrowed my car one day. Sometime after that, a woman said to me, "Mr. Turner, I saw your car, but I knew you were not the one driving it because the driver was not smiling." Here in Toronto, when I drove a bus for the Toronto Transit Commission (TTC), one of my fellow drivers said to me one day, "Every time I pass you, I see you smiling and I feel like giving you the finger just to upset you." Oftentimes we err greatly and cry out, "My God, what have I done?" People are watching and reading our lives every day. Even if they denigrate our faith, they notice the difference or the change in us Christians. I am sure that nonbelievers envy us also because they would like to have what we have. I have been told that also: "I envy you." Other people see in us the radiance described above. They observe it, and they would like to be as we are, without a doubt. They can have what we have anytime, but they do not want to sever ties with the world.

When I and my family lived in our first house here in Toronto on Birkdale Road, in Scarborough, my son lent his shoulder pads to a neighbour's son and we were not able to get them back. My wife went to the neighbours' to retrieve the pads, but she did not succeed in getting them. Then I went to the house. As the mother and I talked, she said that I was the best Christian she knew in the area. I had not met this mother before; I knew her husband, as he and I worked for the same company. We better not pretend or we will be found out, because someone besides the Lord is watching.

Fulfill Our Roles as Christians

My experience has taught me that whenever I start a new job, I should make my stand and my connection right away. Establish yourself right away, right where you stand. Do not mingle with the crowd and later try to straighten things out. Take your stand as the one who does not speak their language from day one. They will shun you all right, but that is better, as sooner or later they will seek you out to pray for a matter on their behalf. Such a thing has happened to me a number of times.

Once when I drove a delivery truck for the old Eaton Company, one of my co-workers said to me, "Trevor, you would not be a bad person if it were not for your religion." He said this after I refused to do him a favour, namely, give him money for cigarettes. Some of those who come to me asking for prayer are people of other religious beliefs too. They know with whom the living God resides: with the Christians. One day as I opened the door to enter the building where I worked, another co-worker was coming out at the same time. His reaction was frightening. His remarks were, with his hands raised, "I don't want to have anything to do with a born-again Christian." I would also hear remarks such as, "Don't worry, Trevor will save you." Of course, these are derogatory remarks. Some other places where I worked, certain people simply addressed me as "Save Trev."

I am criticized often for my boldness in witnessing, but because I know that I have what every person should have, I witness with confidence. If you get to know me after reading *What's Up?* you might say, "I thought he was a saint." I will defend myself vigorously against falsehood and personal confrontation like a man, but I know what I believe and I am trying to live out what I know to be true. We do not go about our business unnoticed. We are observed and read daily. Be careful to exalt our God and Saviour, the Lord Jesus Christ.

Let us also be careful to bring honour to His name at all costs. We are the light and salt of this dark and putrefied world. The faithless need us Christians more than they think. Because of this, we must be careful to live as uprightly and honourably as possible. When I ran my rental business, one tenant said to me that I was the best landlord she had ever had. When I handed back a tenant the $70 she had overpaid in her rent in an envelope, she was shocked. She was a struggling mother of two, so money was tight. She wondered how she could have made that mistake. I did not make a mistake, as I counted the money several times. I was struggling like she was, so I was not going to be out $70. I made sure I was not mistaken.

Some call us arrogant for saying we are children of God, His sons and daughters, and acting like we are. Well, do we see Prince Harry, or any of the princes or princesses for that matter, acting cowardly and shy? Of course not. They are not beggars; they are royals. They must act the part. Act the part, my brothers and sisters. We are royalty also. We are not beggars or paupers; we are children of the King. We must keep our chin up rather than peering down at our shoes. There are too many timid Christians; they are so because they fail to keep a high standard. They fall into the trap of not defining themselves at the start of their relationships. They neglect to do this because they are afraid of displeasing others. They would rather blend in rather than stand out.

As children of God, we are also soldiers of the cross. Our lives have been reckoned lost for the Gospel's sake. Paul declares in Galatians 2:20, "I am crucified with Christ, nevertheless I live and yet not I but Christ liveth in me; and the life which I now live I live by the faith of the son of God who loved me and gave Himself for me." As Christians, we have a new life that cannot be snuffed out by the Enemy. There is nothing to protect, so to speak. We are in Christ Jesus, and therefore we are secure. Those who are kept by God are well-kept.

Worldly wisdom recommends the path of compromise and moderation. Worldly people claim that you should not be too righteous, that you should give in a little, have a drink, enjoy a bad joke, go to a movie, live like one of them. How plausible an argument does that seem to you? Unfortunately for those people, we take our command from our Master, who says otherwise. He demands that we come out from among the unbelievers and touch not any unclean thing. Once we were dancing with the crowd; now we are dancing to the beat of a different drummer. This is the melodious sound we have been longing for all along and never knew it. But now that we hear it, we continue to enjoy it.

Some of this same worldly wisdom is coming from the pulpits as well. If the Gospel you hear does not put you squarely in one of two places, either Hell or Heaven, then it is lamentable, pathetic and spurious. We eat food to replenish and nourish our bodies. If that food does not have the nutrients we need for growth and sustenance, then we starve and die. Similarly, we need sound doctrine to navigate this precipitous pathway. It is fraught with danger, so we need to be ever watchful to navigate it securely.

Where there is a danger zone, you will hear loud and clear, "*Stay clear.*" God commands, in essence, "Stay clear of the world." The pitfalls are numerous and subtle, so stay clear, my brothers and sisters. Purge yourselves of all worldly affairs, even those that seem harmless. We have nothing to gain by dabbling in the affairs of the ungodly, but we do have much to lose. We have our testimony to protect, and that is better than anything else we possess.

After the Civil War in the United States, Robert E. Lee was the defeated foe. An opportunity was presented to him by some businessman who wanted to use Lee's name to promote some product. Lee's response to the proposition was "All I have left is my character and I have to protect it." *We must* keep our heads high. Never should we have to hide our faces when someone is approaching because of our behaviour. For Christ's sake, keep your conduct clean. We need not remember the things we did before conversion, because that was a different life, a sinful one, but now that we have crossed the line to Christ, we must be careful. Look out and do your best to show to whom we belong.

Have you really made the transition, or do people still wonder just where you stand?

As Christians, we must choose our vehicle for travelling on the road to happiness. If the vehicle is not of the highest quality, then we will flounder as we travel. We travel first class, for we are the ambassadors of Christ. We bear His image in our bodies, and we must not defile or distort this image. At baptism, we were buried with Christ and raised to newness of life. Keep that excitement about you always, my Christian friends. We are reckoned dead already in the books of Heaven. Now we are made alive forever in Christ and are given new names. That transaction has already been done. In accounting, such a transaction is called an accrual. Under the accrual system, there are two transactions taking place. One is recording expenses that have been incurred but not yet paid, and the other is recording revenue earned but not yet received. The record shows what is due and to be paid, pure and simple. Likewise, our record in Heaven will have these things recorded. There will be a payday, my friend.

We are piling up one of two things as dwellers here on earth. The sins we commit can be looked upon as expenses incurred but not yet paid. Living for Christ may be seen as revenue earned but not yet received. When the Day of Judgement comes, the accounts must be settled. The books will be balanced and every person will get his or her reward. Every person will get his or her just payment. Need I say more?

The death and burial that we speak of in Christ is no more than a laughing matter to the carnal mind, which ridicules us at these sayings. Remember, brethren, friendship with the world is enmity with God. So whose side are you on? That is the big question. We would be foolish to be afraid of the faces of humans and deny our blessed Saviour. James, speaking to the brethren, said this: "Ye adulterers and adulteresses, know ye not that the friendship of the world is enmity with God, whosoever therefore will be a friend of the world is the enemy of God" (James 4:4).

This is a stinging indictment of the Christians who were dabbling in the affairs of the world. James, a bishop of the church, did not mince words, as we say. He told it as he saw it. We do not hear such stern warnings from the pulpits these days. Why? Because some churches prefer to have a large, thriving congregation than to have a small, spiritually separated one. God help us to deliver the truth always, regardless of the outcome. Is there a price to pay for following the Lord? Yes! There is a price we must pay. We have to leave all and follow Him, taking up our cross. If we are not willing to leave all and follow Him, then it is clear that we are not fit for the kingdom. The way of life now is to align ourselves with the children of God and not with the enemies of the cross.

We have been warned that a little leaven, leaveneth the whole lump. Sometimes we attend church in name only, not in substance. Our church constitution might say one thing, but we may hold a different opinion. We have not the courage today, as Christians did in the past, to follow through and reprimand some believers when the need arises. Instead, we condone or wink at misconduct and outright sin. As with any other organization, a church's rules are the essence of its existence; they must be adhered to. A person must be held accountable for his or her wrongdoings. An individual cannot flout the rules and then expect to remain a part of such an organization. These are elementary principles that are established in even the lowest places, let alone in the Supreme Courts of Heaven.

chapter 9

JESUS THE ENIGMATIC FIGURE

Jesus Christ is the enigmatic figure in the world of religions; many do not know what to make of Him. Some discount Him altogether and say they can go straight to the Father by themselves, others say He was a good teacher; others only consider Him to be a prophet. Many do not acknowledge Him to be an historic figure; they think the story is only a myth.

Now, who do you say that Jesus is? Let me quote a portion of Scripture delineating who Jesus is and showing that God has committed all judgement to the Son. John 5:22–23 reads, "For the Father judgeth no man, But hath committed all judgement unto the son: That all men should honour the Son, Even as they honour the Father. He that honoureth not the Son honoureth not the Father which hath sent Him." If this portion of scripture does not set things straight as to whom Jesus is for you the reader, then you must believe without a doubt that there is no God, for He has spoken here.

My brothers and sisters, how else would we have known these things except they were written for us? The backward or ignorant people in the jungles of the nations around the world have no idea that such revelations exist until someone from another country versed in Scripture brings them to their attention. Do they believe it? Some do believe the revelation. It is these people who have the most glorious transformation in their lives and wear the change on their faces. Those who accept the Truth have a glorious look on their faces; it is something to behold. They will testify that they are amazed that the Creator would reveal Himself to us humans. This knowledge is startling and glorious at the same time. They welcome the good news and are hungry to learn more.

The Lord has children who have yet to be reached. We are responsible for bringing the Gospel to them. Waiting to receive the good news of salvation, they know what the truth is when they hear it. The Spirit of God bears that witness to their hearts when it is spoken.

Recently I spoke to a co-worker to whom I gave a tract some time ago. I asked her if she had read it. She was honest and said it was still in her bus. I took five minutes to witness to her, saying that things are not finished at death and that she will meet her Maker at the Judgement. There was some earnest concerns on her face. I hope she will consider that which I have said to her. I prayed that the Lord would stir her heart. This religion is new to her since her religion is an eastern one.

An amazing thing happened to me recently. First let me say this: it is a command that the child of God be a student of the Bible. Hold that thought dear and never let it go. In 2 Timothy 2:15, Paul writes, "Study to show thyself approved unto God, a workman that needeth not to be ashamed, rightly dividing the word of truth." The operative word here is *truth*. We might know some of the Word of God but not enough for it to make sense, to lay out all the truths. We must know what the Word teaches. And since the teaching of the Bible is all about redemption from the beginning to the end, we must study it. We will never be able to exhaust its truths, but we must keep revisiting the truths of the Bible, as many things can slip from our minds.

Here I am praising myself that I am a student of the Word, yet it was not until the morning of May 22, 2016, when I was in church, that the portion of Scripture reading, "It is the Son who judgeth," registered with me. This glorious truth had been sitting there and I had not noticed it. Yes, I had read that portion of the Bible many times, I was sure, but I did not get the full import of the message. Herein lies the danger. We might know much of the Bible but not enough to convince us that Jesus is Lord.

There are many religions, as you probably know, that have totally discounted Jesus the Son. They attribute no power to Him whatsoever. Some claim Him to be only a man; others believe He is an imposter; and still others say He is a fictitious figure. Jesus has to be Lord of our lives or else we are the Antichrist. If you have been brought face to face with these facts, you are without excuse. You will either submit now or be a castaway. Jesus and no one else is Lord.

The Historical Figure Jesus

While we are on the subject of Jesus, let me bring another of His credentials to you, in case, by any chance, you had overlooked it. John 1:1–3 says, "In the beginning was the Word, and the Word was with God, and the Word was God. All things were made by Him; and without Him there was not anything made that was made." The word spoken of here is the Lord Jesus Christ Himself and no other. Do not be fooled, dear reader. That He did not come as royalty does not mean He is not authentic. He is the genuine article of whom the prophets spoke.

When I was studying for my real estate licence, my class was shown a film portraying the story of a huge business that failed because the secretary judged something incorrectly. The owner of this particular real estate brokerage for years had his eye on a piece of prime real estate owned by a widow who knew him well. She made him the promise that when she was ready to sell, she would list her estate with him. Needless to say, this broker saw the deal as his, no doubt whatsoever. It was a given, as we would say. On one particular day when the broker came in to the office, he enquired if there were any calls. "Yes, sir," replied his secretary. "Mrs. X called, but I did not think she was the kind of person who could do any kind of business, so I hung up on her." The brokerage lost the business and consequently went under.

I am telling you this to point out the following: Jesus is the owner of this world, but He came into this world as an ordinary man. He even had to work to help support his brothers and sisters as He grew up. He had no status. His hands were calloused and rough. He had to go without shoes like all the other boys in the district, wearing, I am sure, patched clothes as they did. Is that a good picture of Him? I think so. The Bible says that He stripped himself of His glory and came as one of us. You would not be able to distinguish the God who grew up in Nazareth from the other boys who lived there. He was simply one of them, living indistinct from any other child in his village. That was his mission; He came to join the ranks of the human race.

Consider Donald Trump's son growing up in a poor country among poor neighbours, not living in any way above their standards. Say he goes with a pail to fetch water from the river or a well, returns to water the goats and the donkey, and washes himself in a basin or a tub. The family he stays with eat as meagrely as the other poor souls in the district. No one can tell that the boy is a billionaire's son.

Then one day there is heard a roar in the village. A motorcade draws near to where this boy lives and then stops at his hut. At this point, everything changes. A motorhome is a part of this motorcade, and it is fully equipped with amenities. Inside the motorhome, the boy showers and changes his clothes, decking himself out royally with the help of the accompanying valets. All of the villagers stand astonished as he emerges from the motorhome to bid them good-bye. They cannot believe what they are witnessing. Mr. Trump himself lands in a helicopter and whisks his son away soon after. Many of the villagers are glad to see the boy leave, whereas others wish he would have stayed. Before he left, he assured them that he would come again someday.

This is the picture of Jesus living among us. He stripped himself of His glory and shared our poverty; it is as simple as that. He ministered to us and then went away to His father after promising that He would come again to receive those who believe that He is who He says He is. "Jesus is coming again." Those who had read the Scriptures and knew what they said about the Messiah were offended by Jesus when He came on the scene preaching that He was the Bread of Life and so forth. They saw Him as an imposter. Many of them refused to believe in Him, although they ate the bread He made through His miracles.

Oh, my friend, have I said enough to convince you that Jesus is God and must be worshipped as God? He is the Creator, as I have pointed out in the Scriptures, and He is also the Saviour. We are nowhere without Him, neither now nor in the future. Wise up, my friend, and bow to Him now. If you hold out, then you are the Antichrist. You are against Him and He cannot plea on your behalf. That is the ABC's of the Gospel. On the other hand, if you have already accepted and are serving Him, be steadfast and faithful, for your reward draweth nigh. Your labour will not go unrewarded, so labour on. We are responsible to bring others into the Kingdom, so be vigilant.

We are afraid to witness sometimes because we will be branded as one of those fanatics. Christians are a diminishing breed here in the Western world. It is Pleasure and Leisure versus God. The world at large has put God on pension, having thanked Him for His services but saying that they are now grown up and can manage on their own—and that He can now take His well-deserved rest. They have not cast Him off altogether though; they need Him close by so they can blame Him when something goes wrong. Yes, when things go contrary to our plans, or there is a disaster they draw Him up on the red carpet. He still has a purpose to many. You have heard it said, "If there is a God, why did He allow this or that?" and "Why did He not stop that?" He is not dead, as some say. He is still alive for many.

Some of the people who blame God for every catastrophe are like the pig. The only time it looks up is when it is turned on its back and has its throat slit. Likewise, these people will never cast their thoughts upward in thankfulness to God for all or any of their blessings. They live on mumbling and finding everything that is wrong.

The Bible warns that as it was in the days of Noah, so it will be in the days of the coming of Christ. People will be lovers of self, more than lovers of God. Why are so many things permissible today? It is because human beings prefer their own rights over God's statutes. We are now coming full circle. God's judgement is at the door because the cup of iniquity is almost full. We are getting there, almost but not quite. Soon, however, very soon God's judgement will be upon us like a great tsunami. The warning sign are all around us that that day is close.

The reason many cannot have a quiet moment in their waking hours is because they are afraid of what might happen if they keep quiet. They cannot bear to think anymore, so they keep up a more than busy pace. In so doing, they drown out the rest of the world and comfort themselves in the business of busyness. They are running scared and they know it.

They will not face up to the truth. Many are already seeing the dark clouds gathering on the horizon.

We are in great danger of experiencing a great upheaval such as we have never before experienced. If that sounds scary, then take comfort in the fact that it will affect all of us equally. God's servant Job found that out, that the world's burdens are ours also. Until He calls us home, we will have to live with the catastrophes and heartaches of life. It is a rocky road for all of us. The way we navigate our path, however, depends on which vehicle we choose. Christ is the all-terrain vehicle that is guaranteed to finish the journey. The door is still open. Will you hop in?

It Is a Big Deal That We Are Warned

You might say that Christ did the hard work, or the heavy lifting, for us already. That is true. He suffered at the hands of cruel men to buy our redemption. It is a great price that He has paid. Many, though, say, "So what? it is no Big deal!"

My first little car was an Austin A40, which was a British vehicle. The man who sold it to me failed to tell me of a problem it had. One of the back wheel lugs would loosen up regularly and I would have to tighten it regularly or else the wheel would fall of. I had to be vigilant to keep the wheel on.

One day a friend and I and his dad went out in my Austin. When we were coming back home, the wheel flew off. My friend said to me afterwards that before we left our destination he had seen the wheel leaning. If he had told me before as a warning, would I have said, "So what?" Of course I would have tightened the lug. By tightening the lug, I would have saved my car from an accident. Thank God none of us was hurt badly. My friend's father got a cut on his face because he was on the side in the back where the wheel flew off. Reader, do not say, "So what that Christ died on the cross?" He died for your sins and mine as an offering to the Father for our redemption. If we accept this gift, we are home free, but if we reject it, then the consequence will be eternity in Hell.

If I have invited you to my home and made you a delicious meal, then you know I have sweated over the stove for hours. Perhaps you know that

I planned the meal for days, including getting all the ingredients. If I set it before you on the table and you told me you were not really hungry, then I would probably ask you to leave. I would not be pleased with you at all. Unless a person is hungry, then even the most delicious meal is of no appeal. Similarly, if you do not see yourself as a person who needs help, you will not accept the offer the Jesus makes. "Come unto me all ye that labour and are heavy laden…." Matthew 11:28.

Here I have the most important news to deliver to humankind, but if you are not even slightly curious, then no gimmick or tactics will entice you. I have nothing to gain by enticing you. You must be hungry for a meal. When it is set before you, I would like to see you devouring it. For all those who think they must entice and allure people by using dishonest means, I say they are doing despite to the Gospel. They will dumb down the Gospel to make it palatable to the unbeliever, but that in itself is dishonesty. Nowhere in God's Word that says we should water down the Gospel to entice anybody. As a matter fact, Paul states in 2 Corinthians 4:1–2, "Therefore seeing we have this ministry, as we have received mercy, we faint not; but have renounced the hidden things of dishonesty, not walking in craftiness, not handling the word of God deceitfully."

Using craftiness to deliver the Word of God has been around since Paul's day. Men wanted to profit from the Word, so they sought a good following. I am sure we are experiencing the same thing today. There are dishonest people who are peddling the good news of salvation and are distorting the truth in an effort to attract converts. Of course, I firmly believe that we should preach not an enticing message but a convicting one. If a person does not see himself or herself as a guilty sinner in need of God's mercy, then he or she would only be a suspect and not a convert.

When I was in the life insurance industry, I and my fellow salespeople were taught to "kill the breadwinner." It is only when the father of a family sees himself as dead, leaving nothing for his family to live on, that he sees the need for life insurance. Normally he would not want to spend the money he needs to support his family on life insurance. But if he sees himself as dead, out of the picture, and can envision that his family will still be able to live and buy food and clothes, then he will agree to buy life insurance. In such a case, he decides to make the sacrifice for his family's future.

If a person wished to buy a policy only because he wanted to do business with us, then we would consider him suspect. Chances are that such a policy would not stay on the books. Before long, I would hear that customer say, "Mr. Turner, me can't afford that thing anymore, you know, sah." Would he catch me off guard with this? No, not at all. I would be expecting it. He bought the policy because he wanted everybody to see me turning into his driveway on a particular day to collect the premium. He wanted to feel relevant and progressive; with others seeing that he also has what they have.

We Christians have something to offer that every man, woman and child should have. We are not adding to our wealth by offering it. We are convinced that as we were won into the kingdom by diligent men and women, we also do our best to persuade people to repent. We know the fearful plight of one without Christ; therefore, we continue to travel the byways and the highways calling them to come. We cannot stop. We will not stop. We must introduce the One who can give life. My burden is that you be acquainted with the truth of your existence.

Too Busy They Are Now

It is not easy to be a missionary, as people seem to be too occupied with other things to bother talking with such a person. It is difficult even getting them to take a tract. Some look upon the tract with scorn, as if I were handing them some contaminated piece of garbage. They refuse it before I even stretch out my hand. A driver who relieved me when I drove for the TTC rebuked me sternly when I left a tract on the bus and introduced him to it. Another time, a person said to me when I introduced him to Christ, "You must have read Marx?" Well, who was Marx and where is he now? All of his so-called brilliance could not buy him an extra day here on earth, let alone make a way for him in the next life. It is haughty men and women who frown at truth and are enamoured of their little learning. They pass on in due time however, some leaving little or no legacy.

One man to whom I offered a tract told me that he did not want it. I said to him, "Take it. If you are a Christian, you can read it, and if you are not, you need it." I don't know what he did with the tract after he left me, but that is his business. I discharged my debt to him. I had given a co-worker a tract, and soon after I saw it in a trash can. He had his chance; it is all up to him. Giving out tracts to educated people and/or rich people is like going into a rich neighbourhood, setting up a hotdog stand and handing out free hotdogs. You might not have any takers. Not many of the neighbourhood's resident would be hungry. Plus, they might not want you in their neighbourhood.

One Kenyan Bible student said that when he was studying theology in Ireland, he tried to witness to a man who rebuffed with "Do you know who I am? I am a professor." The inference was that since he was educated, he was a strong man with no need for the Christian Gospel, which is for the weak and lowly. How will such a man fare in the swelling of the Jordan? That is the big question.

I went into a very rich neighbourhood recently and tried to engage a man I saw outside raking leaves about his standing with God. He told me that he was quite happy with his religion and hoped that I was happy with mine. Further on, he said he hoped that I could find my way out of the area. I was intruding not only on his turf but also in his religious life. He could not tolerate that. Jesus encountered people like that in His day. The indictment is out. "There is none righteous no not one." Romans 3:10.

If we say we have no sin, we make ourselves liars. How shall we escape if we neglect so great a salvation? Jew and Gentile are under condemnation and need the Saviour. It is for all humankind that Jesus died. Christ spoke of the rich that it is hard for them to enter the Kingdom of God. The reason is that they are earthbound. The ostrich will not lift off because it has too much weight. It has all the makings of a bird, but it is much too heavy to attain flight. That bird must envy other birds soaring overhead.

In Noah's day, people's hearts were hard also. They did not believe that there would come a flood. Of course, the fact that Noah was building a huge structure and hoping it would sail when there was to that point no rain, seemed a bit farfetched, so the people thought he was a little nutty. Noah acted upon the command of the Lord and built his boat nonetheless. Since God's Word does not fail, eventually the skies burst forth and it rained and rained and rained. All but Noah and his family were lost. God provided the water to sail this monster boat. Cool, isn't it?

Why are we striving to get the Gospel out in whatever form we can? We believe God's Word, and we know He will accomplish it. Yes, He will perform it. The angels who sinned were cast into Hell, but humankind is given another chance. Here is your chance, reader. Take it now. If you do not, the evidence is stacked against you proving that you will not escape. Though your body be burned and the ashes scattered on the high seas, or though your body be encased in a million-foot-thick concrete tomb, His power will gather those ashes again and His power will burst the concrete and raise you up to face His judgement. You have heard that there are two things that are sure; death and taxes. Not so, my friend. The two sure things are death and the Judgement.

I believe that a person's greatest regret in Hell will be that he had not considered the things presented to him while he was on earth. I urge you, sinner, to consider these things now, for tomorrow might be too late and mercy might be gone forever. You might scoff at these sayings as the thief scoffed at Christ on the cross, but remember that the other man on the other side of Christ asked for mercy. He received it and is now forever with the Lord in paradise. In today's vernacular, I ask, how cool is that? Just two words and you are in: "Help, Lord!" The heavy lifting has been taken care of. You can come just as you are, empty-handed. Walk in and enjoy the banquet.

This is not a matter-of-fact transaction. For the man or woman who has never considered or has never even been confronted with the thought, consider this now. The God who created us wept in the person of Jesus Christ when He saw the stubbornness of His people. He wept because He knew what their end would be. How many parents are weeping today because they see the waywardness of their children in whom they had invested so much and hoped for a good outcome? When we realize that nothing can be fully understood without reference to God's creation and His divine plan, then we begin as human beings to tread on a road that leads to a definite and meaningful existence and a blessed destination.

There is no greater comfort as Christians, than to know where we are at present and where we will be in the hereafter. That is security. Neither a thousand cars nor a billion dollars in the bank can compare to that assurance. We have security when we trust the Word of God and put our faith in Jesus Christ, believing that He is who He says He is.

Ask a born-again Christian if he or she would trade places with the richest person on Planet Earth and he will answer you with a resounding no. There is nothing in this world that can top the serenity, security and joy that we get from serving our heavenly Father. Now we are children, the Scripture says, my friend. We are sons and daughters of the King. Let that sink in. There are many fakes, counterfeits, who say, "Lord, Lord," but in the end they will be rejected along with those who reject Him outright now.

I had a dear brother in the Lord who lived to be over 90 years old. He told me and the rest of our congregation of witnessing to his brother who was rich. The rich brother would say to him, "Clair, if you need anything, you ask your Father. If I need anything, I just go to the bank and get my money and buy what I want." Of course, that sounds like a good argument, until—you guessed it my friend—the roll is called and the rewards that follow are handed out. Beware of that roll call, my friend. Beware. The books are accurately kept *up yonder*. Why, how many people today would say there is no God? perhaps just a small number. They are in the minority. Most will acknowledge His existence, but that is as far as they will go. They believe in God, but do they believe God? Do they understand when He speaks? Do they listen with fear and trembling? Only a very few actually listen to Him and obey His Word.

Reporting for Duty, Sir!

Dear brother or sister, would you resolve this moment that you will be that person who will honour the Lord and His Word? I resolved to do that a long time ago. I have seen and heard too much frivolity and sometimes wondered who is really serious about serving God—serving in spirit and in truth, that is. How very commendable to go as far as acknowledging that there is a God and to endorse Him as existing. People who do this would not claim to be against God. Of course not. Believing that there is a God is not enough. We must believe that He is the rewarder of those who diligently serve Him. If He is not an active participant in our lives, then we know nothing of Him. We must believe Him, and if we believe Him, we must obey his commands. In no way can we be detached and abide only as an observer. We better be in the inner circle. It is mandatory that we take our place there. We signed up for duty to do His bidding.

Saying "No God" and saying "God, God" can sometimes have the same effect. Many give only lip service. These people belong in the same boat as the so-called atheist. If we as mortals can see the hypocrisy of people's actions, then how much more will God, who is the discerner of the heart, see it? This brings me to the place where I must point out that there are but two sets of people: the saved and the unsaved. There are no other categories. I have come across all kinds of arguments as I've witnessed to people. Many have their own version of what God is like. Some consider God to be a benevolent man who could not bear to send anyone to Hell.

Such a belief presumes that we human beings are gentler and kinder than God Himself. We have pulled down God to our level, thinking that if we would not send anyone into torment, then neither would He. That is the argument some people make, and they have won the day, so they think. This is a logical argument, they think. If God is merciful, then He will show mercy even to His rejecters. These are the same people who say miracles are illogical. Since miracles defy all logic, there can be no miracle.

Hebrews 10:31 tells us, "It is a fearful thing to fall into the hands of the living God." I wonder how the unsaved or anyone from the camp of the ungodly would interpret that statement. Would they have any doubt as to what it is saying? My friend, we are inconsistent in our interpretation of Scriptures. What this portion of Scripture is telling me is that we should not be on the wrong side of God, because His punishment will be cruel. God has unmistakably stated that the unbelievers will be cast into Hell. Need I drill it in, that what God says is so? You can reckon it done, my friend. His Word will not return to Him void. That is as much as I would like to say on this matter. Do not fall into the hands of God. Be in His good graces and be safe.

Many people do not heed the forecast of an impending flood and thereby vacate their homes. They would rather adopt the "watch and see" attitude. Well, we know what happens to many such people. Just when they see the flood waters nearing their homes, they make an effort to evacuate, but many times it is already too late for them to be rescued. We will not save anything by waiting to surrender to the Lord, but we might lose everything by waiting. As a Biblicist, I am not here to interpret the Word but to give it to you as it is revealed to me. When I say "revealed to me," I simply mean as I read it and understand it. It is self-explanatory.

I say I am a Biblicist, which means that I will not put a man's word above God's Word. I will search God's Word for my final answer. I will test man's word by comparing it to God's Word. I will reject any belief when the Word of God contradicts it. I will not put friends or any believer ahead of God's Word. I will endeavour to read, know and obey the Word. God's Word is my authority; and I am His ambassador.

History Links Us to the Past

God has judged and destroyed a great number of the inhabitants of this world at different times because of their disobedience to Him. What He says He will do in the future, I have no reason to doubt it. In other words, I look at the records, at history, to distinguish what is factual from what is fiction. God's dealings with His people has always been done on the reward system. When we adhere to His Word and obey His command, we prosper. Conversely, when we disobey and rebel, we are punished. These are rules clearly laid out for us to live by.

Another thing that I have found is that those who know the least about God's Word are those who are more dogmatic about its message. One man told me that his life is better than the lives of most of the Christians that he knows. Simply put, he thinks that he does not have to serve or even believe in God to make it into Heaven. His life is good enough to get him a ticket to Heaven. Such a man thinks he needs no repentance, as he believes he is good—good enough to make the trip upward. This is like applying for a position that you know nothing about but, because you are brighter and more educated than another person who has applied, you are sure you will get the job. We are stubborn, proud and unrelenting in our resistance to the truth of God's Word. We will pay in due time however.

We must be careful to note that Christ came to call neither the righteous nor the good people into His kingdom but the sinners. If you qualify as a sinner today, then you are a prime candidate for His mercy. It is you and no one else that Christ died for. You must come as nothing but a sinner. Of course, the Bible states, "There is none righteous no not one" (Romans 3:10). If we consider ourselves to be one of those righteous ones, then we deceive ourselves and the truth is not in us.

What great falsity that we should go about deceiving ourselves. We must not, we dare not and we will not be able to survive without God at the helm of our lives. If I were to finish on this note, it would be sufficient to satisfy the intent of *What's Up?* Wake from your slumber and be counted among the faithful. No one has more to gain than you. God has provided an escape route for you. It's up to you to use it. The question is, are you convinced that this is the true path you must take?

chapter 10

GET PERSONAL

If you turn to the front of the book, you will again see the title: *What's Up?* Now, I want you to insert your name in the space provided: What's up, _____? See if you can give a factual account of yourself, your true self, at this point in time. I mention your true self because we all have numerous selves. There is the self that others perceive us to be, the self we pretend to be, and the self we really are. The true self is the one that we go to bed with and wake up to face, the one we see first thing in the morning. That is the self that we often fight with. We wake up in the middle of the night and wonder what we will do next with that self. It is hungry, thirsty or irritated? We ask ourselves, "Just how can I quieten it down?"

No more pretences now. We are face to face with reality. Your true self is the same self that you live with when you become sick. You alone know how it can drag you down into the valley of despair and loneliness. This is your true self. No more showy stuff. Give a true account of yourself regarding your relationship with those close to you, an account of your trustworthiness and your progress in life. Ask, "Where am I now in the scheme of things?"

If your life were a clock made brand new and wound up, how much time would there be left on it? Just how much longer do you think it will run? Consider these questions. If you were a child growing up and looking at the person you have become, would you want to be like him or her?

Some of us are in midstream already, but we can change. We can start now to shed an unwanted skin and grow a new one. We only have to resolve to do it. We are able. All of us have tried many new things before and have succeeded. It is not hard. After all, we were created to be masters of the universe, so why can't we also be masters of ourselves? You know more about yourself than anyone else, so you should not find it hard to effect some changes for the better. There are areas in your life that you can improve on, I am sure. None of us has yet reached that state of perfection. When we do, we will have been removed from this scene altogether. As long as we are here, there is some degree of perfection that we can seek to add to our stature. If we could use the word *perfect* to describe a person, that person would be someone who is in control of himself or herself, someone who understands fully his or her standing in relationship to his or her world and eternity. A "perfect" person is fully aware of these realities.

God has said that we all have sinned and come short of His glory. Will you acknowledge that fact and turn to Him, or otherwise dwell in eternal torment? Please believe that. Tragically, at the beginning, that is, as far back as the Garden of Eden, humankind was planted with a lie. Satan told Adam that God did not mean what He said. Certainly He could not be as strict and as rigid as not to allow certain things. That same lie has been perpetrated over the centuries, and today it is more widespread than ever. Man fails to submit to His word.

There is the one-sided view of God as all-forgiving and all-compassionate, but we seldom hear of His justice. That is where He must honour His own Word. He cannot overlook His pronouncement on sin or else He would not be just. Would our teacher be just if he or she gave every student in our class an "A" even though some failed miserably?

The same person who believes only in logic will not follow through consistently. He lies to himself somewhere, and this is one point at which he lies to himself if He does not believe that God will punish the unbeliever. He argues that God, a holy God, would certainly not condemn humanity to a life of separation from Him in Hell. This thinking is well woven into the fabric of our society. To believe that God is all-loving gives us a more comfortable feeling than to think of Him as harsh and intransigent.

He is an unchanging God, my friend, loving and merciful but just. His love provides, but His justice demands. So we say that God is a demanding God. Yes, He is. After lovingly making provision for His children, He now demands that we obey His call. He is the Unchanging One who sets the rules. It is up to us to obey them. Do we really expect to flout all His rules and commandments and then expect Him to bend to us? Frankly, we think too much of ourselves if we think that of Him.

When I and my siblings were growing up, our dad was seldom in the home. When he was not with the men in the field, he would be at the shop (a grocery store) after relieving our mom there. She would then come home to contend with us. She always put up a fuss with us when we get out of line, but the thing we really didn't want to hear from her was "Wait until your father comes home."

When we heard that, we knew that whatever we did or did not do, we would now be paying big time. Our dad was not a harsh man. He was level-headed and had the ability to wait days before calling the alleged offender in for questioning. But he could not let us off when he got a complaint from our mother. He had to act. At these times, he would send us to break our own switch—the twig he would use to give us our spanking.

Today people have come to live without receiving floggings from teachers and parents. The abandonment of scriptural principles has put our minds in a deceptive state. People no longer believe in reality. They are totally deluded into believing that life is without rules and penalties.

Tragically, misinformation, misinterpretation and no information at all, are the path we choose to follow. We would sooner swallow the lie than believe in the truth. After receiving so much information about God, we still remain ignorant of His truths. Many have basically formed their own opinions about the teachings of the Bible. The people who argue that God is good and will overlook our iniquities are those who have perhaps never opened a Bible but have listened to others give their opinion of it. We seem to know everything about everything except for the thing that counts most, the Word of God. It is the Word that shows us our condition and our future and reveals the heart of God.

Why would we not investigate the things that show us our future? We would rather not know and stay in the dark. That is where we feel better about things, in the dark. Is it because we believe that when we know the truth, it will transform our lives—and this is why we are afraid to investigate it? If we learn to feed on God's truth, it is unlikely we will swallow the Devil's lies. There are lots of those floating around. His lies will eradicate God from your life entirely, at which point everything will seem easier, because all things are permissible without God. Where there is no God, there are no rules—and no responsibility either. Where there is no God, we might say we are off the hook.

We drive our cars faster than the speed limit, we run a red light, we make turns where the sign instructs us not to make a turn on red, and so on. Were we never caught doing any of these things, would we say that those rules are useless and that they are never enforced? We would not say that, I am sure. A person can live recklessly, have a seemingly good time in life and think everything is all right, but the records are being kept. One day the books will be opened to reveal all that has taken place in that person's life.

With no strict rules and guidelines, human beings are free to do as they please. And people are doing just that—and are perhaps pleased with themselves. Who would dare say there are no strict rules and guidelines? Not I. There are the strictest rules and guidelines governing our lives, my friend. Everything is being recorded for future reference and application. We think there are no rules now because the Lord is not chastising and punishing us for every infraction as we commit it, so we dismiss our bad deeds as unseen or unpunishable.

The Bible, the Word of God, gives us the truth, some of it as a recounting of historical events, some of it as guidance for our daily living, and other parts as prophecies, events still to unfold. However, all is there for our edification. We must discount none of it lest we will fall into the trap that others have fallen into by neglecting the Word. The Word of God has been preserved in spite of great opposition and attempts to destroy it. The Bible is the best-selling book and the most hated book at the same time. Many have had to read it secretly. By and large, it is good to the last word. It has the power to transform lives and will continue to do so as long as there is a sinner left on earth to be saved.

It is quite common to hear people say that what the Bible speaks of as truth is all relative and opinion-based. It is all about interpretation, they say. What you make things to be is what they really are. There are no absolutes. We do put absolutes to the test every minute of every day. Does true north keep changing? If it did, then the mariners could not find their way. They would be floundering on the high seas and in the skies. There are absolutes and right and wrong. By these standards we live, and by them we will be judged.

We live by natural laws which are truths, and yet we fail to grasp spiritual truths. Yes, yes, the things of God are spiritually discerned and the natural man cannot know them. It is indeed foolishness to Him. O the simplicity of the Gospel, and yet people with a PhD cannot catch its essence. There is a spiritual blindness indeed that lurks in the heart of the proud. One will see the truth only when one approaches it with a humble heart.

Pontius Pilate asked Jesus, "What is truth?" If truth was debatable during that time in history, then how much more is it in question today, when we are so distracted and have wandered far away from the true plumb line? We are as a ship without a rudder on the high seas, floundering and without awareness that we are off course. It is said that when someone is lost, he is suddenly struck with fear and he panics, running faster and faster, notwithstanding, having no idea the direction in which he is heading.

Our condition today could be likened to that lost person. We are running but without direction. We are hastening toward a destination which we do not know. It is not easy to tell—in fact, we cannot tell—when we reach that destination without a map. A map is necessary to take us to our destination. Having a map means also that someone who knows the way has been there before and is now pointing the way. Christ is the Christian's guide and the Word of God his map.

I perceive a lost world heading nowhere in particular, and yet we are busier than a hive of bees ourselves, producing, consuming, discarding and God only knows what else. We are no more than a bored civilization trying our hardest to fill a void. It is so and will remain so as long as we keep God out of our lives. Psalm 27:1 declares, "Except the Lord builds the house, they labour in vain that build it: except the Lord keep the city, the watchman waketh but in vain." We are a stubborn people, fighting against the pricks.

We are hurting ourselves unwittingly, but we do not realize it. We have no idea that we have been defeated. We have lost the fight, but still we fight on needlessly. Have you ever seen a person still dancing even after the music has stopped? It is silly, but it happens. Someone is in a daze and is oblivious of what is happening in reality. In our world, there seems to be an appearance of progress, but it is futile; our efforts are wasted continually.

The wickedness in the heart of a man is set to destroy and tear him down. It is pathetic to see in our time the destruction caused by war. Without the Spirit of God in us, we are a bellicose set, warring against each other continually. In today's world, with so little influence of God in our midst, it is especially hard on the families with young kids who want to train them up to know God. It must be quite a tug on those kids between home and school if the parents want to train the child in the fear of God when the schools forbid it. As such Christian's families find it hard to manage their kids in church.

It is difficult to manage them but there is a price to be paid. Will we the parents guide our kids onto the paths of righteousness, or will we renege on our responsibility and let them grow up with the illusion that all is well? And will we then allow them to engage in the distractions that the world offers, which will lead them into the abyss? Many people, or should I say young couples, have given up the idea of having kids believing that it is too bothersome to raise children in this society without values.

We purport to live in a Christian environment, and yet the laws our politicians make are contrary to the tenets of the Holy Writ. Having a form of godliness but denying His authority quite clearly and absolutely, we live a life of pretence. To put it plainly, we are living a lie. We are literally wandering in the dark of night. It is the same thing with the economy; we are all living a lie. Things are not nearly as rosy as they seem to be. We do not all have oil wells, and we cannot afford anything we want.

The idea or thought that we can have it all is an illusion. We are led on to believe that things will get better by and by. Merchants claim that they can give you your heart's desire, with no credit, with bad credit or on whatever terms you want. Just sign on the dotted line, my friend, and walk out with whatever item you want, be it a car, a motorhome or just a suit of clothes. Judging from what I see, we are an unstable people heading down a road of unprecedented hardship. Reality will set in some day and perhaps sooner than we think.

I believe the world at large has adopted the three-word phrase "mutually assisted destruction" (with the acronym MAD). We can better describe our behaviour in this fashion than in any other way that I can think of. The very things that beset us and are sucking out our lives are the things we embrace. We keep running and seeking after the harmful things of life. We are but shallow people without the restraint of God on our lives. The writer of Ecclesiastes states, "Lo, this only have I found, that God hath made man upright, but they have sought out many inventions" (Ecclesiastes 7:29).

We have turned aside almost completely from our responsibility as human beings toward God and from a natural way of living. We are created to honour and to serve God, but we have fallen sadly short of that duty. Be it those people who are ungodly or those of the Christian faith, we have for the most part gone our own way. We devise new paths to follow every day. We have become very adept at such inventions, but I think they only multiply our troubles.

In some cases when Christians gather for worship, we would rather be entertained than to worship in complete humility and reverence to God. In many cases we are mocking God, feeling satisfied that whatever we bring to Him, He is bound to accept. We offer up Cain's sacrifices. To this I say, may God break our pride and bring us back in humble submission to and adoration of Him. I heard a pianist say one morning as he played the piano, "God must be very proud of me this morning." To think of yourself as being worthy is unsettling to me. God help us to say, "I am nothing at all; Christ is my all in all."

It Is Now the Harvest

"Be not deceived; God is not mocked: for whatsoever a man soweth that shall he also reap" (Galatians 6:7). This verse succinctly speaks of the law of the harvest. We do not gather a harvest of wheat after we have sown thistles, as it is impossible. Likewise, we cannot expect to have fruitful and God-fearing inhabitants when we neglect to teach our children how to discern right from wrong. Established biblical principles and moral values are essential to our wellbeing and happiness. We are deceiving ourselves if we think otherwise. Our rewards are forthcoming; every person will have a payday. After all, a human being does not work for nothing. In my life, there are only two Fridays in each month. The other two are paydays. I look forward to the paydays more than the other Fridays.

Would the judgement be unduly harsh if I said that we are a deluded generation, fundamentally flawed in spirit and in truth? We pretend to be what we are not. We hope to profit from our investment, but we make no land preparation and sowing. It is all a big lie that is playing out. There is a lot of froth and no substance. That is the way I see it. I sincerely hope I am wrong. I know that I am too critical about many things, but on many things I will not give in. I am going to die as a stick-in-the-mud. I am a man of old values, and I know that I have lots of company.

chapter 11

"SIN"—AN OLD-FASHIONED WORD

Some have said there is no such thing as sin; some say there is no God; and others say there will be no judgement. These are people who do not read God's Word. They live in a dreamland where there is no reality, everything is an illusion. It is a safe and secure place to dwell. I would urge those who are there to stay there. Do not wake up to reality or you will get hurt. A person who has not witnessed the result of sin must be from another planet. All around us every day we experience the results of sin, and yet people deny that sin exists. One of the laws that people break frequently is "Thou shalt not kill."

The Puritan John Owen wrote, "Sin, when it presseth upon the soul to this purpose, will use a thousand wiles to hide from it the terror of the Lord." We will whitewash and substitute euphemistic expressions for our condition and reduce the holiness of God to our level. Our depravity will impress upon our hearts that there is no such thing as sin, that is, there is no one thing that God will hold us responsible for. We believe that everything is incidental and is a part of our existence, which allows us to float along, thinking that in the end we will be just fine. Wishful thinking that is all it is. This same idea pervades our society. We argue that if we leave a child alone with his bad behaviour, he will grow out of it naturally. Correction is not necessary; just let him be.

At my interview for my first job, I was given a number of questions to answer and some mathematical problems to be solved. The personnel officer said to me, "Trevor, don't worry. If you do not get the questions right, you can do them over." Once I was finished and handed him the paper, he checked it, saying that if I hadn't gotten the answers right, I would not have a job. He led me to think that I could not go wrong, whatever I did was enough to land me the job but that was not his intention. We must be vigilant at all times and not fall for lies.

In an accounting class, the teacher told us of a practical lesson a father had given to his son on the subject of trust. This son was entering business and the father warned him not to trust anyone implicitly, saying that he was to keep his eyes open at all times; check things carefully and not sign documents blindly. To demonstrate, the father told the son to climb a tree and asked him to jump, saying that he would catch him. The dad did not catch him as promised, which, of course, was to prove his point. Never trust anyone in business implicitly, keep your eyes open at all times.

People deceive others for personal gain as a way of life. If our fellow men can behave in such a way, then why do we think that the Great Deceiver the Devil will give us a break? He is devising many tricks to trip us up. He is constantly planting doubts and lies in our path. This is a thing we must believe, that we are being deceived at every turn. We are being distracted and being pushed off the narrow path which leads to life everlasting.

The Depravity of Humankind

Need I point out any particular atrocities in our day caused by the depravity of humankind? The evidence is all around us. One has to be naïve to the nth degree to believe such nonsense as God will not hold us responsible, and that our turbulent and restless nature and condition is simply unfortunate and we will be fine by and by. History has already laid out the destruction that sin has caused us. Some will believe it, and others will refuse to. We can deduce that a certain comet passed Earth three thousand years ago and is due back in another thousand years, yet because of our sin we cannot see what God has done in the past and what He is going to do again. It is written in the books that Jesus came to live among us 2,017 years ago and that He is due back soon, but we will not believe that.

Are we so daft that we will not take heed and open our hearts to the warnings? We are presuming too much on His mercies. And true enough, He is merciful, not willing that any should perish but wishing that all should come to repentance. Will you heed the warning? God is continually reaching out to us to turn from our wicked ways and serve Him, but we are forever spurning his invitation. How much longer will He keep throwing out the lifeline when we spurn His invitation?

He refrained from destroying Nineveh when, after a warning, the people repented. Sin had enveloped the nation totally. The Lord sent the prophet Jonah to warn them. Once they repented, they were spared. The Lord will keep His word every time. What He desires is repentance from His people. When they repent, they are restored to fellowship with Him. He said in 2 Chronicles 7:14, "If my people, which are called by my name, shall humble themselves, and pray, and seek my face, and turn from their wicked ways; then will I hear from heaven, and will forgive their sin, and will heal their land." Indulgences in sin by the inhabitants bring destruction to the land.

This is a promise thrown out to every nation on earth at every time in history—and to every individual also. God is trustworthy, whether you trust Him or not. He is totally trustworthy; there is no shadow of turning with Him. Those who serve Him in spirit and in truth find Him steadfast. There is no wavering. In Psalm 117, the psalmist declares his gratitude publicly toward his faithful God. "Praise the Lord, all ye nations: praise him, all ye people. For His merciful kindness is great toward us: and the truth of the Lord endureth forever. Praise the Lord."

Christ Our Peace

Should there ever be a miserable Christian? Only if he wanders from the assurances in the Word of God. Isaiah 32:17 states, "And the work of righteousness shall be peace; and the effect of righteousness quietness and assurance for ever." This is the guarantee laid out for the Christian's life. Hers is not a hit-and-miss proposition. It is a good life, one of quietness and peace. What more can a person ask for in his sojourn down here on earth? Not much more. We are given a program guaranteed to get the best results, yet we look elsewhere, continuing to search. The liberals clamour to water down the Christian doctrine in order to cater to the masses. They claim that rigidity is not an essential element in serving God, saying that we may loosen up a little, dabble a little and so on.

In Isaiah 32:6, such a one is called out and exposed. "For the vile person will speak villainy, and his heart will work inequity, to practice hypocrisy, and to utter error against the Lord, to make empty the soul of the hungry, and he will cause the drink of the thirsty to fail." The liberal person has nothing to give; in fact, he empties what is already there. A liberal Christian leader is simply the blind leading the blind. Watch out for this type of person. Shun him, because he is dangerous. When a person makes light of the Word of God and discounts it, that person is a deceiver, a rogue and a dangerous person to be around. He is capable of robbing you of your birthright, your soul's salvation.

Generally a bill of deception has been sold us and we are paying for it. We have now entered a state of decadence, dissolute in morals; we have broken free from our moorings of moral rectitude and are heading into a disconsolate realm. This is our plight. We are already into the rapids; there is no turning back. It is so sad that I feel it. As a matter fact, we have been heading toward the rapids since sin entered the world. The difference is that today we have a greater sense of freedom to flaunt our depravity, and we do it with a great deal more sophistication. We literally create the atmosphere to hide our depravity. All is only a façade. Nevertheless, our sins are still within us. They are only covered with seeming respectability. Look at the sinners go! Most are heading to the abyss with no inclination that it is very close.

Jesus in His day, likened a certain sect to a "whited Sepulchre, full of dead men's bones" (Matthew 23:27). Such a sepulchre is fancy-looking on the outside, but within, it stinks. We live and say we have no sin or that there is no such thing as sin, and we simply bury our heads in the sand and think we will not be held responsible. That is a clever move. That we may remain unaware of our sinfulness is one of the deadliest lies we could have ingested. There is neither help nor hope for the person who is unaware of his sinfulness.

If the fire is raging around you and you cannot feel the heat, then the rescuers cannot get you out. The frog in the boiling water does not know when to jump out of the pot because it does not feel the heat.. May God burden us with our sins to the point where we run to Him for cleansing? May we see ourselves as unclean before a holy God.

If we could see our sins as a crime against the holy God, then we would be moved to make amends. Until we reach that stage in life where we see ourselves in light of a Holy God, we might not take steps to remedy the situation. Many preteens who have not committed any gross sins have come to that realization that they need cleansing from their sins. The reason is that they have been made aware of their sinfulness in light of the Gospel and the need to be forgiven is made clear by a teacher or a preacher. Everyone, big or small, Jew or Gentile, needs to be forgiven or cleansed from sin.

The Righteous Sinner Abounds Today

After church one Sunday morning, I saw a young man wearing a certain type of headgear which identified him with another religion and I asked him if he were converted to Christianity. His reply was "I have just come here to lend my support." How very kind of that young man to leave his church or whatever he calls his house of worship to come to our church to lend his support. I spoke earlier of the our respectability. We have no need of Christ, but we will not fight against Him either. After all, He is innocuous and can do no harm.

Some people speak ill of Christ and despise Him as God, but they come to present an offering nevertheless. Malachi 1:10 reads, "I have no pleasure in you, saith the Lord of Hosts, neither will I accept an offering at your hand." How fitting a description when Jesus told the Pharisees that they were like whited sepulchre, full of dead men's bones. We do not need any moral support from the ungodly. We do not.

All of us, some more so than others, have fallen away from the rectitude that would make us worthy of commendation in one way or another. This is a fact that need not be rubbed in. It is a truism. We have all fallen short of what we would like to be, and we know it. We need to get right with our Maker. He is waiting and calling, but we are not listening.

"Some other time, perhaps," we say. For every Christian reading this, I urge you to stand tall and be strong in the power of His might. Do not go about accepting sympathies from the ungodly as though we were without help.

In today's society with its sophistication and wealth, *sin* is a word that has practically fallen out of use. Even many preachers rarely use the word. As a matter fact, one preacher I knew (who is now dead) once said that the word *sin* is not profitable for the Christian enterprise. His philosophy was, "You are good and I am good." Sin, therefore, is a disruptive term. Such a preacher would invite you to his service on the terms that you can come as you are and be assured that your equilibrium will not be disturbed. You come just as you are, and you will leave just as you came. That was his deal.

Until we are disturbed by the Word of God, it can do us no good. It is declared in the Holy Book that all our righteousness is as filthy rags in the sight of God. There is nothing we can do to gain an interest in the work of God. We must come only as a sinner needing forgiveness by the finished work. The cross is the symbol demonstrating the accomplished work of redeeming humankind to our Maker.

"It is finished," Christ cried out on the cross before he gave up the Ghost. He poured out His life as He said He would to redeem us from our sins. It was part of the plan of God since the foundation of the world. It represented part of the blueprint, if you will. It was not something concocted as a contingent plan after humankind sinned, but instead it was part of the plan long before. Understand that to be so. Some would teach that it was a miscarriage of justice and that Christ was wrongfully convicted and crucified. In such a case, we are saying that God was caught off guard, that He could not foresee what was coming. There goes His sovereignty down the tube. Not so, not so. He is sovereign and controls all things.

Find the Hand of God

Minnie Louise Haskins wrote the following:

> I asked the man at the gate to give me a light

> That I might go out into the darkness
> And he replied; go take the hand of God
> That shall be to thee better than the light
> And safer than a known way
> So I went out and found the hand of God
> He led me toward the hills and into the lone east.

God is always taking us eastward where the sun rises when we find and place our hands in His. That is His plan for us, a bright future. Without the hand of God holding ours, we walk in eternal darkness and on an unknown path. Security, then, is to walk with God. It is likened unto a child holding his father's hand and walking through a cornfield with the corn stalks way above the child's head, yet he is not in the least perturbed or scared. His father is holding his hand, and that is all that matters to the child. Security is present. We in turn are only secure when the Lord holds our hand.

We are still on the subject of sin and the consequences of sin. The consequence of sin is death and the judgement. Those are the two things that await humanity.

Jonathan Edwards writes: in "Hand of God"

> Every natural man that hears of Hell flatters himself that he shall escape it,
> He depends upon himself for his own security,
> He flatters himself in what he has done,
> What he is now doing and what he intends to do.

Salvation is not about doing but about what has been done by Christ for us. All our righteousness is like filthy rags in God's sight. Isaiah 64:6. We can only do acceptable works after we have first submitted to Christ.

How shall we escape then if we neglect so great a salvation? None can. The only escape route is through the narrow gate. That gate is the Lord Jesus Christ.

A person's very ability to distort, deface, debase and kick against the truth makes him or her a responsible person. You might say you are not responsible for distorting the truth and not believing anything—"I am free to do whatever I feel like doing without any dire consequences"—but you are woefully wrong. We are accountable, and as such we are responsible for all our actions. The idea that one is not responsible and therefore free to do as one pleases is an entirely false notion. There is falsity all around us. In my long life, I have seen and experienced so much of it that I know I must not trust anyone implicitly. Humankind was created—and here I reiterate—to worship God, Jehovah God the Creator, and any deviation from this command leads us away from the truth. It's simple: if we do not believe and adhere to this dogma, then we have swallowed a lie and the accompanying consequence will be dire and irreversible.

Perhaps at this point you are bored with *What's Up?* Since you did not buy a book to hear a sermon. But I implore you, my friend, to take it in, as this just might be your last sermon before you are called to enter His presence. The person who does not embrace the truth of God and acknowledge a judgement is described in Psalm 14:1: "The fool hath said in his heart, there is no God. They are corrupt, they have done abominable works, there is none that doeth good." People like this claim to be wise, but they are fools. It is only fools who say there is no God. You have got to be a fool to think after all the declaration of the heavens and earth that there is no Designer. "The heavens declare the glory of God; and the firmament showeth His handy work" (Psalm 19:1). These who cannot see have willfully cast God from their thoughts. It has to be that they are willfully ignorant and therefore refuse to see.

His Glory Will Not Be Denied Him

John Bunyan wrote, "Whether to heaven or Hell you bend, God will have glory in the end." Nothing that humankind does can thwart the plan of God. He will be honoured in the end. In the end we will see how intelligent those who claim that there is no God are, or how they are intelligent by the way they take. I have a dear brother in the Lord who would give as a reply, "How about that!" I would say the same here, brothers and sisters: how about that! Human beings cannot and will not thwart God's plan, period. His truth marches on regardless of the barking dogs. There are many things in life that are of little consequence in the scheme of things and carry little or no weight, but other matters are weightier—and this is one of those very weighty matters. We will be held accountable whether we believe it or not. Let us get a hold of this fact before it is forever too late.

People have gone to great lengths to educate or to bring to people the Gospel of Jesus Christ. Many great and noble individuals have given up their wealth and profession to spread the Gospel in the hope of lifting the falsehood and the lies perpetrated by the Devil. We cite here such men as Dr. David Livingstone, who left his family in Scotland to live and evangelize the Africans, and men like Count Nikolaus Ludwig von Zinzendorf, a German who gave his wealth to spread the Gospel in the West Indies. In the eyes of the world, these men were fools, literally wasting their lives. Dr. David Livingstone had a brother who was a medical doctor also but who has ever heard of him? whereas David Livingstone remains a household name.

One day, Count Zinzendorf visited a museum in Britain and saw the figure of Christ hanging on the cross and the caption underneath: "I have done this for you. What have you done for me?" The count was deeply moved and convicted of his inaction in the Lord's vineyard. From that point on, he used his wealth to start the Moravian movement. That church is still going strong. I visited a crusade at a Moravian church in St. Elizabeth, Jamaica when I did some evangelical work in 2015. Twelve people came forward when the altar call was given that night.

It was in that same church that all my ten siblings and I was christened. It was there that our mother and father were saved also, although that occurred when they were much older. The famous John Wesley who travelled to the United States to preach to the Native Americans was not even converted until he met a group of Moravians on a ship in distress at sea as he returned to England on one of his voyages. The ship was floundering in a storm and Wesley was panic-stricken and thought they would die. Judging by his reaction to imminent death, he knew he was not ready to die. In the midst of all this, there were some Moravians who were singing and praising God. God was truly their Father. Knowing that fact, they entrusted their lives to Him. Wesley had an encounter with these brethren and found Christ for the first time. A preacher not saved! That is as common as the sighting of a flying saucer. Death to the Christian is only a gateway from this life to the next; a glorious life with Christ.

The two preachers I mentioned are real men who gave their lives for a cause they knew was worthy of their time. They could not rest until they had discharged their responsibility to their fellow human beings. Every person needs to hear the good news of salvation, and every person who hears will be held accountable if he or she rejects it. These people who served in foreign lands are possessors of eternal life themselves, as they literally gave their lives to enlighten and enrich the lives of countless others through the liberating news of the Gospel. There are many, far too many, who belittle the Word and the messengers of the Word. They denigrate it and relegate it to nought, but in the end they will cry out, as every person will, "Lord, be merciful"—but for some it will be too late, they would have waited too long.

Right now there is a great prayer meeting going on in Hell. People are crying out for God's mercy, but it is too late. In fact it is forever too late for these people, as God's mercy is gone and His judgement has come. You, who are reading this, please do not make that mistake; do not let pride rob you of your rightful place in the Kingdom of God. Repent and turn to Him for forgiveness. It is His good pleasure to give you the kingdom. Luke 12:32 reads, "Fear not, little flock; for it is your Father's good pleasure to give you the kingdom." I personally love to use the word *relax* when speaking to my kids or my wife. Everything is going to be all right, there is no need to worry.

Is it so that we do not have to fight for anything, even to get into the kingdom? Yes, it is so, as it is our Father's good pleasure to hand it over. We all have our own key to our mansions. That is something else, my dear brothers and sisters; that is something else altogether. There are those keys awaiting us upon arrival. How marvellous is that feeling?

Although I was brought up in the church as a child, I drifted away in my teenage years. When I was saved as a young man of 22, I had many worldly friends, many of whom thought I was only moving up in society by aligning myself with the church. But, my friend, thank God, my conversion was real. Every day with Jesus is sweeter than the day before. My conversion was over 50 years ago. I am learning to trust Him more and more.

While I was in Jamaica on my mission trip in the summer of 2015, I witnessed to two men on one occasion. I entered the home where they were standing outside talking. I knew the father of one of the men; as a matter fact, his dad worked for my dad for many years as I grew up. The last time I saw his father, he said he regretted leaving my father's employ. Anyway, when I told him that I had been serving the Lord for over 50 years, he was quite surprised and asked, "And you are still serving Him?" I replied with a question myself. I said, "If you have a business and it is prosperous, would you give it up?" Of course he would not. I am now in the most comfortable position I have ever been in, period. I am happy and settled. I could be likened to an old oak tree with deep taproots and sturdy branches whose limbs barely bend in the breeze.

The Scriptures remain as attractive and intriguing to me today as they were on the day that I was saved. I wanted to know them as well as other Christians do—and why not? I had access to the Word, and my desire for it grew and grew. As a result of studying the Word, I grew as a branch feeding from a fertile vine. The Word of God is literally my life support. I do not understand how anyone who has a connection with Christ could have no appetite for the Word. I have watched as many who were saved the same time as I was faded away. They faded because the Word was not as important to them as other things, I am sure. Not many from my class are still standing. An involvement with the church is crucial to maintaining contact with the kingdom. I have had many assignments in the Church from Sunday school Superintendent to Missions Committee Chairman.

I am on my fourth Bible today as I write these words; the others have been tattered and worn because of use. The Word of God is indeed an inexhaustible treasure. For those of us who believe, it is the power of God unto salvation. There is a reality that rings stronger and truer every day to the Christian when the Holy Spirit bears witness with a child of God that he or she is a son or daughter of God. I would relinquish everything to see the conversion of a person's soul. The joy on a person's face after he or she has received salvation is a sight to behold. A soul that was once held captive in Satan's grip and is now set free is indeed a miracle.

Upon salvation, the person who once abideth in death is now made alive in Christ Jesus. He or she has been quickened or made alive, as the Bible says who once was dead in trespasses and sin. Who can understand it except the person who has experienced the transformation? That is the reason the fact of Christ's living within cannot be reasoned away. The new birth is experiential and real. The Holy Spirit bears witness simultaneously with our spirit that we are the children of God. Who are these who would dare say otherwise but the agents of Satan? We are now secure in Christ, and to us that is all that matters. Those who are kept by God are well-kept; that is security personified.

Land, houses, money in the bank, stocks and bonds, jewellery and so on are the things that the world seeks security in, but what they offer is far from security. While some people who seek such things, many of them perhaps, live miserly lives to accumulate these so-called valuable possessions, the quality of their lives is diminished. Many of these people's values are misplaced. When I distributed aromatherapy oils, I was hard-pressed to find a wealthy person who would spend $300 on a lamp and some oil that would do him or her a world of good. Why, wealthy people would sooner spend hundreds of dollars to change the oil in their car and whatnot than to take care of their own bodies properly. Certainly, external show is better than inward strength. It is an attitude with us human beings; our values are misplaced, placed in the wrong things, things with diminishing value most of the time.

chapter 12

A TRAGEDY

The most unfortunate thing in the entire world and in the course of humankind's existence is that the Light has come into the world and yet the majority of humanity still gropes in darkness.

A person would not walk in darkness if he or she trusted in Jesus Christ who is the light of the world. When this is known, witnessed and scrutinized and yet no action is taken, it is sad, to say the least. That a person would wander off into the dark of night without a light is madness, yet some do exactly that every day although a light is available.

D. L. Moody, an American evangelist, said on his deathbed, "This is my triumph, this is my coronation day! It is glorious." He got a glimpse of his eternal home and saw that the glory of it outweighed any hardship or suffering he endured down here. He rejoiced even in his sick and dying body. His expectation was made a reality. About to reap his rewards, he was now ecstatic.

Whether we declare those words or not, every dying Christian can echo the sentiment. The reality will not be anything short of our expectations; as a matter fact, it is far beyond anything we can imagine. Paul states in Ephesians 3:20, "Now unto Him that is able to do exceeding abundantly above all that we ask or think, according to the power that worketh in us." We cannot imagine anything as beautiful and as glorious as what awaits us as the redeemed of the Lord. It exceeds anything we know here on earth that we would be in awe of. Heaven is real. It is a prepared place for a redeemed people.

The man or woman who has this assurance of eternal life is the same man or woman who believes implicitly that there is one God and no other. He or she cannot waver by an iota in knowing that the God we serve has no rival. He is absolute, and what is written about Him is the absolute truth. There is but one God and there is but one absolute truth. Those who claim that all roads lead to Heaven are imposters and deceivers. They are not possessors of eternal life. Pluralism can only be held if we reject absolute truth. That doctrine is literally linking an ox to an ass to plough a field. It cannot and must not be done. The ass will drag the ox off course every time.

Those who preach that there are other gods and that Jehovah will wink at us for so believing are false prophets and deceivers. These are heretical or spurious doctrines designed to keep us out of Heaven and shunt us to Hell instead. There is no nearness as far as the mark is concerned. We either hit it right on or we miss it and are lost forever. The angle of re-entry of a spacecraft into the Earth's atmosphere is perfectly calculated. Otherwise, the craft will burn up or float off into space. An astronaut cannot miss that angle upon re-entry; it has to be dead-on. Those who command space crafts are not novices; they are experts. They do not leave Earth with limited knowledge and hope to take a chance at landing the craft after their mission. They are proficient to the nth degree.

The Christian better have the expert on his craft or else he could have a sharp re-entry, burning up or slipping away into outer darkness. If Christ is not his guide and pilot, then he is in for a rude awakening; he is headed to the furnace. The unbeliever who thinks that all these fanciful notions are in our heads will be shocked when their place turns out to be just the one described in the Judeo-Christian Book. We all have a destination whether we will live or die. We will all keep two appointments: death and the Judgement. These are two appointments that are unavoidable, inevitable. We would do well to acknowledge them now. The sooner we acknowledge them, the sooner we will prepare to meet them.

As I witness, I come across some people who do not want to hear of death. One man said to me, "Tell me about life, not death." Even the person going into battle not knowing how he or she will fare is willing to prepare him or herself for a good outcome, and yet we who are free to investigate and turn from our sins and unto the Saviour would rather wait and see. A great king was dying when his clown, or his jester, came in to see him and said, "Your Majesty, you are going on a journey. Have you made any preparation for that journey?" The answer was no. Then said the clown, "You are a greater fool than I am; you can keep that present that you promised me."

The clown was so good at entertaining the king by making a fool of himself, that the king felt that there could not be a greater fool and promised him that if he could find a greater fool than himself he (the king) would give him a great reward. Ah, my friend, we cannot judge a book by the cover. Here was a man who was good at his job and who fooled the crowd, concealing his true identity. Clowning around for the king was his job and not his life. He had a life to live, and he lived it in view of eternity. That is wisdom, my friend. Many of us are doing just that—clowning around. It will do us little good in the end. It will be dismal for many of us who do not see the lateness of the hour.

Not knowing that we are on a journey puts us squarely in the camp of the foolish. Death is scary, but we experience it often. It is around us every day. Given this fact, we should face death head-on. We should know what lies ahead and in this be prepared for when it overtakes us. A person is afraid to speak of death because he is not ready to die. No one can be ready to die outside of Jesus Christ, as He is the only one who can get us ready to meet that enemy. He has the keys of death and Hell. He can close the doors to those monsters so they cannot get at us.

"The man that wonders out of the way of understanding shall remain in the congregation of the dead" (Proverbs 21:16). Where are you today, my friend? Are you embracing the Truth, which inevitably will lead you to eternal life, or are you still skeptical of the Truth? Christ has not promised, nor is He now promising, eternal life, but He possesses eternal life and will hand it to whomsoever will ask for it. He is God and does whatsoever He wills. Even now He is crying, "Come to me all ye that labour and are heavy laden and I will give you rest" (Matthew 11:28). Rest for your weary soul, my friend, is near—real rest. Consider the Great Creator crying with a loud voice, saying, "Come! And I will give you rest." He offers rest for the weary soul that is longing for comfort and security, longing for serenity and approbation. He comforts totally with specialized security. This is our Lord.

We must be very important if He has so great an interest in us. It is so, my friend. The great God of the universe desires to have fellowship with us and delights in us when we submit to His authority. We must know that in spite of His desire to have fellowship with us, He is a self-sustaining God. He has existed long before we were created and He will exist without those who choose not to embrace His love. It is not He that will suffer loss; it is us who will.

We all seem to say we are seeking the best for ourselves, but is that really so? That is not true. We might know what is good, but we do not pursue it. For the most part, many would rather remain ignorant of many things than to face up to the truths. Some simply do not want to know what the noise is all about. They are not curious. Sitting at a table with a co-worker one day eating, I spoke to him about the Gospel. His remark was "I did not come to discuss religion. I want to enjoy my meal." He said that he wanted to enjoy his meal, and he did enjoy it, I am sure. I have come across him regularly and we greet each other. I see him as a miserable and pathetic man, heading nowhere in particular. He is just biding his time before making his exit. I pray that God will bring him the light before he makes his exit.

Still Loving This World in Death

Many know that there are a few rich people who have paid to keep their dead bodies in freezers with the hope that if scientists at some point in the future are able to find a way to inject new life, they will be resurrected or resuscitated. So very dear life is to these people, yet while they lived, they neglected the most precious of all gifts—and what's more, it was free. They have left large sums of money as endowment to pay for their trite fantasies. These people were likely astute businesspeople who made a lot of money and yet knew not that eternal life was available after this life—and gratis at that. Those same people would tell you that they were too busy or that they did not mix business and religion so as to dismiss you if you tried to witness to them. What would they not mix right now if they had another chance?

Some do not mind being consigned to Hell, they will tell you, because most of their friends will be there. Quite some consolation to the foolish soul, isn't it? Have you ever imagined anyone trying to save someone else in a whirlpool after they both fall in? They expend all their energy trying to save themselves. In Hell, everyone will be so tormented that they will not be quiet for a single moment of the eternity they have to spend there. They will not know who their neighbours are. If they could get comfortable long enough to see who was next to them, they might be surprised to see that so and so is there too. The only comfort these people might have in Hell is to know that so-and-so who pretended all along that he or she belonged to God was now their neighbour.

Think of it: you cannot wear clothes in Hell because the fire will burn it off, and you have to dance in your bare feet since your shoes will be burnt off also. The media gives us a mental image when there is an inferno, saying it is living hell. The reporters may not believe in Hell, yet they know what it is like already. Of course they know. The image is imbedded in us. Eternity has been planted in us; it is only that we erase it conveniently. Some cars have a voice recording talking to us when we do not fasten our seat belts, but after a time we get disgusted with it and disconnect it. Such is our nature. We are free agents and will do as we please.

The Lord of Heaven Himself has pledged that we can have eternal life just by asking for it. The provision has been ratified on Calvary's cross. Our gift is already paid for; it is ready for pickup, my friend. Any time night or day, at home or in the field, we can have it. I hope you will pick up yours today. Many people have only come to accept this truth after exhausting their resources and time in labouring to disprove the authenticity of the existence of Christ. They will gladly or readily believe other historical facts, but when it comes to spiritual matters, well, they cannot grasp or will not be coaxed to accept those. This I call the most unfortunate tragedy. The light, the truth, and the peace are all accessible, but still we keep searching.

The Gospel, says Jerry Bridges, "Is not only the most important message in all of history, it is the only essential message in all of history." This statement affirms that all other messages—and we get many of them each day, on the billboards, on the streets and in the media—take second place to the glorious news of the Gospel. The Gospel is the only message that can give the comfort and security that we seek. Just as Christ said in John 16:24, "Ask, and ye shall receive that your joy may be full." Is it that easy and accessible? Ask.

Every person dreams of happiness and living a life of eternal bliss, but people also like their sins. Some revel in their sins for some time and then turn, but others die while they revel, not getting the chance to turn. We do not know the minute or the hour we shall go in death or when the Lord shall come, so we are admonished to be ready. We must keep our lamps trimmed and burning; that is the watchword. The Light has come, but we are still living in darkness. How very unfortunate; how very sad is this reality. Will you turn today and dwell in the light?

The Christian is maligned and shunned in our society, especially as sin and immorality increases. Our fellow citizens decry us, but were it not for the Christians, who are the salt of the earth, the preservative if you will; the wrath of God would be poured out already in its fullest measure. Whatever restraints are left in our society today are in place because God's Word resides in the hearts of many.

A total rottenness and an unmitigated disaster will overrun our times and societies when the Christians are removed from their places and spheres of influence. The world will not know our worth until then. That time is coming, I dare say. To add to the urgency of this message, it is fast approaching, even at the door. To what advantage is it to you to wait to accept Christ as your Saviour? There is none. The graveyards are full of men and women who thought they had time. They left much unfinished business in their lives because they had plans. Death was not part of their thinking. Personally, I live on the edge. It used to be that I brought all my affairs up-to-date when I planned to take a plane trip but now I keep things relevant from day to day. I keep short accounts. Death is ever before me as more and more I have less and less use for this sinful place called earth.

To live safely and securely, we would be well served to live with all our accounts with humankind and God up-to-date. Do not live in such a manner that you are left begging for a few more days. Be ready; be ready to go when death comes. There are many men and women like myself in their seventies who have gotten their allotted time here on earth, and yet when death knocks, they hesitate, asking for a few more months or years. How very careless it is to live our lives while leaving things in an unfinished state. It is rather odd, but it is true, and without a doubt, that the things that are worthwhile and wholesome are always a hard sell to the public. People have a built-in resistance to accepting healthy and worthwhile ideologies. Often people are left adhering to the lies and embracing the destructive ways instead. We have evidence of this all around us. Healthy lifestyles have to be forced onto the public, whereas taking the easy and destructive route is natural. It is easy.

Our Guilt Is Already Established in High Places

When you come to Jesus asking for forgiveness, you will not have to prove your guilt. You will be taken at your word as soon as you verbalize your position. If you pray, "Lord Jesus, I confess that I have no standing before You. I am a sinner asking for forgiveness, please forgive me," it will be done as you asked. There used to be an ad by a certain company promoting a particular product that ran like this. "You can pass up [our product] now and pay for the consequence of losing an engine later." Such a cost is inconsequential in light of the value of your soul. If you pass up the opportunity to repent, you will have lost everything.

There are a lot of big gamblers in the world, but to take a chance with your soul makes you the most reckless of all gamblers. Do not chance it. There is too much evidence to support the claim that God exists and that He is coming again. ``It is a fearful thing to fall into the hands of the living God.`` Hebrews. 10:31.

A man will not profit if he or she gains the whole world and loses his soul. A soul is the most valuable of all possessions; please do not gamble with it. Bow now to Christ, or else you will bow later—but then it will be forever too late. God's Word is weightier than all the planets, galaxies and stars, and whatever else you can imagine, put together. It will not be diminished by anyone, however important that individual thinks he or she is. God's Word will not be voided by anyone.

Get this sentence—do not gloss over it—because it will come back to haunt you for all eternity if you do not: "For it is written, As I live saith the Lord, every knee shall bow to me, and every tongue shall confess to God" (Romans 14:11). I must admit that as I typed this passage of Scripture, I shuddered at the statement. Having been saved so long now, I know the teachings of the Bible very well, but to hear the Lord Himself speak has a humbling effect on me. I am weakened by just looking at these words. It was not an audible voice that I hear, yet it has its effect. The words reach into the inner parts of my being. I know them to be true now as I did the first time I heard or read them. God has spoken; no one will void His Word.

In the natural realm, a person can disagree with his leader and even leave his country in protest. People can even band together to depose their leader. The case with Jesus is that He is not affected by our opinions and actions. We either fall in or fall out—it is up to us—but His authority and power is unaffected and undiminished, pure and simple. He is the anvil on which all hammers are crushed. He is the sun that melts the butter and hardens the clay. Choose wisely and decide whose side, Christ's or the Devil's, you would rather be on.

Who Will Be Exempted?

Every knee will bow and every tongue will confess that He is Lord. What are the implications here? *Every* means just that: every one. That statement is all-encompassing; it takes into account everybody. There will be big bodies (600-pound bodies), small bodies (50-pound bodies), short bodies, tall bodies, bodies with numerous post nominals, and bodies with no learning whatsoever. There will be lazy bodies, swift bodies, slow bodies, poor bodies and rich bodies. There will be a gathering of the bodies for bowing, what a day of bowing that will be.

It will not be like the days of Nebuchadnezzar, when some refused to bow to him. This time, we will have no choice. It will be an automatic and all-encompassing event. This time there will be no exceptions. Every person will be fitted with a good pair of knees for this colossal event. A lot of these bodies have already bowed and are bowing every day, but those who are still resisting, some with rather stiff knees, they, perhaps for the first time in a long, long time, will be bending at the appearing of the Lord Jesus Christ. It will be interesting to see how flexible those joints will become once they get a glimpse of the Crucified One. It will be so, regardless of your thoughts or mine on the matter. The Lord has spoken it, and that is why it will be.

Bowing the knee to the Savour is a natural thing to the redeemed. So compelling it is that one man's story is hilarious. The story is told of a soldier who every morning was seen by his roommate looking for his boots under the bed. The mate then asked, "Jack, why don't you leave the boots somewhere in sight where you can get them easily in the morning?" "Well," answered Jack, "while I am down on my knees looking for the boots, I just stay down and pray." Jack had devised a plan that compelled him to pray. This soldier knew the value of connecting with his Father and did not want to miss an opportunity, so he devised a strategy to ensure that such would happen.

The Christian knowing that the greatest need of the heart is to connect with his Maker, grasps every opportunity to keep in touch. Christ succinctly stated that He is the Vine and we are the branches and that we will have to abide in the Vine to keep relevant and productive. We know that our strength comes from this connection. All things come from the Source. We would do well to keep connected.

Many times we try to intervene in God's plan for our lives and we plan our own affairs with striving and worrying, demonstrating by so doing our lack of faith. We learn to relax in Him at times, such as when we come to the end of our rope and recognize our helplessness. It is only during that time that we seem to be able to rely on and trust Him totally. He should be our peace and guide from day to day in good times and bad. We should learn to abide in Him totally. He desires more than anything else to have fellowship with us. Let us join Him at the table.

chapter 13

WHO SHOULD READ THE BIBLE?

Just who should read the Bible? The answer to this question may seem quite easy to the ordinary person, but in today's complex society, the answer would be quite divided, with perhaps half the population taking one side or the other. There are perhaps as many reasons for reading the Bible as for not reading it. The Bible, which is the Word of God, is literally God speaking to us. When we read the Bible, we have the mind of God revealed to us and the condition and destiny of humankind laid bare before us. Given the value and the riches, or should I say treasures, encased in the pages of the Bible, I recommend that every sane person should read it, those who have the chance to do so. In some homes the Bible is not read, and for different reasons, some of which are as follows:

- The religion of the home prohibits it, since the Bible contradicts the teachings of their particular religion.
- The people flatly deny its message as unrealistic and farfetched.
- The people simply feel that they are much too intelligent to adhere to the teachings of tradition.
- The people say the Bible is human-influenced and written like any other book.

From my experience, some see the Bible as a dangerous book, influencing and captivating the minds of their most valuable possessions, their children.

The Bible has basically four thrusts:

1. It is a history of humankind.
2. It is prophetic, having foretold of things that have come and of things that are to come.
3. It reads as current news. Yes, it is abreast of things happening right now.
4. It lays out the future of the world and the future of humankind.

Who would not want to read a book that is so valuable? Well, I would answer, "Nobody!"

The Bible is greatly despised nevertheless. People everywhere are curious to know what their future holds and will pay grand sums to find out, but of course they cannot be told the truth by any soothsayer or fortune-teller. There is only one book that can make accurate predictions, and that is the Bible. Its pages are full of accurate predictions made hundreds, sometimes thousands, of years before the events happened.

Many children, however, are brought up without the knowledge of the most important guidance manual of all and live in a delusionary world where there are no absolutes. Without the teachings of the Bible, these people, at death, will perish eternally. Sad, isn't it?

I read recently where the police department of Houston, Texas, issued a leaflet giving rules for raising lawless children, as follows:

1. Begin in infancy to give the child everything he wants.
2. When he picks up bad words, laugh at him. This will make him think he is cute.
3. Never give him any spiritual training. Wait until he is 21, and then let him decide.
4. Avoid use of the word *wrong*. If you use it, your child may develop a guilt complex.
5. Pick up everything he leaves lying around – books, shoes and clothes.
6. Let him read any printed material he can get his hands on.
7. Quarrel frequently in the presence of your children.

8.   Give a child all the spending money he wants.

It is interesting to note here that in today's society of conspicuous consumerism, many parents spoil their children by doing for them too much that they should do for themselves and allowing them free reins in the name of love. In the end, these parents are contributing to lawlessness, selfishness and dependence in place of godliness, self-sufficiency and fruitfulness. Our priorities have been turned upside down. We now have the cart before the horse. Even in Christian homes, many parents are not willing to separate their children from the activities of the outside world. They indulge them in many of the ungodly things as though these things were the norm. We Christians are called to be separate. In this, we must obey.

The children of some parents might be denied access to the Word of God. These people, once they reach adulthood, would be wise to investigate its pages. A German professor, a Christian man, once told me and my fellow students in a class that he was told that every educated person should read the Bible, saying that it contains a great deal of history in addition to its spiritual contents. This professor said that every person would be better off knowing its contents. Actually, to be educated, one must be versed in Bible truths. It is from the Bible that wisdom and knowledge are derived. How could anyone not be versed in such truths unless one were mentally handicapped? Without some of us realizing it, our " Common Law" is derived from its pages.

There is no other book that has the array of wisdom, guidance and governance that the Bible has. It is there that equality is taught. Racism is frowned upon and gender equality is proclaimed and reinforced. The Bible as the only book could be a survival kit. If we follow its directions and instructions, we will land safely in the haven of rest.

Commodore Matthew Fontaine Maury (1808–1873) of Richmond, Virginia, USA, was on his sickbed and called his daughter to read the Bible to him. She chose Psalm 8, which includes verse 8, "Whatsoever passeth through the paths of the sea." When the commodore heard "the paths of the sea", he repeated the line several times and then said that when he got out of bed, he would find those paths. Having begun his deep-sea sounding as soon as he was strong enough, he found that ridges extend from the New York coast to England. He made charts for ships to sail one path when travelling to England and another path when returning. It was in the 19th century that he discovered the paths, thereby confirming that statement of the Bible as fact. Can the skeptics dispute this? They have tried, but history is against them. There is a monument erected in Maury's honour in Richmond with a plaque describing the history of this discovery.

Consider the great river that runs in the sea that keeps its own water separated from the seawater. That great river runs through the sea as though it had banks, the fresh water and the saltwater not mixing, the warm and cold not fusing. That great river is the Gulf Stream. Consider this great mystery, but then still some would say there is no Designer. It was only recently that scientists discover a black hole that sucks up stars, but the Bible speaks of such a thing. The scientists thought that they had made a startling discovery, but there it is written clearly in the book of Jude. This description is not delineating a scene or pointing out the mysteries of the universe but pronouncing a verdict on the ungodly, the sinners and the God rejecters. It reads, "Raging waves of the sea, foaming out their own shame; wondering stars, to whom is reserved the blackness of darkness forever" (Jude 12–13). This is an indictment on the person who does not have the covering of the blood of Christ on his or her life. It does not get any darker than that, my friend.

The Bible is foundational and helps to develop a person's character even when a person does not delve into its deeper truths. The books of Proverbs and Ecclesiastes are sufficient to assuage the soul. Therefore, for the person who wants to develop normally, with personable behaviours, the words from the Book are just what are necessary. From the Bible, one develops functionality and stability, which propel people further than any other book they can read. The Bible is truly the basis for all knowledge. The laws of the Western world have their roots in the Bible. In court we swear by the Bible, and yet we think it unhealthy as a textbook in schools and discard it at every opportunity we get. How very hypocritical we are. Again I will reiterate that we are irrational beings. Like the monkey, we will eat the banana skin and discard the banana.

Who can deny the truths of these words I have penned? No one, except those who dwell in the congregation of the dead. Every adult owes it to himself to own a Bible and investigate its truths. Within its pages are the treasures of life. I am bewildered at the thought that for lack of knowledge, many are perishing. Eternal life is within their grasp; nevertheless, they go a hungering and thirsting, never to be quenched and satisfied. I will mention here again that the great tragedy is that light has come but we still grope in the darkness. The living water is available, but we go thirsty. There is a greater power at work in such lives.

Right here in Canada are some of the darkest places on earth. People are blind to the truths of God's Word. Many have cast it off completely. If they do believe in God, they give Him last place on their list. How very unfortunate. Men and women stand up as honourable members of our government and know nothing of God. We sing in our National Anthem that He shall have dominion from sea to sea but we deny Him the privilege of dominating the space from ear to ear.

Lip Service Only Occasionally

Yes, we pay lip service to God, but in essence we are God rejecters. That is the sad state we are in. In the seventies when I worked in a factory, I heard a Polish man say there were more churches in Poland than there were here in Canada. Poland then was under communist rule. We Canadians are busy, much too busy playing with our toys and gadgets, to consider the Word of God. There is certainly nothing more regrettable and disturbing than that. In Hell, souls will cast their eyes upwards and cry, "Dear God, why did not I listen? Why did I allow myself to be deceived by religion or disbelief?" Parents will cry out for depriving or denying their children of that privilege.

For every unbeliever, it would be better that a millstone was hung around his or her neck and that he or she be dropped in the depths of the ocean. It would be better still if that person had never been born. Never will a person who is ushered into Hell be given a second chance to repent, as his or her fate will be forever sealed. At the closing of such a person's eyes in death without the Lord, mercy is gone and the Judgement comes. The time to do anything, as we all know, is during the day when we can see clearly. The time to seek the Lord is while we are alive and can reason. We must not wait until we are on our deathbed, if we ever get that chance.

In Deuteronomy 4:29, it is stated, "But if from thence thou shall seek the Lord thy God, thou shall find Him, if thou seek Him with all thy heart and with all thy soul." From my vantage point, I will tell you that this portion of Scripture is worth its weight in gold. This seeking is worth every effort we can muster. In our searching and seeking, He will make Himself known—and it will be worth it all when we see Him. He will be the pearl of great prize that we heretofore never knew existed.

Do not be fooled; "from thence" is not referring to any other place than where you are now. It is in no way talking of Hell. That is not where you can call from and be heard. How flippantly one who has read these pages will say, "That is your opinion" or "That is your interpretation."

When one begins to doubt established truths, he or she starts to believe the Devil's lies that there are no absolutes. Self-centeredness is at the heart of such thinking and he or she set themselves up as their own god.

My friend, I beg you now, believe the evidence. As the Bible says, there is a cloud of witnesses attesting to the fact of His existence. If the Lord speaks to you now, harden not your heart.

What you give to the Lord, you cannot keep. What He keeps, you cannot lose. Now, that is a deal you would be out of your mind to pass up. Therefore, as a sober-minded person, bow now wherever you are, in spite of your surroundings and your company, and settle the matter as I did so long ago and as many are doing even at this moment.

People everywhere are coming to their senses and recognizing their need of God. It is only today I read in the *Baptist Daily Bread* that a friend visited his friend at his apartment to give him the news of his conversion. As he entered this friend's apartment, he noticed that he was busying himself to leave. The friend asked his guest what it was he wanted. By the look on his guest's face, the man knew it was big news, not ordinary news. When the news was divulged, tears ran down the other friend's face because he had the same news to share. He too had been saved a short while before. Men and women everywhere are seeing the light and are basking in the realization of sins forgiven. At the cross they have their burdens rolled away. There is no greater joy that can infect a person than to know his or her sins are forgiven and that he or she is now reconciled to the Maker. Sins and burden of sin rolled away at the Cross.

There is a little thing within us call pride that would hinder us from gaining this great prize, but we must subdue that voice and let freedom reign. Let freedom reign in your life for the first time. If you are not saved, you might think that you are now free, but that can't be. Your present master cannot liberate you from death. He is hoping and even fighting against you right now. His purpose is that you will not see your need of salvation. The more he keeps you comfortable here, the better it is for him. For he has possessed another soul.

Some of us Christians are branded as arrogant, but I beg to differ. We cannot be arrogant once we have recognized our insufficiency and have bowed to the lordship of Jesus Christ. On the contrary, it is those who refuse to bow that are arrogant. Hubris rules supreme in their lives. In many instances it is the which has prevented them from bowing. Now we get the name-calling right. It is rightly placed. Why is not every person bowing the knee to his or her Maker, as everybody will? The answer is simple: arrogance. "I will not have this man to rule over me" is the cry.

The child who rebels against his or her parents is arrogant. He will not be subjected to their rule. I heard a youth say one day on my bus, "I love my dad, but if he ever put his hand on me, I would kill him." My friend, how terrible is such a statement or a feeling toward ones parent. A child with murder in his heart? The Bible says, "As a man thinketh in his heart, so is he." So it is. They want to be fed and clothed and schooled, but they show no respect. If such minds will think in this way toward their parents, what will they think of God, whom they hear of only vaguely? Proverbs 22:15 tells us, "Foolishness is bound in the heart of a child; but the rod of correction shall drive it far from him." This is the teaching of the Bible. If children are corrected early, then they will not grow up to beat and kill their parents.

Where the home is an ungodly one, one where children are not corrected, they will have no fear of their parents, as anything goes. Can we afford to raise our children like this? Can we plant a garden and not weed out the intruding weeds? We will not get much from that garden if we do not do our due diligence, weeding the garden and fertilizing those plants if we wish to get a good harvest.

On the school bus I would constantly encourage the kids to be courteous and kind to each other and to use words that are edifying, and to discard words that are debasing. How children were brought up can be clearly observed in their behaviours. When some of the children on my bus use profane words, I say, "You cannot use those words on the bus," but they tell me that at home they are permitted to use such words. They learn quickly, though, because once I correct them, they readily refrain from using those words. We are all in the process of learning, whether we are schoolchildren or adults. If we cease to learn, then we are as good as dead.

When I worked in the hardware department of a Canadian Tyre store and I was pulling up to a door in my car to load an item for delivery to a client who needed it urgently, the security guard said to me, "You can't pull up here." I tried to talk to him, but he said, "I don't listen to anyone." After much ado, we sought things out. My point is that we must not say things like "I don't listen to anyone," because it is mighty foolish.

Children today are dictating the terms on which they should be raised. Of course they have the backing of our shadow governments. How will they fare in the end? The future seems bleak to me for such children. Our young are being neglected in favour of wealth. Many mansions are empty and even haunted, devoid of any semblance of love and duty. Parents are away on business trips and the children are hungry for love. On one occasion, I went into the apartment of one of my tenants and found her daughter, who was about 3 years old, crying and begging me to hug her. The parent was there, but she showed no desire of fulfilling her role as a mother. May God help us to prioritize and bring us to see our errors? In the end or near the end, once it is too late, many will see and regret their behaviours. They will throw up their hands and cry out, "Why was I so foolish?" It will be too late then, as the damage has been done.

We cannot live recklessly and walk blindly in this world. We must live with our eyes wide open and with our wits about us at all times. The world is a dangerous place to be in. Those who are oblivious to its vices will be either swept under or run over. We are literally swimming with the sharks. Other people are not afraid to make mincemeat of us. Some who delight in scamming us make it their life's work to do so.

The Devil is the biggest scam artist there is. Many lean on him daily as though he were a friend. He whispers suggestions that, if we reasoned them out, would not make sense, but we listen to and obey him nonetheless. He entices you into doing things that will be to your ruin and demise. He is not your friend. Christ, on the other hand, is the friend of sinners who wants a good end for us. He will not entice you to do wrong. He offers you what is good. You must decide for yourself whether to accept it or not.

Christ is patient and long-suffering. Micah 7:18 lays it out for us: "Who is a God like unto thee, that pardoneth inequity and passeth by the transgressions of the remnant of His heritage? He retaineth not His anger forever, because he deligeth in mercy." The God we serve delights in mercy. He does not dole out mercies sparingly or grudgingly but abundantly. He does it with great pleasure. How about that, my friend? There is simply no other god besides our God; blessed be His name.

If you were applying for a job and had been recommended to work for such a boss, why would you hesitate to apply for a job at his firm? He is not a hard taskmaster. Employees would not be afraid to make mistakes; they would know that they would likely still have a job if they did. How very assuring this kind of boss is. His patience with us makes our load lighter and our burden easier to bear. Our God delights in mercy. Psalm 37:24 states, "Though he fall, he shall not utterly be cast down: for the Lord upholdeth him with His hand." How very gentle is our Father; He picks us up with His hand when we fall. "Never mind, Son; never mind, Daughter." He even soothes our wounds with a gentle touch.

Surprisingly, there is another boss. He pays harsh wages, yet almost everyone is rushing to work for him. He works you to the bone, and his task is rigorous and cruel. His overseers are tyrants and at his place of business exist the harshest conditions. You get few or no breaks from work. The comparison is made here, and the evidence is clear: people prefer a harsh taskmaster over a kind and compassionate one.

Someone to Help with the Load

"Come!" the Lord Jesus Christ cries. "Learn of Me. My burden is easy and My load is light." It might not have occurred to you, but in foreign lands many are pouring into the kingdom daily. Some are hearing of Christ for the first time, and many are coming in from other traditional religions. People everywhere are embracing the truths taught in the Bible. Some of them testify that there was always an emptiness within them and a longing for something better; their former religion could not fill that emptiness they felt. Now they have found joy and satisfaction in the Lord Jesus Christ. They are feasting at the fountain that never runs dry and eating the manna that satisfies.

Just a few hours ago, I stopped in to Canadian Tyre on my way home from work to get two items. The cashier told me that my bill was $19.19. I mentioned to her that in 1919 my dad was 8 years old. I said, "He is gone home now." I went on to say that everyone thinks that when they die there is only one place they are going. I asked this beautiful woman, who was very pleasant and around 60 years old, if she knew of both places. She said no. Just then another customer came up, so I could not keep the conversation going, but before I left the store, I told the cashier that she should find out.

In Angola many years ago when the communists went in to aid the suffering people there, they told the Angolans that there was no God. Years later, the Christians went in and told the Angolans of God. The Angolans said they knew that there was a God, they just did not know His name and they were actually waiting to hear of Him. The big question they asked the missionaries however, was: "What took you so long to come to us?"

If we are made in the image of God, then we have a spiritual connection with Him and instinctively we know that we are not alone. Every person has that witness within, but some put Him out knowingly and wilfully. That is our position here in the West; we have been inundated by His Word and it has now become passé. Humankind was created with that homing instinct, if you will. As St. Augustine said, "Man is restless until he finds his rests in God." We see the restlessness all around us every day.

We know that people are labouring under pressure as they go about their businesses. The burden of life is imprinted on their faces. The stress of life takes its toll. We often hear of people succumbing to strokes or heart attacks.

We must learn to relax and find rest for our souls. Rest is available, but we are simply seeking it in the wrong places and in the wrong things. It is said that while half the world worries about what to eat and cannot sleep, the other half worries about how to spend their money and, as a result, cannot sleep either. If only we were our brother's keeper, we could all have a good night's sleep.

Heaven is our home. We would do well to find the path back. We have lost our way, but a Guide has come to lead us home again. The allure of earth and its pleasures and treasures is keeping many earthbound, even some Christians. The reason is that they are not storing their treasures in Heaven as they should. All that exists here has only a diminishing return. It will all be lost eventually. The real value is in the things we cannot see with the eye. The things we can see and touch are but an illusion and will not last. They are like the mist we see in the morning that vanishes as soon as the sun comes up. The everlasting dimension, which is the most important, is that which is seen by faith only. May God help us to see it clearly?

Not Ready Yet!

In a church service, the pastor asked those who wanted to go to Heaven to raise their hands. All but one man raised their hands. After the service, the pastor went down to greet the congregation and asked this man: "Brother Joe, why didn't you put up your hand? Don't you want to go to Heaven?" "Of course, Pastor, I want to go, but I thought you were taking up a trip now." Too many even in the church are hanging on tenaciously to the things of this earth. They do not seem to see another life as being better and more glorious than this one. They do not want to leave this life now. They may wish to leave it later, perhaps, but they want more time with their things here. The allure of earth has kept too many weighted down. They will not make the flight when the time comes, either. Many are going to miss it, even some of those who thought they had a ticket.

Many years ago when I was a boy, the thatch roof of my grandfather's house caught fire. A ladder was placed at the side of the house with one man on the roof and others handing him buckets of water to douse the fire. The water tank was close by. Everyone was frantically doing what he could to help. One man fell into the tank. Now the problem was multiplied. One man was on the burning roof, and another was drowning in the tank. That night I will never forget.

The Lord did save both men and the house, praise His name. The next day, a man came to my grandfather's home and said to him, "Distress on top of distress, Uncle Sala," describing the position my grandfather was in. I want you to imagine the situation that night with no electric light to see by, only flashlights and the burning roof. I mention this incident to show you that we are in a plight right now similar to the one that night at my grandfather's house. Many of us are in mortal danger and need to be rescued. Without the hand of God intervening, we are going to burn.

"Ready or Not, Here I Come"

In the parable of the five wise virgins and the five foolish virgins, we see the importance of readiness. We must remain in a state of readiness because we do not know at what time the Bridegroom will come. Many will be left behind at His appearing because they were not looking and watching for His appearance. Many will be bogged down by the affairs of this life. How unfortunate that will be, after we were warned to be ready and waiting.

Warren W. Wiersbe in his book *Live Like a King* tells us, "One of the essential differences between mere outward piety and true holiness is that piety makes you conform to a system, while true holiness conforms you to Christ and develops your own individuality." The "beauty of holiness" (Psalm 29:2) is not by imitation but by impartation and incarnation. "Christ liveth in me" (Galatians 2:20). This is the hope of the glory that is to be revealed in the other life. This is the one that fadeth not away.

We mentioned that possessions are keeping many Christians

earthbound, but we better think that we will be leaving earth sometime and somehow anyway, so we might as well empty our purses now so that others can hear the Gospel and eat a decent meal. I urge you to immerse yourselves fully into the work of the Lord. The harvest truly is plenty and the labourers are few. Join the ranks, dear reader, either personally or with your money, but get totally involved in God's kingdom and His vineyard.

chapter 14

NEVER ADD TOMORROW TO THE EQUATION

Tomorrow is but an elusive word and cannot realistically be added to our plans. Today is all we have. In a great sense, we cannot live without making tomorrow a part of our existence and plans, but the point I wish to stress here is that for some of us there will be no tomorrow. One person is struck dead suddenly by a heart attack; another has a gun placed to his head; another drowns; and yet another is the victim of a car, train, or plane crash. In each case, the person's life is over unexpectedly and immediately. Considering untimely deaths is part of our reality check.

Here is where we abide, in the midst of danger. *Unexpected* or *shocking* should not be words in the wise person's vocabulary, as he or she knows that tomorrow is not certain. Given that tomorrow is not promised, the wise person should be prepared and ready up to the minute; living in constant readiness for the eventuality of death. The prudent person knows that there is no certainty in life. Calamity is just a part of our existence. Life can be snuffed out any minute, leaving us to wonder why. As I mentioned before, our lives are like a wound up clock. No one knows when it will stop. There is a time limit on every head. We must not squander it.

In my lifetime, I have witnessed many tragic deaths. I will recount some of these here. On my first job, I had training as the first aider in the plant, in addition to my office duties. (a mining operation). One morning I was called to the scene of an accident. A worker had been run over by an earth-moving machine and killed. Strangely enough, when I drove to the deceased house and before I broke the news, his sister said that her head was exploding. She was already aware that something had happened to her brother.

The previous night, the brother had cursed his mother, bringing into play the biblical principle that children are to honour their mother and father so that their days may be long upon the land. Another time at the same company, two men were killed on a trolley on the railroad tracks. Their trolley hit a train head-on. It is said that one of those men also had been in a fight with his mother the night or week before.

Going out one night, I came across a dead man who had been thrown from his car when the door flew open and he tried to close it. When I worked at Federal Pacific here in Brampton as an assembler, on two different occasions three people drowned over the weekends. One of these events involved a single man. The other involved two brothers, one who worked at Federal Pacific. I had previously witnessed to one of these brothers. He had shrugged off the suggestion of a God and his responsibility to Him.

At TTC, one of my co-workers was making his way over to Newfoundland when he fell asleep and was thrown from his car and killed. He was certainly not wearing his seat belt.

Personally, before I turn the key in my ignition, I fasten my seat belt. The seat belt is one of the greatest safety features in a car, yet many of us choose not to wear it. I was in an accident where I hit and pushed a car 50 feet. The impact broke my headrest. I wondered if there hadn't been a headrest what the result would have been. Is the brake in a car a safety device? Of course it is, as it stops the car, preventing lots of tragedies. You would not drive without brakes on your car, yet you ignore other features. Am I trying to show the inconsistencies in the human psyche? Yes, I am.

Another sudden death of one of my co-workers occurred at Vaughan Transit. One day, this rather healthy-looking mechanic had a massive heart attack and died. Also at Vaughan Transit, as I recall, another supervisor moved to a new house one weekend and died in his sleep after the move. The last of the bad or sudden deaths came on April 18, 2016, when my namesake and long-time co-worker was shot and killed at his daughter's home in Jamaica. I will stop here, because the list of sudden deaths never ends.

From all appearances, it is only a small proportion of us who will be cut off suddenly. The rest can live with no fear of dying prematurely. Nevertheless, since we do not know the length of our lives, we should not be careless and wait, hoping that when the time draws near we can repent or ask for forgiveness. Remember, if we liken our lives to a wound-up clock, we do not know just when that spring will unwind completely and the clock will stops. Let us be careful then to live in constant preparedness and remain, as we live, vigilant about taking care of ourselves, especially our eternal welfare. Find rest for your soul, dear unsaved person. Find rest. May God help you to find His rest?

chapter 15

OUR TWO-DIMENSIONAL LIVES

Perhaps half the world right now does not know of the afterlife. A great number of those who do not know are likely here in the Western world, a seemingly more civilized part of the globe. That is because we have drifted away from our moorings and have indulged so deep into frivolous distractions that we could not care less about eternal things. We might realize that there is life after death, but we say, "So what?" We do not bother to look into such matters.

There are others who acknowledge the existence of God, but they want a personal miracle before they will believe in Him or consider having a personal relationship with Him. Some are looking for that kind of proof before they will budge.

A colporteur of the Bible Society in a European country came to an orchard with ripe fruits. He introduced the Word of God to the farmer at a low price. The farmer replied, "You tell me that your Book is the Word of God, but you do not prove so." To this, the man of God made no reply. He merely stood admiring the trees laden with ripe fruits. Then he said, "What fine-looking pears! But what a pity they are of such poor quality." "What?" exclaimed the orchardist, "Of poor quality?! It is quite plain that you have never tasted them. Pick one or two and try them." The man of God did as he was invited to do. As he ate, he relished the pears. He then said to the farmer, "You must deal with my Book as I have dealt with your pears. ``Taste and see that the Lord is good." Psalm 34:8.

Many people are jumping to conclusions without first checking to see what is written in the Book. Most simply do not know what it contains, but they develop a prejudice against it nevertheless. Such assertions run contrary to logic. We cannot simply judge a book by its cover; our judgement must be based on the book's content. There is an invitation to every person in Psalm 34:8: "O taste and see that the Lord is good: blessed is the man that trusteth in Him." If we fail to accept the invitation, then our demise will be the result of our own neglect. The onus is on us, not on anyone else. As intelligent men, women, boys and girls, we must know these things for ourselves. We all have access to the Bible. No home should be without one. It is the most informative book you will ever read.

If we were heading out on a long road trip with our family, or even alone, we would be careful to map out our journey to see where the eating and lodging places were and, more importantly, where we could fill up our cars with gas. We also would be sure to take a spare tyre and a jack. We would not play the fool and be so optimistic as to leave things up to chance, hoping against hope that we have enough food or gas and that we will not get a flat tyre.

We would rule out none of those things, yet as intelligent human beings, we will not even look at the possibility of the next leg of the journey after this life. Our God has spoken, but we do not want to hear Him speak. He has written letters to us, but we leave the envelopes unopened. In some circles, He is relegated to nothing while we have elevated ourselves to deities. Our God is still high and mighty; His worthiness is not devalued or depreciated one iota, regardless of how we feel about Him. God stands high and mighty still.

His Mercies Do Not Cease

Inspite of the stubbornness and waywardness exhibited by human beings, God is still merciful and would seek to find and heal us of our iniquities. God's revelation on this matter is clear, but we will not listen. We remain stubborn and resistant to His calling and reasoning. Here in Isaiah 1:18, the Lord Himself wants to talk to us as a father would, sitting with his wayward son or daughter and having a chat. "Come now, and let us reason together, saith the Lord: though your sins be as scarlet, they shall be as white as snow; though they be red like crimson, they shall be as wool." He has promised our total transformation if we will return to Him. This does not sound like a God who is waiting for us to sin so He can then send us straight to Hell.

He is long-suffering, compassionate and not willing that any should perish. Instead, He wishes that all should come to repentance. That is the God of the Bible. And yet with all His pleading, some brand Him as rigid and intransigent, ready with the axe, so to speak. One of my professors at York University, where I obtained my BA degree, said that he could not believe in a God who would send men to Hell. After God's pleading and coaxing, it is clear that if we go to Hell, we will go on our own accord. We will have earned our stay in Hell if we neglected so great a salvation.

I have had similar encounters with other professors in different classes. There is only one, whom I mentioned before, who really believes in and serves the God that I know. The others are lingering in the congregation of the dead. These are the people we entrust our children with, the one who will educate our children and equip them for life's journey. These are the people who scoff at the realities of our existence and seek to introduce some superficial paradigm of their own.

When we write an essay, the introduction includes the thesis, which is a position that you advance by means of an argument, in which a particular view of a subject is set forth with supporting evidence following. The professor will review your paper and make the following comments, among others of course. He will cite the fallacy of presumption, for example. Fallacies of presumption are arguments that are unsound because of the following reasons:

1. They overlook the facts.
2. They evade the facts.
3. They distort the facts.

Now if we brought into a court of law the same professor who base his unbelief on the claim that God is partial, how well would he fare? The evidence is stacked against him, in that there is a mountain of evidence to support the claim that God is a just, forgiving, compassionate and conciliatory God who is forever reaching out to us. He is ever pleading for us to come home. He is literally chasing us as a police officer chases a thief, but we keep on running. The judge would rule against the professor for failing to investigate and collect more information about God before making his decision and denouncing Him as unfair.

I met another professor who claimed to have grown up in the church but who now did not believe. I asked him how he was going to fare when he came to the swelling of the Jordan. A third unbeliever was presented with some evidence, but he forthwith rejected it. After his initial rejection, I pulled out a testimony of Shakespeare who was a believer and started to read. The professor rebuked me sternly, saying, "Trevor, put that paper away." I heard another student asking that professor if Christ was a myth, to which he quickly agreed. "Where shall the sinner and the ungodly appear?" You be the judge.

After being surrounded by so great a cloud of witnesses, how do we know where they will appear? Christ spoke of them. He said that they not only shut themselves out of the kingdom but also were barring others also from entering. These are wicked people whose spirits are arrayed against Christ and His good news. These people are like those who would bar the door of a burning building while people were trying to get out. I have already said that it is sad. I will say it again. It will be sad, and sadder still, when such a one comes to meet his or her Maker.

One man I spoke with claimed that he was a believer. When our discussion turned to the story of the Israelites coming through the wilderness, he refuted the claim. He said, "How could over two million people with cattle travel for forty years without a single person ever seeing them?" I cannot remember whether it was on this account or because of something else, but I asked him, "How can you call yourself a believer?" They are simple not enlightened. Everyone can read about the wonderings of the Israelites in the wilderness.

My friend, we would do well to investigate the world about us ourselves and not rely on anybody to do it for us. Consider the adage "There is none as blind as those who will not see." Christ is the most central figure in all of history, and professors deny his existence. What else do they not know? Our calendar started at the birth of Jesus of Nazareth. Here we are marking the 2,017ᵗʰ anniversary of His coming into the world and some so-called educated people do not know that. It is because some hate Him so intensely that they would suppress every truth about Him. To them, He never existed, but to us who believe, He is the power that keeps and moves us.

The History of the Israelites Coming from Egypt

The book of Exodus starts thus: "Now these are the names of the children of Israel, which came into Egypt; everyman and his household came with Jacob." The other books are Leviticus, Numbers, Deuteronomy and then Joshua. All these books provide the history of the Israelites over the 40-year period as they journeyed from Egypt to Palestine the Promised Land. After the Israelites travelled for 40 years in the wilderness, Joshua settled them in Palestine. Finally, God said in Joshua 24:13–14, "I have given you a land for which ye did not labour and cities which ye built not, and ye dwell in them; of the vineyards and olive yards which ye planted not do ye eat. Now therefore fear the Lord and serve Him in sincerity and truth."

This portion of Scripture is simply an historical account of the Israelites, just as we read today of the refugee camps in the Middle East, of which our children and grandchildren will read later on in the history books. A great part of the Bible is simply history. Many professors are the so-called great minds that are confusing the minds of our young people. Our students go in to universities sane and promising, with great expectations, but they come home hemorrhaging, wounded, bewildered and despondent. Some do not make it out alive. I know of a friend whose son hanged himself after a short time as a university student. Perhaps he could not cope with the curriculum but the world does not end if one does not have a University Degree. There is no shame there. Many brilliant and successful people never darkened the doors of higher learning.

College professors are people who pride themselves in having great book learning. These are the erudites, right? They have chosen the books they want to read but have aligned themselves against God's Word. God is angry with these rejecters but still extends His mercy; He is waiting for them to turn. In Isaiah 9:21, God declares, "For all this His anger is not turned away, but His hand is stretched out still." My friend, the patience and long-suffering of God is beyond human understanding. Like Job, I know that the Lord knows the way that I take, and that is good enough for me. My times are in His hands, which is more than comforting to me.

Life as an Adventure

I have viewed life like an adventure, forging through the forest, so what is next I cannot tell; however, whatever comes must not surprise me. A long time ago, I learned the following, a poem written by Samuel Ullman. I must admit that I made it a part of my life.

> Youth is not a time of life
> It is a state of mind,
> A spirit of the imagination
> A vigour of the emotion
> A predominance of courage over timidity
> Whether six or sixty
> There exists in the heart of every man who loves life
> That insatiable appetite for what is coming next.

We must find something in life on which to lean, a hiding place, if you will, where we can relax with tender repose. Some even lean on a Chevy. Whatever it is, find it. A person must have a study, a quiet place to relax. The individual might only be using it to hide from a wife or a husband, but it is necessary.

Christianity is more practical than one might imagine. It involves record-keeping. I remember my first job as a records clerk. It is interesting to see how often in the Bible the books are called for. Lest someone misinterpret something, the books are called for. Every word, every deed and every action is recorded and will be brought as evidence against us if those records still exist. I say "if those records still exist". For the Christian, they are wiped clean. We can have a clean slate when we appear before God, but only if our slate has been wiped clean by the blood of Jesus Christ. Therefore every born-again son or daughter has a clean slate before God. Not now, not ever, will any sin be brought against us, because there is none.

I know a brother who had a record—a criminal record, that is—and went to jail for aggravated robbery. He was later pardoned by the Queen. One day he said to me that he had asked someone who works in the criminal department to see if a record still existed for him. The person did not and could not find any such record. It no longer existed. It was as if he had done no wrong. It is the same for us Christians; nothing is recorded against us anymore. We are working with a clean slate, praise the Lord. How shall the sinner plea, my friend, when an array of evidence is brought against him? Isaiah 29:18 states, "And in that day shall the deaf hear the words of the book, and the eyes of the blind shall see out of obscurity, and out of darkness." The deaf will hear and the blind will be made to see, but you who can hear and can see now will not see.

If the things we did as kids were things we did not want our parents to know about, those done as adults are things we do not want our wives or husbands to know about because they are despicable things. How then will we feel when the sins are laid bare before us in front of a holy God? Personally, I never again want to hear about some of the things that I have done. No, sir. I am happy that those things, or might I say those records, are buried in the depths of the sea. God Himself knows nothing of my past. How free can I be? It is exhilarating that with God I have no sinful past. Now that is freedom personified.

In Isaiah 43:25, the Lord says, "I, even I, am He that blotteth out thy transgressions for mine own sake, and will not remember thy sins." Imagine yourself as the accountant in the firm who is an embezzler. You have defrauded your employer of millions of dollars over the years, and now you are caught. You cannot deny it, because you cannot account for buying the things you have on your salary. You are forced to admit the truth. Your boss calls you into his office and offers you a seat. Very politely, he says, "Good morning, John. Nice to see you. I hope everything is well with you and your family."

He proceeds to make small talk. By now you are screaming inside because you know he is going to fire you, or worse, send you to jail. He has found out, you know that; the auditors were in a few days before. At this point, you wish he would tell it as it is. You wish he would tell you what he thinks of you, calling you the names that fit you—"scoundrel," "low-down rotten vermin," as they say in the movies—but instead he says, "John, I know all about the embezzlement, but I forgive you. And on top of that, I want you to continue working in this same capacity for me. I will be going away for a little while. Take care."

Unable at this point to face your boss, you turn away your head and cry, you sob audably. Nothing more need be said. At the end of the day, you cannot wait to get home. As a matter of fact, you do not know how you got home. You cannot remember if there were traffic lights or not. Your wife, who knows of everything, cannot wait to see you. After relating to her the events of the day with your boss, you go to your room and put your head under the covers. You are not hungry. Your heart has stopped beating, you have no pulse, and for a time you are out of this world. The events of the day cannot be true. It must have been only a dream.

God has done the same for the repentant sinner. He has pardoned all his sins and reinstated him to full partnership in His kingdom. This accountant has even been compensated after his actions; he is now given a position of greater trust than he had before. Unbelievable! How can that be? Our heavenly Father has done no less for us vagabonds.

Come to Know Him Now

There is a deceiver at work. His name is Lucifer, a.k.a. the Devil or Satan. He is vying for your soul, and he has deceived many into thinking that it all ends here when our eyes are closed in death. It is not so. You do not want to find this out when you land on his side of eternity. At that point, he will mock you then, and there is nothing you will be able to do to correct your error. It will not be like the other mistakes you have made while you were on earth living through time. Time is now gone and you have stepped into the eternal dimension. There, things remain static; nothing changes. "He which is filthy let him be filthy still" (Revelation 22:11).

May God soften your heart to the point where you will make some enquires, even silently, even secretly, and search for Him. He has said,

"Those that call upon Him he will not cast out. A humble and contrite heart he will not despise" (Psalm 51:17). That was Christ's mission here on earth, to call sinners to repentance. In Heaven, Christ continues to plead for those who believe in Him. How can we not be humbled by the attention given us, my friend? How could we cease to praise Him for all He has done and is doing? As the songwriter says, "I will praise Him till eternity rolls."

To live for Christ is not fashionable these days, as a believer might be scoffed at. But as it is said, your friends may laugh you into Hell, but they cannot laugh you out. Many a bad decision has been made to please friends. We know the consequence of deciding to abandon Christ is dire, irreversible and detrimental. Consider yourself and your wellbeing. This is a decision you will later rejoice in having made.

Speaking of rejoicing, you might not know it, but it is said in the Good Book that when a sinner repents, there is rejoicing in Heaven. Consider that, my friend: a celebration when you come to Christ, probably a marching band playing for you, a sinner who has come home. Yes, the return of the prodigal son is a picture of one sinner coming back to God. It is a monumental event in the Bible, worthy of celebration of the highest magnitude. Why will there be rejoicing and celebration? Because there is a great value placed on your soul, that is why. There is a great price on your head, you might say: "Wanted alive."

chapter 16

QUESTIONS, QUESTIONS, QUESTIONS

A myriad of questions are being asked when one witnesses to an unsaved person, questions that cannot be answered. And even if the questions could be answered, the answers wouldn't affect the person's thinking. Most times, I have found out, people to whom I witness ask questions only to be smart alecks, as we say. One such question that someone asked me was "Why didn't God make us with the capacity to obey Him only, and without the ability to doubt or disobey Him?" To this question, I provided an answer consisting of a hypothesis (a proposition made for the basis of reasoning). Before I went into the hypothesis, however, I said to the man, "When I get to Heaven, I will ask the Lord, but you better be there so that I can give you the answer."

By virtue of his attitude, I doubted that he would be there. But thank God, this will not be the case. Since I wrote this account, he told me that he now believes in God. Glory to God, the truth is marching on. In reply to his question "Why did God give us choices?" I said, "Say that one evening you came in from work; dinner was on the table; you sat at the table, called to your wife, and asked if she was not coming to have dinner; and she replied, 'Dear, I am not feeling well, but if I feel better I will eat later. I had a terrible day. I only forced myself to prepare dinner for you,' just imagine how you would feel seeing that she forced herself to please you or simply honour you. If you are a tyrant, then you will think: ``Good, she is obeying me. That is what she should be doing regardless, having my meal prepared.``

"On the other hand, let's suppose that you came in and dinner was not ready. You ask, 'What's happening, Dear?' and she says that she is not well but as soon as she feels better she will start dinner. You will object to that proposition, surely, and then you will either get in the kitchen yourself or tell her you will go out and buy dinner. The question of waiting until she feels better is out, absolutely. In the first scenario, your wife feels obligated or compelled to have your dinner ready, regardless of her feelings. She has grown fearful of you and is unable to face the consequence of not having your dinner ready. Here you are her boss and must be satisfied at all costs. In the second instance, she feels free in the marriage and can skip preparing a meal if the circumstances warrant without losing a moment's peace. Here is love manifested, where your wife enjoys the marriage and can relax in it with a great deal of latitude."

Certainly, God could have made us as robots doing only what we were programmed to do. I cannot say what things would be like living without sin, but if I compare it to something I have experienced, I know that it is more satisfying to be in a position with choices. If, for instance, one were never hungry, one would never relish a good meal. It is the being in both camps that makes for an interesting life. God knows better than we, and as such He has given us a choice. That is more meaningful to me, that we are equipped with an intellect. Choices put a burden on the chooser in that he has to accept the one and reject the other. It is the world we live in, a world of duality where we are given choices in every aspect of life.

We have the faculty of reason, and as such we can be held responsible for things we do. Isn't it interesting that while on one hand we are proud to be able to say we are great intellectuals who have the capacity to fathom new concepts, to reason and to develop ideas into working prototypes, fashioning gadgets that do amazing feats for us, yet on the other hand we cannot grasp the things that we have to face up to eternally? Our destiny with God at the judgement that is. Is there a gap or a gulf between the natural things and the spiritual things so that even the idea of a Designer of the universe cannot be grasped by many? There is that gap indeed.

Another question that comes up when I witness to people is "Why will God send us to Hell if we do not accept His Word?" My answer is that when Adam sinned, we were all separated from God through his sin, and as such we all belong in Hell. Christ's coming into the world was the only means of reconciling us to God. A way has been made back to God through Christ. Acceptance of that Way is our responsibility.

If we neglect so great a Way, then we remain in our sins. The soul that sinneth shall die, and here we are in the congregation of the dead. These are the two men in our lives, the first Adam and the second Adam, Christ Jesus. The first Adam gave us the burden of sin, and the second Adam removes that burden and sets us free again. Which Adam are you leaning on, my friend? As they say today, this is a no-brainer. You have choices, but will you choose wisely?

chapter 17

WHAT ARE YOUR ASPIRATIONS?

What is it that you are aspiring to? What is it you want to be, to become, to accomplish in your allotted time here on earth? That you have bought *What's Up?* means you are thinking and not just living. You are engaged in the process of living, fully engaged in the ongoing process of living and engaging yourself in life itself. You are not lying around eating, drinking and watching TV. You are at least trying to improve your status in life like other enterprising people. By just reading, you are being entertained, improving your vocabulary and engaging in the conversation that started so long ago in the Garden of Eden with our Father.

Seeking and searching are the goals all of us have, seeking with the hope of finding and landing a lofty one, be it a fish, a job, or even the car or house of our dreams. That lofty dream is what keeps us going, and rightly so, for without a dream, something to aspire to, we would find it impossible to keep getting up day after day. It is the dream that serves as that magnet pulling us ever farther away from mediocrity. We want to be something, not just an ordinary person. We want to be the best in our field. We certainly do not want to be at par with the lowest denominator of our clan or team. We want to excel and stand out from the crowd. In essence, we want to be the best person that we can be. We are satisfied when we know that at the end of the day, we know that we have given our best to whatever we are occupied with.

We must learn to become managers, first of ourselves and then of the activities we engage in. Knowing what you want out of life and where you are in the pursuit of that thing to which you aspire is an essential element of the process. Ecclesiastes 9:11 states it simply: "The race is not to the swift, nor the battle to the strong … but time and chance happeneth to them all." As long as we are in the fray and keep at it, our chances of success are good. It is by being there with consistency and tenacity that we will see some progress. Sometimes progress is slow, but in essence things are happening. Sometimes it is only laying a foundation—and then putting on the frame and building gradually.

A man with a sledgehammer pounds a rock and sees that nothing is happening for a while, but as he keeps at it, eventually the rock yields to the hammer and it crumbles or splits apart. Is it the first blow or the last one that did the job? It is all of the blows. Everything takes time to effect measurable progress, so be patient and you shall be rewarded for your efforts as you persevere. A brother and preacher called it *sticktoitivity*—that is, tenacity to the max.

Someone has said: "*No one can climb your mountain it is for you to pick and climb in your own time and space.*" The race of our lives can be a lonely one. There might not be another soul on the track, but we must not be discouraged. If the Lord is beside us, we can jog happily along. View life as an adventure to travel through and not as a problem to be solved. Lighten your load; do not run with a lot of baggage. If you keep the journey as light as possible, then winning will be a breeze.

When my daughter Kathy was in elementary school, Grade 4 or 5, she would say as she grasped new concepts that it was *cinchy*. She meant there was nothing to it. I myself have come to favour a similar word as I travel through life. It is *salubrious*. What if we could live our lives like this, seeing things optimistically and saying, "There is nothing to it"? It is easy after all. Life is not meant to be burdensome; we are burdening ourselves with this life unnecessarily. Life is not always a walk in the park but it is not a maze either, where we have to fight to keep on track. We can take time to smell the roses frequently.

Sir Winston Churchill was a man who solved many great problems during the war years. He was not overwhelmed by seemingly huge problems. He saw large problems as many small ones added up, so he set about solving them in the same way as one strips an onion. If we would see life in a similar manner, then we would enjoy our lives more, much more.

The Thought Principle

One principle that works for me is the thought principle. The thought life is most important. We must strive to drop off any negative and unprofitable thoughts so as to make way for healthy and productive thoughts. If we can cultivate and maintain healthy thoughts regularly, then we will succeed in maintaining healthy bodies as well. The thought life can be as enriching as any energy bar; it will buoy you through the storm and through the flight. In many of the books written by men and women from time immemorial, there are countless gems to make us wise and keep our minds healthy and vibrant. These books are not necessarily religious; they can be ordinary books with healthy content. And remember, big names do not mean a thing. Authors with a lot of post nominals can produce as much fodder for the fire as a kindergarten kid.

A contented spirit is a thing worth cultivating. Why can't we have it all? Good looks may evade some of us, but apart from that, we can be happy with what we have to work with. I was driving my bus one day on Finch West coming into Finch Station when I heard a commotion between two women. The younger woman came off the front steps in such a flurry at the next stop that I thought she flew off the bus. At the station, I asked the other woman what had happened between them. She laughed and told me that she had looked at this young woman, who asked her, "What are you looking at?" She said that her reply was "I am not sure. Give me a minute and I will tell you." That is how the argument started.

It goes to show that many people are not sure of themselves, they are not well adjusted to face the world. We have to learn to manage ourselves and we practice on ourselves as managers, and then we go on to practice on others. Amidst all the confusion, we should be able to keep our cool and triumph over all the problems. If not, why not? We must take charge and learn to master our own selves at least.

When I studied architectural drafting at the Delehanty Institute in New York City, I was travelling on the train one morning looking vaguely across the aisle when one man said to me, "Don't look at me." Well, he did not know me. Whereas I had not seen anything in particular looking across the aisle, now I had a target. Why are we so terrible as human beings, using every opportunity to denigrate others? Why can't we embrace others as equal and not make a fuss every chance we get? We expect teenagers growing up to act in such fashion, but grownups should be more conciliatory toward each other.

My elementary school teacher who travel by subway in New York City would tell us that on the train everybody would be reading a newspaper. Everyone would *have* a newspaper, that is. Some didn't read the newspaper; they would have it only to hide their faces. Why, when someone looks at me I give them a smile. Quite often I get one back. How cool is that? That makes for a cool trip instead of an unpleasant one.

Many people fuss over themselves before they leave the house in the morning. If someone stares at them outside the house, they get upset. How odd is that? Why would we not think that our effort is paying off and that we look good enough to catch someone else's attention? Why don't we learn to be our own guardian, keeping a charming, confident and serene countenance, and attracting rather than repelling others? You can cultivate such a countenance by controlling your thoughts; keep them pure and enlivening. Good thoughts add vigour to your steps and contribute to the overcoming of life's vicissitudes. Keep on your toes and keep your chin up, my friend. Do not be brought down by the burdens of life. The things that you are not able to remedy or even fix, leave them alone. Do not be burdened by them unnecessarily.

I know someone who makes every other person's problem hers. The other person might not think he has a problem, but this person sees the other person as having a problem that she must fix. That is her mission in life, I am sure. That person is quite close to me and will certainly read this book and know who I am talking about. You might read of her reaction in my next book.

Love your life, be kind to yourself and be the best person you can be. Learn to live with yourself and then pass the love on to whomever, your kids, your spouse, your neighbour and every one else for that matter. As you grow older, let your life tower above the rest of the crowd. Show that you have been an overcomer, a victor and not a victim. Do not let the cares of this world pull your shoulders down to your knees and your face from the sky. Keep life positive and keep your optimism alive as long as you live. "Live as long as you want to and want to as long as you live." Let that slogan be your motto. With a good attitude and outlook on life, you are likely to arrest many of the hardships that might otherwise overtake and subdue you.

The mind is our greatest strength and asset, so cultivating it to withstand all the rigours of life will be a worthwhile endeavour. There are many things we have to contend with, pain, disability, and all kinds of debilitating injuries and diseases as we grow older, but keep your focus. At the point of death, look back with a smile and with gratitude that you have been able to glean enough from life to see you through thus far.

Many minds are so weak that they cannot withstand bad news, a little pain or disability. They are broken by any sad news. At the first sign of these things, they are ready to make their exit. I encourage you to make your plans and work those plans to make a better life than the one you have right now. Don't make plans only to neglect them. If you follow through on your plans, you will end up being a better person and not a sad and bitter one. If you do not start on your plans right now, you will end up looking back at the things that you should have done but did not do, and the result will be bitterness. No one wants to be around a bitter person. You do not want to be around a bitter mother, father, brother, sister, husband, wife or child. Emit a sweet fragrance all the days of your life, starting right now.

Be a successful person. And know that success is not an accumulation of goods and so on; it is self-management. Being able to live free from the encumbrances of this life is a masterful achievement. It allows you to pass up on many of the things that easily beset and upset us. We see the distress on the faces of so many as they force their way through life. Many of life's allures to them are must-haves, and in the end tragedy strikes. We see these things, we know these people. Let us move away from the things that bring them such unhappiness. Pick your own fight, the one you can win. Be the kindest, gentlest person there is, particularly to yourself.

Do not overlook yourself; you are worth the best treatment. You will enjoy the switch in attitude toward yourself, and it will extend to others effortlessly. Just try it. You want to be able to examine yourself in the mirror and sum up your life, being able to delight in the person you have become and not seeing yourself with disgust as so many see themselves. You have within your grasp the potential and creativity to produce a good and wholesome person. I say that you should go for it, starting now. Prioritize and watch yourself grow. In another year or so, you will be amazed by the progress you have made.

Creating and growing the inner person is worth more to your complexion than all the cosmetics in the world. Enjoy a joke and laugh often, as that is better as medicine than a lot of pills. Instead of being oneself, some people are busy trying to emulate someone else. You see them on TV all the time, saying, "I want to be like so-and-so." They undergo surgery to be like someone else. The confusion is all in the mind. Be comfortable with yourself. If you have not cultivated a good spirit and character, then you will forever be miserable and will not be an attractive person. At least you will not feel it, you will always be walking away from the mirror seeing a horrible person.

If your only desire is to imitate someone else, then you are out to lunch. By so doing, you show that you are unhappy with your Creator. Thank God for the person you are, as you are a unique person. There is no one like you. You should feel the impact of this every day. A gigantic problem some people have is how to live with themselves. They will skip from job to job, from marriage to marriage and from place to place not knowing that the problem lies within themselves. They are waking up to the same old self every day, notwithstanding a new this, a new that, or in a new this place.

Be a Four-Dimensional Person

Start developing yourself as a four-dimensional person. Develop the intellectual, the spiritual, the physical and the financial aspects of your life. By this time next year, you will surprise yourself. You will assuredly be the rounded person you never knew you were capable of becoming. Lord

Tennyson wrote: "Made weak by time and fate yet strong in will to seek to find and not to yield." These are not words that I use frivolously. This is my life, and anyone who knows me, knows that I am a four-dimensional man. I never sit on my laurels. It is said that laurels are like your pants: if you sit on them, they wear out.

The poet William Henry Davies writes: "What is this life if, full of care, We have no time to stand and stare." This is a hint by Mr. Davies to relax a little, take time to smell the roses and carry on. One should not give himself entirely to his occupation even as some do today. I once knew a man who ran a Gas Station in Jamaica and he lived at his station. He had help but nevertheless he had every item he sold in the station under lock and key. Anything you want had to be removed from a cabinet with a key. Some time ago I went out to Jamaica and visited him but he was out of it then, I mean he was dying and yet he was still in the business. He was barely or literally hanging on to the counter and he still would not stay home. He died shortly after I saw him then.

It is said that there are three types of people in this world: the type that watches things happen, the type that wonders what happened and the type that makes things happen. Each of us falls into one of these three categories. I urge you to be the mover and shaker, the one who makes things happen. You will be happier for it.

When we analyze things and see how much there is to be acquainted with around us, we must confess that we know very little about the world. We are virtually overwhelmed by all the information around us, but we need not be if we are fully engaged in our world and our future. Possess something for yourself and own it literally. There are too many things going on for you to be left behind in this busy world. Get engaged fully and reap the rewards.

chapter 18

HOW MUCH GOODS DO WE NEED?

It is always good to stop and take stock. Ask yourself the question "How much of what I need do I have now?" If we do not have a destination, then we will keep on running, running more marathons than are necessary. There is a Chinese proverb stating that if we do not reach out, we will lose both mule and horse, and if we overreach, we might also lose both also. Having a balance in life is prudent. If we strive aimlessly, we will not have anything to settle for. We will become restless unnecessarily and wear out ourselves unwittingly.

Why is it that some people seem to have an indomitable spirit and are the epitome of success? They wear the confidence but are neither haughty nor offensive. They never tire, nor are they worn out. They show us simply that they have the bull by the horn and not by the tail. They grow with their eyes wide open and distinguish the good from the bad. They know what flowers to pick and which must be left behind. They are not gatherers of all things; they are selective men and women.

It is said that there was a rich man who called a real estate agent to put his house on the market. He had grown tired of his house and wanted something different. Not long after listing the house, he summoned the same agent and showed him the listing of a house he wanted to purchase because it fit all his requirements. "Well," the agent said, "Mr. M, this is your house, which I have listed." It goes to show that we might be just where we want to be but do not know it. We keep struggling and for no good reason. Knowing what we need, and knowing how much of what we need we already have, is a great blessing. We do not know when to stop and enjoy our winnings. Most of us have far too much of everything anyway. When it is time to lock shop, we find it difficult to close the doors because they bulge from too much goods.

Many of us already have far more than we need to live happily, and yet we run after more. This is because there is greed within us that we have not learned to control. We kill ourselves to have more and more, but in the end, whose shall these things be? Living purposefully is an insightful phenomenon. It alleviates needless worry and hassle and great pain. Elementary Watson! But do we get it.

In general, we must learn to travel much lighter than we are travelling right now. By lightening our loads, we will travel much farther and become happier campers. I encourage you to try it. Give more to charity and receive a blessing, a great one. I suggest this because I know from experience the joy of giving and the blessings that come with it. The topic for this chapter is "How much goods do we need?" Yes! How much do we realistically need for a good existence here on planet earth? Should we look down and not up, we might fare much better than we are right now. Look and see how many are managing with little and not on those with their abundance.

For transportation, people used to use the horse and buggy, that is, one horsepower. Such a transport was able to carry a family of six or eight. Today we feel that we must have 400 horses under the hood just to go pick up some groceries. People's homes used to be 1,100 or 1,200 square feet. Today they feel they need 4,000 square feet for a family of four. Most times it is two or three children living in a huge place since the mother or father is often away. This is simply extravagance magnified.

People are caught in an evolutionary vortex where bigger is better. Bigger is better, and why not? Why must not we take from life just as much as we can get. So that we can show our neighbours that we are something, that we have attained success. It is nothing more than an all-consuming rapacious nature and an urge that we cannot subdue. It has taken control of us; we fall victims to our appetites.

One man moved to the country and after seeing how much things the new dweller brought, the old settler went over to greet and welcome him, saying to him, "If there is anything you do not have, come over and I will show you how to get along without it." The new neighbour had not the vaguest idea how to live simply.

Realistically, we do not need much to live comfortably. The way I see it, many of us could live on one-quarter of what we have today. We could give three-quarters of what we own away and our lives would not be any different nor would we feel deprived. It is a whirlwind, a cyclone. We are caught up in it and cannot extricate ourselves now. We cannot release ourselves from the madness and, more often, the stupidity of it. We are paying too high a price for our greed. In some cases we are paying with our lives.

I urge you, dear reader, to settle down and triumph over the avarice that besets you in this age. Do not pay a high price for being here; you will grow to regret it after it has become a burden to you. After a time, you will experience the same effect as overeating at a buffet. You must learn to curb the insatiable urge for more and more. Exercise prudence in your desire for more or even new things. After having the urge, sleep on it for a week. If you must have the item after that week, then give it a try. This is one of the tactics I have used myself. It works splendidly.

chapter 19

WHAT IS THE PURPOSE
OF OUR EXISTENCE?

How far do we think we can go into life, or how far do we think our lives will extend into the future? Will our life extend interminably, or is it for a brief period? The Bible says our lives are like the mist, which vanishes as soon as the sun comes up. That is how fragile and transitory our lives are. We are only a breath away from death. In light of the brevity of our existence, we ought always to be mindful of that fact.

Being the possessors of something so fragile, we ought always to be careful of the handling of our lives. How much care do we really give to ourselves when we know of life's frailty? We do not treat an egg as we would a baseball or an orange. We treat an egg with greater respect than we would the other two items. The thing that we were given is irreplaceable; it cannot be regained after we have lost or abused it. Often, we do not treat our lives as something worth taking care. The way some of us treat our lives carelessly, one would think we could get a new one on demand anytime.

May God open our eyes to see that this precious thing we are given called life is worth taking care of. If we truly recognize the value of our lives, we will be careful to plan our activities around the Creator and His divine plan for us. We would live in constant consultation with the manual that is supplied for the care and maintenance of our bodies. *Sobriety* and *watchfulness* would be our watchwords. We would not live as carelessly and as wretchedly as some of us do. We would be more careful if we placed the proper value on our lives.

As we look around us, we see the flagrant abuses. One of the many abnormal things I observe is the excessive stuffing of the body with food. People weight 200 pounds, 400 pounds and so on. It is outrageous, to say the least. Another thing is the desecration of the body with markings and piercings. I heard a young man say that he resisted being marked for some time but that now he wanted to be different, so he yielded. I don't know what kind of reasoning that is, when everyone is doing something, you do it too in order to be different. That is absolute nonsense.

Collectively, we have lost sight of what we are here for but individually we must make the effort to get back on track. It is our personal responsibility to seek after righteousness. It is not the collective effort that we will be held accountable for; it is ourselves we will be held accountable for. God has given each of us a responsibility and He is holding us accountable. We cannot lose sight of that fact. Our bodies are temples of God. It is in the human body that God dwells. We repulse Him when we defile our bodies in any way.

The purpose of our existence according to the Word of God is to serve Him and to have dominion over the earth. We have discussed this already. The conclusion was that we neither serve Him nor take proper care of the earth. We have become vagabonds upon the earth, roving and plundering it, making dereliction of it, when we should be good stewards instead.

Getting back to basics is a fundamental necessity for all of us humans. We must search ourselves and see where we are right now in relationship to God and His dictates. It might seem a reasonable thing to do just to get lost in the shuffle, but that is not good, as it is not the indulgences that will bring us rewards. Let us stand tall as humans and get in the fray, get our faces bloodied if necessary but get in and fight to produce the kind of world which the Maker will be pleased to be a part of. His blessing or His curse is incurred whatever we do, so why not incur His blessings? Let us invite Him to be an active participant in our activities as long as we live, starting now. Frankly, God cannot be left out of our lives without dire consequences. It is tantamount to forbidding the architect from coming into a building he designed. Things will get chaotic if he is forbidden to be on-site.

The purpose of our existence is to occupy the earth until Christ comes again. He has made us stewards and keepers of His vineyard. We are expected to perform our role in harmony with His rules, but we are doing just the opposite. How shall we fare then when the Master of the vineyard returns? That is the big question we all must answer, my friend—the how.

chapter 20

ATTITUDES ARE SUFFOCATING AND EFFACING

Why do I say that attitudes are suffocating and effacing because they are. I know the difference between being proud and being humble. I know the difference between striving for the first place and accepting second place or any other spot other than the first spot. All the aspiration for the top spot is vanity of vanities saith the preacher.

—Ecclesiastes 12:8

The quotation above expresses the conclusion of the whole matter. All is vanity when we have spent our lives in self-gratification and self-aggrandizement, neglecting our service to humanity and God in particular. We are now the proud people independent of God, hurtling down the path of destruction unknowingly, extricating ourselves from His Majesty's service almost completely. We have already crossed the point of no return and our destruction is imminent. Our behaviours are causing us much grief, too much grief.

Many brilliant men and women have come to the end of their productive lives with the realization that they strove too valiantly for themselves alone and failed to extend themselves to others. These people settled with the hard truth that they did so at their own peril. It is more comforting to lift up others along the way than to strive to promote and elevate oneself solely. Hence the biblical teaching that: "it is more blessed to give than to receive." We cannot circumvent sound biblical principles; they will catch up to us.

I know from personal experience the joy of singing as I go because Jesus has lifted my load. A load, my friend, is all we have to show. We bear a heavy one at times. An unmanageable load is what we needlessly carry on our shoulders as we traverse the road of life. Life's load and the guilt of sin can only be lifted when we come to the cross of Calvary and place our burden at Jesus's feet. There it will be lifted, at which point we can sing a song as we go through life. It is an experience you will have to have to know its truth. You must drink of the Water of Life, which is Jesus Christ Himself, to have this experience.

Having not known is one thing, but now that you have been introduced to the One who satisfies, you have no excuse for not drinking. I must warn you now, and I hope you will follow my train of thought: this world and all its attractions is a buzz of confusion and delusion. It is a madhouse of distractions pulling and luring us away from our main objective and purpose. That purpose is to serve the living God. This is the purpose for our existence. If we miss that purpose, then we go off on a different trajectory, one that inevitably leads us away from the target and into the abyss.

The path we are on can be very alluring, seemingly bright and affluent. Embracing a lifestyle that is rose coloured, seemingly lined with beds of roses, we follow it leisurely until suddenly we realize we are lost, like Alice in Wonderland, unable to find our way back home. Surely many are on that road of ease and comfort, not realizing that they are travelling on the wrong road. They are unaware that there might be another way, one that leads to eternal life.

Minnie Louise Haskins wrote a poem about a man who wanted a light so he could go out into the darkness. I quote "The Gate of the Year" as follows:

> I asked the man at the gate to give me a light
> That I might go out into the darkness,

And he replied, "Go take the hand of God.
It shall be to thee better than the light
And safer than a known way."
So I went out and found the hand of God,
And He led me into the hills and the lone east.

In the east is where you will find pure sunlight, which purges all impurities. To be there is to bask in the vast expanse of God's holiness and blessings. Where God dwells is where we are headed when we hold God's hand. With our hand in His, we can never get off track, my friend. That is security personified, to be held by Him. He or she who is held by the Lord is secure and well-kept. Thank God for that blessed security and that is when we are safe, my friend, when our hand is in the hand of God. That is where the light is, in the presence of God. I believe that the greatest tragedy in our world today is that the Light has come and yet we dwell in darkness. We are still groping our way through life, when in fact we could have perfect direction and peace. The Prince of Peace is in our midst, but we strive for and settle for a substitute or even a false comfort. We would rather comfort ourselves with the thought that we have done things our way.

Self-sufficiency is only a thought, an impression imbedded in the human psyche, but it is far from being the truth. "We think we know what's best for us, and we plan and plot to reach the shining goal we have in view, but often times we have to dream another dream and build another castle in the blue."

For us to have a finality that is comforting and secure with assurance, we must hand over the reins to God. He is willing and able to take care of us. Christ has said, "Take my yoke upon you, and learn of me; for I am weak and lowly in heart: and ye shall find rest unto your souls" (Matthew 11:29). Leave your cares at the cross and roll then upon Jesus. He is quite happy to carry your load for you. Millions have rolled their burdens upon Him throughout the ages. He is strong enough to carry them all, including yours.

These are not mere promises but actual deals that have been concluded. Millions can testify to this fact. As we say in today's vernacular; it is a done deal; you can bet on it. Those of us who have surrendered to Christ will testify that His invitations are not empty words. They are real, substantive and obtainable; they are there just for the asking. After striving all their lives, many men and women have wondered at the ease by which they were able to obtain the peace and security that they sought. It was there in the Book all the time for the taking. "Ask and it shall be given" and "Knock and it shall be opened" are the invitations of Jesus. Matthew 7:7.

The Lord Jesus Christ came to the earth for no other purpose than to redeem the lost, which includes all of humanity. "All we like sheep have gone astray, we have turned everyone to his own way; and the Lord hath laid on Him the inequity of us all" (Isaiah 53:6). We might not want to acknowledge this position, but it does not negate the fact that we are lost. We are on the broad road to Hell, but we can be lifted off that conveyor belt on which we ride. There is no specified time, It can be now right, this minute. It is all in your grasp. Jesus cried with a loud voice, saying, "Come unto me all ye that labour and are heavy laden and I will give you rest" (Matthew 11:28). He made that emphatic cry because He wanted to stir the people. He wanted to get their attention. This was not a circus call to entice you to risk your money on some fancy game. This was a call for men and women to answer, one that would change their lives eternally. Jesus agonized over His calls, my friend. Christ knows what the alternative is. It is Hell, literally.

This is the greatest call men and women from all ages will ever hear, made by Jesus Himself: "Come unto me." Many times I hear people say that they have been made an offer that they cannot refuse, maybe of a purchase, a job or something else. But here is an offer that we dare not refuse. Those other offers are important and worthwhile, but they do not come with a penalty other than, perhaps, a monetary loss. The offer of salvation, however, is of eternal consequence. Forever your soul will be tormented if you do not accept this offer.

We cannot fathom all that has gone on for the Everlasting Father to give up His Son to redeem us from our sins so that we can be reconciled to Him. We can revert to our original state and status with the Father when we heed the call. We can enjoy fellowship with Him now and live with Him eternally. "How cool is that?" some would say. Very cool, I am saying now. To be able to address the Almighty God as Father is beyond me. Here is a command we should count as a privilege and an honour to obey: "Be ye reconciled to God" (2 Corinthians 5:20). We are commanded to be reconciled to God. It is an order to get back to basics. Will we spurn that order?

Unfathomable to Be Able to Call Him Father

Some religions count it blasphemy to address God as Father. We might have felt that way ourselves until we saw it written in God's Word that we can say, "Abba, Father." God wants to have fellowship with us. Because of this, He is saying, "Now you are My children. There is no longer a formal relationship. You are now part of the family." I liken this to when a woman or a man gets married. The mother and father do not lose a daughter or a son but gain a daughter or a son. Whereas each was a stranger before coming into the family, things become different at marriage. We understand that concept easily, but the idea of God being our Father is too farfetched for many of us to grasp. Each child will easily grow into the realization of having the Great Creator as his father.

I do not have to understand it all; but because I accept it, I am benefiting from the relationship. More and more as I grow older I find it essentially so. He who commands everything and holds everything in His hand can take care of this feeble life. I praise Him every day for that assurance. I speak to Him as my Father on a continuing basis; literally we chat throughout the days and nights.

In spite of the vastness of this universe, there is nothing here of more importance to God than you and me. We are more important than all the planets put together. We are the apple of His eye. Think of that. You have often heard people say that their struggles will be over when certain events take place or when they reach a certain milestone in their lives. We know that there is only some truth to that belief, because once that event takes place, additional troubles will be brewing. Our troubles are not over ever, not even as Christians, but we can rest in our troubles when Christ is at the helm. We know that as far as searching and finding goes, we have put that matter to rest. We no longer wander in the valley of indecision. We are now anchored to the Rock, which is Christ Jesus our Lord and King.

As the hymn writer, Martin Luther, puts it, "A mighty fortress is our God." He has written of Jesus as the Mighty Fortress, and we have found Him to be just that: mighty. He is mighty in saving, mighty in keeping, mighty in protecting and mighty in justifying. Who is like a god unto our God? He Himself has made the pronouncement in John 17:3: "And this is life eternal, that they might know thee the only true God, and Jesus Christ, whom thou hast sent."

The world is full of falsities—false hair, false teeth, false jewellery, false or faked paintings, false hope and false gods galore—but it is made known unto us that there is only one true God. He is the God of the Bible. He is not found anywhere else. It is here that He is revealed to humankind. A person can suffer great losses when he invests in a false painting or a false business, but that loss is only of material value. On the other hand, if one is trusting in false gods, then his eternal soul is at stake. There is only one true God amidst all the false gods and He is the Almighty God. Through Jesus the Son, we can obtain eternal life from that God. In failing to come to this God, we embrace a false hope eternally.

chapter 21

A TASTE OF THE INFINITE

Have we now a sense and taste of the infinite? Does the hope that we have provide us with a sure and confident expectation? Are we now as the little kids are, anxiously looking and unable to wait for our arrival to an anticipated place? Often, as you near your destination on a road trip, your children will anxiously ask, "Are we there yet?" As Christians serving Christ for many years, we also get caught up with such great expectations, looking anxiously for the day when He will come or we will go to be with Him. Or are we like many who are looking forward with great trepidation upon the prospect of His coming or their departure? God help us to look with great expectation toward our glorious day, the day of our departure or the day of His appearing.

Friedrich Schleiermacher wrote, "The essence of religion is the sense and taste for the infinite." How very true a statement that is. If our religion cannot give us a taste of the infinite and a sense of the realty of its promises, then our religion is flat, lacking the zest and mobility needed to lift us up. With a religion like that, one remains as all other unsaved people are, hopeless and staid. The Christian religion is the religion that brings hope and quiet confidence to the believer. It produces faith, which is the driving force of our life. We have a synopsis of what faith is: "Now Faith is the substance of things hoped for, the evidence of things not seen" (Hebrews 11:1). By faith we are already experiencing the blessings. We are already living in heavenly places in Christ Jesus.

No assurance; well, that is not the way we must live as Christians.

We have assurances in so many things, yet not absolutely. When we leave for work, we are assured that our place of business will be there. We are assured that when we turn the key in our car's ignition, it will start. More often than not, it will start. To a certain degree, we live in a world of assurances, yet when it comes to eternal matters, weightier matters, we are not sure. Ask people of a different religion where they are going when they die and they will say they are not sure. How can a person invest in such a hit-and-miss proposition? People want to know just where they are heading once they leave this life, yet they are not willing to embrace the religion that gives that assurance.

Within the ranks of the Christian religion there are skeptics, those who practically make Christ a liar. They do not believe that He gives eternal life upon the asking. We are what we are from the beginning, fools—at least the majority of us are. Lot and his family had to be dragged out of Sodom by the angels. Although they were told not to look back, Lot's wife did. Consequently, she was turned into a pillar of salt. Is God's warning not sufficient to get us moving? Many of us are going to suffer a great loss because we have not listened to His Word. "Get up and out." We are living in a danger zone, a very dangerous one that is due for total destruction, and we are well served with lots of warning. *What's Up?* might be your last warning newsletter. Get ready to vacate this world. God has said it: the end of the world is coming.

We know by faith that what is promised is already given, because the One who has promised it is God Himself. He is totally trustworthy and capable of fulfilling all His promises. Those who trust in Him will have eternal life. Even though we die, we will be raised again to everlasting life. At His command on that Judgement Day, some will be resurrected to everlasting life and others to eternal damnation. Who can speak against His judgement? No one. It is stated, and we embrace it as truth as we do all the statements made in our Bible. "Behold, what manner of love the Father hath bestowed upon us, that we should be called the sons of God. Beloved, now are we the sons of God, and it doth not yet appear what we shall be: but we know that, when He shall appear, we shall be like Him; for we shall see Him as He is" (1 John 3:2–3).

Such a statement is not up for discussion, because the things of God are spiritually discerned and the natural person (the person who is outside of Christ) cannot understand them. We cannot discuss how it is possible for these things to be, because the natural man or natural woman will not be convinced. These things are all foolishness to such people, and rightly so, since their eyes are cloaked in darkness. Until their eyes are opened, they will not perceive them. There are things that the Christians know because we fear the Lord. These things are not revealed to the world. We are in the inner circle. Only those who are in the inner circle are made privy to what is happening and is to happen.

Indeed, there can be no bigger thriller for the Christian than this coming event. The coming of Christ, or our departure to be with the Lord, is an expectation like no other. There is nothing on earth like it, and there should not be anything here that is nearly as attractive. This is our hope and treasure. Heaven is where our sights are set. This is where our attraction is. The things of earth grow strangely dim the more aware we are of this event. This is what I consider to be a taste of the infinite. As I write these words, I know that this earthly tabernacle is fading away. I eagerly look forward to receiving a new body, one that defies gravity and the ravages of sickness and old age. A new body is promised me. I can't wait to trade in this mangled one. This is indeed a magnificent hope to live with and for. The God who made the first body can make a better replacement, which will be the latest and final model. There will be no depreciation on this one, which will also require very low maintenance. You can trade in yours too.

chapter 22

WEARY AND EXHAUSTED THESE REVISIONISTS

There are those who are running befuddled and bedazzled among us, trying to play the part of God. They call themselves revisionists. That which is settled, delineated and established as truth is what they try to undo, ridicule and treat with disdain. Confused and weary of the truth, they seek to make a name for themselves. In so doing, they damn their souls eternally. One of the things they deny is the Virgin Birth. Any alteration or amendment to the Lord's Word is defamation and is condemnation to their souls. The revisionists do not fear God and are numbered with the unrepentant sinners. They can be termed fools. That is what they are when they try to add to or subtract from God's written Word. Psalm 119:89 states, " Forever, O Lord, thy word is settled in Heaven." Do such statements give us any room for manipulation? No. Who do we think we are, anyhow, when we try to change His word.?

The revisionists can add nothing to God's Word to make it more effective. Still, many are trying to do just that. They are busy doing all manner of projects and trying all manner of tricks in an effort to attract more people into the church. A person needs to hear that he will be held accountable to God for his deeds and that if he does not repent, then he will die in his sins. All are under condemnation because of sin; we bear its marks in our bodies. We are on death row—all of us, not some of us—until we repent. It is as simple as that. Any change in that status comes from our kneeling at the foot of the cross in repentance. God will honour His Word if a sinner comes in repentance to Him. He will not cast such a person out.

Like the thief on the cross, we all should bow our head in humble submission and ask for forgiveness. It is a place of honour in society that people are seeking when they try to reinterpret God's Word. It is the pride in them that causes them to stretch as far as they do—and that to their destruction. Until we humble ourselves, we are absolutely nothing. It is only on our knees that we gain strength and stability. The great and mighty things are not wrought or accomplished standing tall with strong lungs and a clenched fist fighting the air but with a humble spirit while on our knees. It is on bended knees that many wondrous problems are solved and glorious victories are won. We will be better served when we adopt that posture.

Slipping Away Precipitously

Where are the great tear-inspiring sermons these days that show us as we are, naked and undone before a holy God? Where are the ministers of the Gospel who move as holy people of the truth? Where are they? You would not recognize them in the marketplace or in the sanctuary. They are not to be found anywhere, because they are not there. They have all become careless and disrespectful of the things of God. Where are the suits and ties, the shiny black shoes and the King James Bible? I know where some of those things are. They are kept new, reserved for worldly events, perhaps if an unexpected invitation comes from the Prime Minister or the Queen.

The congregation is being entertained but not upbraided for our sins and our shallow standing before a holy God. We can run from the pulpit into the market and mix with the crowd. No one is the wiser as to whom we are. If people have a spiritual need, they do not know on whom to call to meet that need. Some ministers perform their task and leave the service as unnoticed as anyone else. "Who cares?" they say. "I have other things to attend to right away anyhow. I do not have to go home and change before I attend to those things because I am in my running shoes already. I do not have to loosen my belt since my shirt is out of my pants already. These are time-saving devices which I have adopted to simplify my life. I hope no one has a problem with it," or so they reason. Where are the holy people of God these days, I ask? Where are they? This is certainly not an umbrella assessment. Thank God that in His house, where the pulpit should be found in such a state, as to give honour to the Lord by its appearance.

Heed the Warning and Live

I remember reading of a farmer ploughing in his field and as he saw an itinerant preacher passing on his horse fell to his knees right there and cried out to God for forgiveness. He recognized a man of God doing the most important of all businesses, winning souls, and saw his plight without God. Therefore, the farmer surrendered to God without a word being spoken between the two men. Does a man not know his state before a holy God? Of course he knows. He fools himself to think otherwise and hides his unworthiness in pleasure.

Jesus Christ cried out in Matthew 11:28, "Come unto me, all ye that labour and are heavy laden, and I will give you rest." Here for example is a rich man seeing a poor boy looking across his fence. The rich man goes out to speak to the boy. "Son!" he says. "If you want to come and live with us here, you can." Well, my friend, do you think that that man could not afford to support the little boy and did not mean what he said? He would not bother to give the invitation if he did not mean what he said. For him to have uttered those words, he would have first counted the consequences and all that might be involved in giving that invitation. The boy coming to live with him would not put him out in any way, as he would have ample room and food to accommodate a thousand hungry boys. This little one would pose no hardship. Similarly, when the Lord calls us, He has ample provision for us. He will make the resources available to us out of His abundance.

Those of us who have ever watched *Undercover Boss* know that the willing and faithful workers receive unexpected windfalls from the undercover bosses. At our posts as Christians, all that is required of us is faithfulness. We might not seem to have any success at times, but we must stay where God plants us and remain faithful. If we do, then we will be rewarded in due season. Our reward is guaranteed, if not here, then in Heaven for sure. We might receive only a little here, or perhaps not even an observable amount, but according to the Bible in Psalm 37:16, "A little that a righteous man hath is better than the riches of many wicked." Coupled with that is this other verse in 1 Timothy 6:6: "But godliness with contentment is great gain." When we live godly lives, we are rich men and women. We praise the Lord constantly for the smallest of mercies. We thank Him for the half loaves we receive daily. Our satisfaction comes from the Living Stream.

The poor Christian is the one who still has a foot in the world. As soon as he steps off the world, he begins to increase his wealth and does so exponentially. Wealth is wrapped up in you, in your thoughts, your pursuits, your joy, your character, your peace and your outlook on life. All these things are the ingredients that make for a good and wealthy life. You and only you can gather the ingredients to bake that tasty cake, as it were. Our lives can be aromatic and sweet-smelling all our days, producing healing qualities for all the people we come in contact with.

The people who encourage me the most are those poor saints who have little or none of this world's goods. They are the ones who speak mostly of the grace and mercies of God. This is our position in the Christian realm: we are not paupers living like underdogs. We are wealthy inhabitants enjoying and praising our God. During my mission trip to Jamaica in 2015, I encountered one of the severest droughts ever to hit the district where I once lived. There were hardly any crops, except those catch crops hydrated by way of irrigation, which is done at great expense to the farmers. There was great suffering with all the gardens failing, yet I did not hear one person crying. They were all optimistic, sure that better days were ahead and that the Lord would provide. That is a sentiment that runs throughout the island: "The Lord will provide."

Some people have that saying on their vehicles and their businesses. But "The Lord Will Provide" is not the official motto of the island. The motto on the coat of arms is "Out of Many, One People." The existence of God is well engrained in the people of the island, and anything contrary to the teachings of the Bible is frowned upon. The Jamaican people are a God-fearing people. Although some may hold views different from the mainstream doctrines, yet they are a people dedicated to their God. Salvation, the judgement and Christ's Second Coming are central to most Jamaicans.

Who will tell them otherwise, no body.

chapter 23

HONOUR TO BE HONOURED

In God's kingdom, we honour Him and then we are honoured by Him. It is that simple. When we recognize our status in the kingdom, knowing that we are but subjects, we begin to grow and be promoted in the ranks. We cannot usurp any position in the kingdom. It is folly in the scheme of things to think that prosperity and godliness come without first submitting to the highest authority. We must first realize that nothing can be fully understood without reference to God's creation and His divine plan. Many of us drift along through life without knowledge of this divine imperative. He is Sovereign and He is in charge, and His plan unfolds with the passage of time. We are anxious about many things, but God has a timetable that is being followed in spite of our anxieties. His will, will be done in due time—in His time, not ours.

It would appear that some loyalists have slipped away from the kingdom and are trying to fill in the gap in places where they think God is slow or has failed to change as they suppose He should. They are making the changes on His behalf, although He has not sanctioned the work and does not approve of these changes. God is being helped from every side by compassionate loyalists who are anxious to see the work done. You be the judge, dear reader, as to whether anyone should be adopting the revisionists' policies.

The Bible discloses the character of God and His sovereignty. The trouble is, only a fraction of those who claim to be His followers adhere to His dictates. The rest of us make our own paradigm. Off we go on our own tangent and feel that if we are wrong, God will understand because our motives are sincere. Not so, my friend. It is His way or no way. In all that we do, we must remember Cain. Some are running the way of Cain, first satisfying themselves and if in the process God gets something, then so be it. God is not given His rightful place in our lives. God gets the leftovers most times. If we have spare change at the end of a pay period, He gets something; if we have nothing better to do, then we will attend church service; and so on. My friend, we forget that God is the discerner of our hearts and our intentions. We cannot fool Him. We only fool ourselves.

God knows where He is on the scale of things. We do not need to tell Him where we put Him. It is better if we just come clean all the time. Let us pour out our hearts to God. Let us confess our deceits to Him before our sins find us out. Remember Ananias and Sapphira in the book of Acts chapter 5. Our relationship with God is a reciprocal one. He has promised to honour those who honour Him, but this starts with us. We take the first step to honour the Lord, and then He fulfills his part of the deal. In 1 Samuel 2:30, the Lord said, "For them that honour me I will honour." God will not deal with us deceitfully, the way we would deal with each other.

When the Lord states that He will honour those who honour Him, He is implicitly speaking to the disobedient too. He has told them that they will not share in the blessings of those who honour Him. The unbelievers are simply outcasts. Revelation 20:15 states, "And whosoever was not found written in the book of life was cast into the lake of fire." Young man or young woman, do not let your parents tell you that this is scaremongering. In Hell you will not get the chance to accuse them of being liars. You will not be able to harass them as you do here on earth. Open your eyes and see for yourself what is written, and what your lot will be without Christ.

Will a Person Rob God?

In Malachi 3:8, the question is asked, "Will a man rob God?" Malachi 3:9 goes on to read, "Yet ye have robbed me. Ye are cursed with a curse; for ye have robbed me." Yes, we can rob God! And we have done just that. If we come to that realization, then we should correct the situation.

We should repent and start on the road to getting out of the horrible fix we find ourselves in. God expects us to be honest men and women, not robbers. We neglect to do that which is required of us, and then we move along without addressing the situation and while pretending that all is well. But we know all is not well.

God help us to recognize our neglect in His serve. Little wonder that we strive and strive valiantly without any tangible results. If we are careful to pay our bills to our creditors at the end of the month, why would we not consider giving God what is due Him at that time also? How do we expect the church to be run, salaries to be paid, hydro and gas bills to be paid, repairs to be made, insurance to be paid and so forth? Do we honestly look to others to do it for us? We must know that these things take money, real money.

God our heavenly Father is to be treated as a real partner in any business. For lack of trust and stinginess on our part, we have kept the Lord away from investing more time and interest in our affairs. Enough is said on this matter of trustworthiness. I urge you to be as trustworthy as the other partner you are in business with. You know what the Lord has said in the dealings He has with you. His words are "Bring me all the tithes into the storehouse" (Malachi 3:10). The irony is that we will shout and sing and raise our holy hands to the Lord, while at the same time, secretly defrauding His treasury.

People who fail to tithe have deliberately made falsehood their way of life; they have submerged their conscience in deceit. Falsity cannot be profitable for the sinner, let alone for the child of God. These are the people Isaiah speaks of. "When the overflowing scourge shall pass through, it shall not come unto us: for we have made lies our refuge, and under falsehood have we hid ourselves" (Isaiah 28:15). These are the people inside the camp speaking in this manner. They have determined to resist any plea for fellowship and goodwill with the Creator. They are rebellious and shameless and have settled their own destiny.

Proverbs 21:2&8 reads, "Every way of a man is right in his own eyes: But the Lord pondereth the hearts. ... The way of a man is forward and strange, but as for the pure his work is right." We cannot wander out of the way of instruction or else we wander out of *the way* completely.

It is strange, but here it is: a person will arrange his or her own demise for failing to follow the instructions given him or her. No one will be able to stop such a person. No amount of coaxing or allurement will entice such a person to change his or her ways when he or she is bent on self-destruction.

Some people are in our midst functioning as Christians, when indeed their hearts have not been changed. They will go to their graves hiding themselves under falsehood. It will be worse for them in the Judgement, since they have been privileged to be part of the company of God but stopped short of total commitment. Even as we live now, we have certain regrets; we chide ourselves for not doing this or that or for not trying a little harder.

God has my hands and my resources to use in the propagation of His Gospel. Will you join in too, dear brother, dear sister? Jesus said to His disciples in Matthew 9:37–38, "The harvest truly is plenteous, but the labourers are few; pray ye therefore the Lord of the harvest, that He will send forth labourers into His harvest." Get engaged in this plea for workers in the Lord's harvest. If you cannot do anything personally, then let your money do the work for you. There are many who are ready and equipped, just waiting for the financial backing. Let us answer the call by whatever means we can. I urge you to be fully involved from this point forward.

chapter 24

RIGIDITY OF CHARACTER

The Christian is viewed as being many things that are inconsistent with the world's view—and rightly so, because our orders are rigid. They are strict and must be obeyed. We are soldiers in the King's army and must not backtalk our General and Commander in Chief. We must obey His commands implicitly. He does not take advice from His soldiers; we follow without objections or questions, and we follow obediently and willingly. God is not losing the battle as some might think. As such, He has no contingency plans just in case something does not work out; everything follows according to His original plan and fits in perfectly. We might believe that the battle is being lost or stymied by the devils disturbances but we think this because we do not fully understand the sovereignty of God. When we grasp this concept that He is sovereign, we know that no one can override His plans or thwart them.

Whatever goes on, it is because He allows it.

If as Christians our allegiance is to our Lord and Saviour, then He has the right to give the orders. In the beginning, He tells us that friendship with the world is enmity with God, and that he or she who sets out for the kingdom but then looks back is not fit for the kingdom. Is that demand harsher than some of the rules laid down by some military leaders? I know that it is not. In the Second World War, there were suicide bombers in some militaries who dared not grumble about such a mission. Having joined the military, they voluntarily gave up their freedom and their lives.

Christians are no different. We are literally slaves owned by a Master.

Of course, this Master does not rule with an iron fist. We serve Him with delight and willingness. We have handed over to Him the reins of our lives freely, and we know that which we handed over was impossible for us to keep anyhow. He keeps us in perfect peace as long as we remain loyal to His command.

The Christian's life is not a two-tiered system, the religious and the secular. Every aspect of our affairs—as we play, as we work and as we worship—must be conducted as if God Himself were peering over our shoulder. Our business with the world must reflect the Master we serve. This is our new mandate, to honour and obey Him.

At a factory where I worked, a number of us would go for lunch occasionally. One day, somehow my lunch was not paid for. The next day, when I returned to pay, the cashier was shocked that I returned to pay for it. One Christmas I came home from the supermarket with an extra turkey. Accidently I bagged someone else's bird. When I went back to the supermarket to return it, the rightful owner had just missed it and returned to the store to enquire about it.

The world is a strange place. I mean, the people of the world are strange. They have a high expectation of the Christian, and when we fall short of that expectation, they condemn us. They know that our standard is not the world's standard and they admire us for it. Nevertheless, they expect us to compromise on so many fronts. It is hypocritical of them, really, knowing what the new life is and expecting people to deviate from it. We must endeavour to keep our standards high. The world has a high standard also in many aspects of its operation.

It is interesting to note that for certain government positions, the applicant has to be squeaky clean. No stone remains unturned in selecting the right candidate for such a job. The person who fills the spot practically has to be from Heaven, without any vices or any criminal record. Some standards are high and should be kept that way. Many people want to know that the people they elect to public office are of good character.

Returning from a certain shopping mall where I returned something to a business there on my way home from work, I realized that the mall, which I had been to several times before, now struck me as the most serene place I had ever been in. Every shop had items laid out perfectly and with such order that I wondered if they were only on display or if people really handled those goods. Of course, the things were for sale to everyone.

I am not shabby, by no means, but at one point my car broke down. As I was walking, I saw one of my co-workers and asked him for a ride in his bus. I did not have on my safety vest then and was on the roadway when this occurred, so I had to identify myself. It was not a driver I knew. His remarks were, "Look at you how well dressed you are. I would not think you drive a bus." I told him that when we work with children, we have to be especially careful to be modestly dressed. I mention this only to say that when I went into the mall I spoke of a few sentences ago, I was coming from my job as a school bus driver and I felt that I did not belong in such a place because it was so sterile. I literally felt unclean and unfit for such a setting.

Human beings can make things appear perfect on the outside, my friend. Sometimes we fall for the glitter, but all of that glitter does not mean much in the larger scheme of things. The world sees this glitter as a measure of success, but what do the Christians do or show? Many times we cover our faces in shame and say, "O Lord! O Lord!" for the things we portray and say.

Christians are warned not to be contaminated by the world. Instead of striving to emulate the world, we must live the unadulterated life that pleases our Master. I have heard it said, "Trevor, you would not be a bad person if it were not for your religion." I would fit in wonderfully but for my religion. It is the one thing that many other people cannot stand, and it is the thing that removes us Christians from full participation in the world. I have not ceased to praise God, bowing the knee when I do. I warn people daily through the Word or by a tract, hoping and praying that they will see the light also.

chapter 25

OBJECTIVITY VS. SUBJECTIVITY

Our progress is being hampered when we build on subjective impressions and behaviours rather than on objectivity. We are a people who fall prey to falsehood. Oftentimes we have our doubts, yet we go against our better instincts and fall for the scam. I say scam, which can be from an outsider or even from our own desires. Some ideas forced upon us are induced by our own unsound thinking. Yes, we are deluded daily by our subjective thoughts and behaviours. In spite of being an educated set, we do easily swallow a lie. A lie is told us or we ourselves make up the impossible and convince ourselves that it can be or that it is so.

We read and hear daily about people getting scammed. These incidents are not on the wane; they are on the rise. You hear things like, "I trusted him. He sounded so sincere when he said he loved me," and so on. One doctor revealed how he was scammed out of $200,000. He might have scammed himself into believing that it could not happen to him. He did not see things objectively. He did not read the world as a sad and cruel place to live, with dangerous people who will make mincemeat of you.

Someone has rightly said, "Build your life on what is real, rather than on what you feel." We often overextend ourselves in many ways. It could be in a job posting we want to apply for, which is a position far beyond our sphere of expertise or knowledge. Or we attempt a feat far beyond our strength and stamina and in so doing hurt our prospects for anything good. Of course, in some circumstances it is good to set our goals higher than we can reach and then reach them. In doing this, we strain our abilities somewhat to grow. If we did not do this, then we would remain stagnant and become passé. In such cases of goal setting, if you fall short of your goal, you will not have lost anything except an ego boost.

Build your life on what is real rather than on what you feel is worthy advice. Doing this removes emotions from the equation and implants reality squarely in your lap. We must remain free from many of the induced encumbrances that surround us that seek to suck us in. Many things are unholy alliances designed to weigh us down, preventing flight.

Discipline is the word we need to embrace. Without discipline, the river becomes a swamp and the rut becomes a grave. Are we digging our own graves by engaging in a certain lifestyle? I think we are. We must strongly embrace the self-management enterprise as a foundation and then build on it. Let us be frequent stock takers of our lives and activities. We should set our affairs in proper perspective as though we were leaving this stage for another and everything must be cleaned up on this front. If we looked at our lives in this light, then we would find an easier path to tread. Who is averse to ease? Nobody, I am sure. To enjoy the good life, then, is not difficult. Stay within your limits, know your boundaries and push to expand them when the opportunity arises.

As Ella Wheeler Wilcox wrote:

> One ship sails east,
> The other sails west,
> By the same self-wind that blows
> Tis not the wind nor the gale
> But the set of the sail
> That determines the way they go.

There is a stirring of the wind for all our sails, but the direction we take is determined by the setting of our sails. If we do not have a direction set, then the wind will be of little value to us. We will not benefit from it. If a course is set, and then we can be greatly helped by the force of the wind. Directions. Directions we must have—not all directions but a certain one.

We cannot be like Stephen Leacock's horse. After he mounted it, it galloped in all directions. A direction is like a value system that we adopt and follow. There is a positive and compelling reason for setting those sails for the direction we want to travel in life, and an equally compelling one for taking the direction that we take. To begin with, the desire to launch out is propelled or driven by some provoked unpleasant and unsettling conditions at the point of departure. Things are not where we want them to be. Our rejection of the surrounding conditions sometimes forces our departure.

There is, however, a tide in the affairs of humankind that is set in motion by the Great Creator and there is nothing one can do to stop it. He has it all planned out. We take that wave and are buoyed high above the crest, where we might still not know to lift a thought to Him in gratitude. We might think that we have created the opportunity that we embrace and thereby fail to give credit to whom it belongs.

Never mind what we think things should be like. It is what they are that counts. In real estate, I sometimes encountered buyers who wanted to list their house for a very high price. Such people, are sentimentally attached to the houses, thought that if someone else wanted to own their house, then that person better pay whatever the asking price is. I would tell people like this that the same type of houses in their neighbourhood sold for X amount, but they thought their houses were the exception. If a real estate agent is foolish enough to take such a listing, then he or she will only waste time, because the house won't sell.

We are in that stage of our existence where we think that we can discount the Word of God. Whatever we think a situation to be, it is that which will influence the outcome, we believe. We are dead wrong, just like the property owner who sets his price way above the selling prices of the other houses. If he wants his house sold, then he had better be objective and accept the going price.

Each of us would do well to see the reality of our world in essence. Recognize just which way the wind is blowing and profit from it.

chapter 26

YIELDING TO GOD

Yielding is one of the traffic laws in our world. Yielding becomes frivolous in some places and seems unnecessary on some streets because there is so little traffic. However, on the highways, people dare not ignore a Yield sign because doing so places ones life in mortal danger. We know the results of careless driving when rules are ignored, be it a sign, a speed limit or our neglect to wear a seat belt. All these laws have consequences when they are ignored. Some of them have deadly consequences. How many times we hear or see horrific crashes with lives lost because someone refused to stop or yield. Some one's life is snuffed out because someone could not spare an extra second and yield or stop.

When God's signs says. Yield, we would do well to heed and obey them or the consequences can be as deadly—even more so since the consequences are eternal. "Seek ye first the Kingdom of God and His righteousness; and all these things shall be added unto you" (Matthew 6:33) is not a sign that can be ignored without a penalty. It is laid down as a guide to everyone who would live a godly life in this troubled world. Christ Himself gave this command so that we can get our priorities straight. Putting first things first that is.

This command will help us keep the horse in front of the cart where it belongs. Christ has not condemned us for wanting things of this world, but He is warning us to attend to the most important thing first, and that is to be aligned with Him and His Word. If you or I have not done just that, then we are still in the camp of the unbeliever and can expect no further growth than they. In such lives, which lack the certainty of a final destination, there will continue to be an accumulation of grief and sorrows, and in the end frustration and bewilderment. The will not experience a good outcome.

There are sequences of events in the tide of humankind. We must not confuse them. To ride the waves comfortably, we must obey the rules. When the Master Himself says something then we better obey. The Lord has given us this guideline so that we can get our priorities straight.

In a nutshell, we must let the Word of God guide our desires. Are the things you pine after sanctioned by God's Word? Are the things you are setting your affection on earthly or heavenly? Does what you seek threaten to possess your heart, your mind, your soul and all your energies? Remember, "Where your treasure is there will your heart be also" (Matthew 6:21).

The Word of God confirms our desires in light of what is right and what is wrong; it becomes our working conscience, the pulse, if you will, of our very essence. It is necessary and most vital to protect the most important part of our being: the heart. It is in the heart that the decisions are made for good or for evil. What is done there will drive our destiny and determine the quality of our journey to our destination.

This might not make for easy reading for some, but if I neglect to point out the importance of these two places, I will fail in giving you honest guidance. In all of life, and in whatever we devote ourselves to, our destination will be either of the two places without fail or deviation. If we fail to keep those two destinations before us, then we are like the ostrich burying its head in the sand, which basically supports the pretence that all is well and that it is safe. There are two roads and one leads to Hell and the other to Heaven.

When I mentioned to my optometrist that I was writing *What's Up?* he said that I should fill it with scandals, because that is what sells. Well, writing about scandals may make some authors money, but if I did so, it would condemn my soul. I certainly would be selling my soul, if you will, for silver. Most of what is written herein is repulsive to most because they do not want to hear of their responsibilities to their Maker, but I am obliged to write about them nevertheless, because *What's Up?* is intended to be used as a witnessing tool and a guide to a better future for all who open its pages. Making a profit is my secondary aim.

It is easy to dismiss these two realities of Hell and Heaven as myths. Some people view the idea flippantly, agreeing with the majority, but in no case is the majority right. It is the few that have the truth at any time. The popular view is never the correct one. The tumult and the noise have proven always to be the *de facto* element. Christ has said, "Broad is the road that leads to destruction and narrow is the one that leads to life and few there are that finds it" (Matthew 7:13). Which road are you on right now dear reader?

Before the Second World War, there was a vigilant man, Winston Churchill who saw and warned people of the danger of the German buildup that threatened the stability of the world. The then Prime Minister of Great Britain, Neville Chamberlain signed a peace treaty with Adolf Hitler and waved his paper in Parliament to show that at last the two countries had achieved peace. Sir Winston Churchill scoffed at it and warned continually of the deception and the danger that the world faced, especially Europe. Today, history has proven him to be the true voice that rallied the troops to defeat the ugly reign of Hitler's terror.

Many people have denigrated the Gospel and in turn have exalted themselves. It is easy for us to slip into that trap and think that they must be right. Many too are among the ranks of the Christian denominations that are leading millions into a fiery furnace where the worm dieth not.

Sometimes when I hear people scoff at Hell, I advise them to take dancing lessons because they are going to have to be fleet of foot to navigate the fire. My friend, do not take the chance and find out. Do not line up behind these God-denying mongers. Don't do it. Let them perish without you. If they deny the existence of Hell, the Virgin Birth or Heaven itself, then get out from among them, as they are not shepherds but butchers. If after reading *What's Up?* you find yourself in Hell, you will have no one to blame but yourself. Benjamin Whichcote rightly said, "The longest words, the strongest lungs, the most voices are false measures of truth."

Truth needs no embellishment and no defence. It stands the test of time and will exonerate itself. There is a sea of confusion about truth.

Every person thinks he or she has the truth, but truth is not an opinion. It is established facts, and it will break all the hammers that are struck against it. It is steadfast and sure because it emanates from God. When we learn to lean on the truth instead of on humankind's wisdom, we are surely supported throughout time and for eternity. Why can't we all see the truth? Is it because the Intruder has blinded our eyes and poisoned our minds? I think that is why.

Elizabeth Barrett Browning wrote as follows:

> Earth's crammed with heaven,
> And every common bush afire with God
> But only he, who sees, takes off his shoes,
> The rest, sit round it and pluck blackberries.

Why can't we see the truth? It is because we have blocked it out of our minds so we can get on with the business of sinning? "We are busy planting right now. We have no time to bother with you and your scare tactics," people say to those who witness to them. "If I am free, then perhaps when I retire I will listen to you. I promise I will remember my date with you." Surely people like this are their own keepers, so they will be there to listen to us when they are ready.

When I was in the field of life insurance, I and my co-workers were told of a man who was approached many times by an agent to buy life insurance. Every time he refused. He would not budge, as he did not see the need for life insurance. Later, realizing that his health was deteriorating, he one day called an agent and said to him that he was ready to buy. "Well," said the agent, "that is fine, but you will have to have a medical examination." The man did have a medical examination, but his chance for getting an insurance policy was nil. The only thing he could buy then was a coffin from the undertaker. There is a tide in the affairs of humankind that we must be ready to ride when it presents itself. If we miss it, we might miss it forever—and that would be regrettable.

Some of us are so conscious of the consequences of these weightier matters of life that we dare not take chances with even temporary things. We will not drive if our car insurance lapses. We are terrified that we would have an accident that day if we drove. As the saying goes, we would rather be safe than sorry. Why then would we gamble with eternal matters? I must confess, it is beyond my understanding. People say nonetheless, "Let us feast and have our fill of pleasure, and perhaps someday we will consider your call to look up toward God."

There is a dearth of the knowledge of God that pervades the home, the houses of Parliament and all the institutions of learning. God is relegated to the sidelines or benched. There is a distraction of mammoth proportion that is robbing the homes and even the house of God of the glory and majesty that is due Him. Parents will not forbid their kids to enter church without their pacifiers. Little Johnny likes his toys and will not come to church unless he may take them. He comes and disrupts the service by distracting others. He enters and exits without learning a single thing about God. He is either reading a book or fidgeting with a gadget. He must be busy with something other than the Word of God.

When I brought up my kids, we went to church as a family every Sunday. And why not? That is the place to go, God's house. One of my kids, Stephanie, although she could barely read, would not let me find the passage of Scripture for her. She would say: "I will find it myself, Dad"— and she did. How else does anyone learn except by doing?

Many parents will have much to account to God for. Many in their poor state have bargained with God and pleaded for opportunities to fight and conquer poverty and have had their wish granted. Somewhere in the midst of prosperity, they have forgotten their plea and have become like the rest, neither hot nor cold: worthless. In Revelation 3:16, God says this of such people: "So then because thou art lukewarm, and neither cold nor hot, I will spew thee out of my mouth." We become unpalatable and insipid when we reject God's commands and fail to live up to His standard. We are unworthy to approach God's throne. Because of this, we need to repent.

If we do not repent, then we must pay—and we will reap our rewards. Galatians 6:7 says, "Be not deceived; God is not mocked: for whatsoever a man soweth, that shall he also reap." There always comes harvest time, my friend. Harvest time can be a refreshing season when our fruits come to maturity and we can enjoy those sweet fruits of our labour. That is nice indeed, to say the least. On the other hand, some of us will be eating but sour grapes. It will be a sour harvest indeed.

Many parents have failed like Samuel to correct their sons. Woe to those who neglect to discipline their children, as they have negated their responsibilities. In so doing, they have failed to be good fathers and mothers. I know. As a parent, I know how unpopular I can be to my children when I use the Bible as the guide. It is a struggle. But as I grow older, I am pleased with—or should I say that I have no regrets about—the effort I put into raising my children in the nurture and admonition of the Lord. They have a foundation on which to build a sound life. If they go astray, I do not carry a burden of negligence. I am satisfied that I did my uttermost to give them proper guidance. If they side with the world, then it is their doing. It is not I who helped them. Certainly, if they choose to follow the *via dolorosa* (the way of sorrow), then it is their choice and I have no part in it. My resolute intentions were to steer them in a godly path so they would grow up to be God-fearing men and women.

Fighting to provide food and shelter and the other necessities of life is a laudable accomplishment, but if we stop short of helping our children to see the big picture, then we have failed miserably. I salute all you parents who take the time to be with your children in church on a Sunday and at other times. This principal foundation surely is the best security that you can ever give them. It will be better than money or property. Let them have nothing of this world, but give them Jesus and your joy will be full.

We can fight and struggle as much as we want, but the way to success is to be obedient to the dictates of God's Word. Again you might scoff at this, saying that many are making headway in this life, which is success. Success is intrinsically linked to happiness. "Happiness," wrote Samuel Taylor Coleridge, "Can be built only on virtue and must of necessity have truth as its foundation." Without truth as our guide, we are floundering and are bound to be dashed on the rocks of despair. We will realize sometimes that we are lost, but we might flounder before help can be summoned. Help is at hand now. Ask for it.

Happiness is an elusive thing today because we seek it in odd places. Happiness is found only in truth. Truth is facing up to facts, not falsities. A person lives falsely and hopes to find happiness, but he knows truthfully that he will never find it under the cloak of falsehood. Why are we not happy, why can we never be happy, outside of Christ? We are wealthier and healthier than our parents were, but we are more miserable. We have houses full of trinkets, garages packed with cars, and things in storage and in basements. We cannot find a clear path to walk. We pride ourselves in having things. We have things, things, everywhere. Where do they get us? Nowhere. We are in the throes of despair and uncertainty. Our rapacious nature is getting the better of us.

One of my co-workers had so much stuff in his basement that you could hardly find a path to walk. He pointed out to me, "No one knows how much these things are worth." I know. Another man is such a hoarder. Coming home with his wife one day, he saw a fridge placed at the curb and he put it in the trunk of his car. Well, he got part of it in the trunk. He asked his wife to drive while he walked behind the car holding the fridge. He told me that he has a property in Newfoundland with a truck full of things. I believe that this is a situation where one spouse would want to die before the other. I am sure that this wife would be glad to go first. That kind of inheritance is something she does not want to be partaker of.

Another person I know paid storage fees for many years for some items that she would have been better off throwing out, since the storage fees amounted to thousands of dollars over the period, far more than the things are worth. People like her have their priorities backwards. They put emphasis on nonessentials. If we have all the things that we could ever hope for, then why aren't we happy? Well, happiness is not found in things, pure and simple. Happiness is linked to a relationship with our Father.

Why is it that a person who built a career and reached the top of an organization would suddenly quit in disgust? Because the person has come to the realization that he is fighting the wind. All is vanity, vanity. Of course, there is an emptiness that pervades the hearts of humankind that can only be filled by Christ Himself. He is the living water and the Bread of Life.

Building a life without God at the centre is like building a structure on the sand. It cannot be done. If there is no proper foundation, when the wind of life blows, as it certainly will, our house will fall. We need to build on the sure Foundation, which is Christ Jesus the Rock. We need to make hard choices at times, but when we make them, even if sometimes they are costly, they will add greatly to out wellbeing and happiness.

When Joshua was leading the Israelites through the wilderness, he met with some strong opponents, but he challenged them with strong words. He gave them an ultimatum: "Choose ye this day whom ye will serve" (Joshua 24:15). They had the opportunity to choose life or death. It is hard to think that anyone would choose death over life, but that is what the Christ rejecters are choosing today. It is what you will do if after you read *What's Up?* You reject its message. Jesus is still pleading. Won't you let Him in?

Does God Need Anything from Us?

We ask the question "How much of what we have does God require or need?" None. He owns everything and needs nothing from us. He is and has been self-existent from eternity past and will be throughout all eternity to come. In spite of His greatness, He created us to have fellowship with Him. He delights in us when we seek to restore the broken relationship caused by sin. God still loves us; He states it in His Word. I still cannot fathom it, but I accept it as truth because He says so. My soul is at rest in this simple but glorious truth. No one can tell me otherwise. Some smart alecks have said that Christians' beliefs are in the head, meaning we are a bit nutty, but they long for what we have. They are even jealous—and rightly so—but they deny everything we say and relegate our faith to fantasy.

Many unbelievers on their deathbeds are tormented and frightened when they know they are going out into the darkness with no certainty of what's out there. They are afraid. And yet because they have lived a lie for so long, they still will not bow. They would rather postpone the bowing until it is a worthless bow. They will bow when mercy is gone and the Judgement comes. It will be too late then, too late, because mercy will be gone.

A man had been preached to and witnessed to, and yet, occupied with other things, he rejected the Gospel, hoping that someday he would accept it, but in his own time, when it was convenient. He fell sick and sent for a preacher, who wondered: *"What can it be this time? "* since he could not tell this man anything that he had not hear before. The preacher went to the sick man's bedside and listened. The dying man wanted a word of hope, which the preacher then gave. But the man said, "I cannot receive it. It is too late. I cannot believe it anymore." The Spirit of God had left Him for good. He was conscious of his end and destination, but he was helpless to change it. He had waited and had spurned the Holy Spirit for too long. This warning is apt even now: "If today you hear His voice, harden not your heart" (Hebrews 3:8).

The way of blessing and success is simply the way of obedience; that is so without a doubt. In utter submission, the hymn writer Augustus Toplady writes: "I can only spread the sail, Thou, Thou God Almighty must breathe the auspicious gale." Inherent in this saying is the great truth that we can plunge into an act but that the ultimate outcome will be determined by the hand of God. He can still the storm for our benefit, send a gentle breeze to fill our sails, or magnify the breeze to a destructive outcome. Whether we acknowledge Him in it or not, He is there directing the outcome all the time. All things are upheld by His omnipotent hand. Can we truthfully ask for more?

Eternity is planted in all of us. It is like the life that is in every seed. Each is capable of germinating and becoming fruitful. Once a person is born into the world, he or she becomes an eternal being. Death cannot extinguish the soul, which after death carries on in a different realm. It moves from time to eternity. Do not wait and see, dear reader. Act now to secure a place in God's kingdom.

Seneca, philosopher and tutor to Emperor Nero, said, "The body is the prison of the soul and death is praised as release, as the birthday of eternity." This is a statement of tremendous truth. Every word here can be substantiated by the believer. We have a witness from above, bearing witness with our spirit that eternity is planted in us. As a Christian nears the end of life, he can sense or even feel the eternal breeze cooling his sick body and encouraging his eternal soul.

Many have gotten a glimpse of their eternal inheritance even before they closed their eyes in death. My own father tasted the bliss of entering into the presence of God before he died. On the morning before he died, his facial features were transformed into the likeness of a young man. Although he was 92 years old, his face shone like that of a 20-year-old man. He had already experienced the transformation from time to eternity while yet a sojourner down here on earth. He felt it, he knew it and he was going home. That is the place he longed for. His experience is not unique. Every believer dies gloriously. God has set eternity in us, but some, instead of nourishing and nurturing the great potential for a better and more glorious life in the hereafter, stifle the thought and kill the germ.

God has planted signals in the animals, the birds, the fish of the sea and every living thing on earth. They all survive using the instinct within them. Some have accomplished such astounding feats of survival that it staggers the mind. How can one account for the fact that the Rufous hummingbird travels 5,000 miles to winter in other lands and then returns to its starting point in spring? There is a GPS in every creature. The designer and engineer who puts it there is God.

If you are reading *What's Up?* it is more than a coincidence. God has given you yet another opportunity to awaken your senses so that you fall at His feet, acknowledge Him as Lord of all and ask Him now to be Lord of your life. Let Him supply the GPS that you need to navigate your life. Recently I witnessed to a co-worker who said that she had not been educated in Christianity. From another country, she speaks English very well. She must have arrived in Canada in donkey years and had the chance of entering a church. I gave her some literature to read and begged her to read it.

I often believe that the greatest regret of the lost soul is the wasted opportunity while on earth. A person who has squandered all opportunities will, for all eternity, mourn the chances he or she had. The reason for *What's Up?* is to do my part in pleading with the lost to find the Way. It is knocking at your door. You can get connected on the radio, on the TV and through literature. Of course, some people think that there are more pressing matters to take care of, but there is no matter more important than your relationship with God. This is the only essential matter there is. We can survive the loss of everything else, but not this. This loss we cannot get over.

Napoleon Bonaparte thought the most pressing matter he had was to conquer the world. One day his friend asked him, "So what, then, when you conquer the world?" "Well," he said, "I can sit and rest." The friend suggested that if that is all he wanted in the end was to sit and rest, he should do it now and forget about conquering the world. Ego, ego, my friend, supersedes everything else. Ego is at the top of the priority list for too many. The thought is: *"When I have satisfied my ego, then I will do the lesser things, even the good and commendable things."*

People say, "I will help the poor and needy of the world, but only after I have paid for my new BMW and my million-dollar house. After all, these things are necessary to bolster my ego, which is the basis of my existence. How could I ever feel good about myself if I did not indulge in the toys of the wealthy? I must satisfy the urge, or else I cannot rest." People like this will not rest because things such as expensive cars cannot give the rest that they need and are contrary to the rest that the Lord promises to those who will put their trust in Him.

As the children of God move closer to our priority, which is the new home in Heaven, and realize that we are moving out of earth's orbit and into the heavenly realm, we are comforted by the fact that God is in control. I had a Baptist pastor who would assure us that whatever was happening, such as the threat of nuclear proliferation, should not concern us, because nothing can happen until the Lord says so. I have comforted myself with those words, knowing that we must believe totally that there is a set time for the Lord to act on certain matters and that no one can thwart His plans or expedite them. Nothing can happen before its time, as the saying goes. He rules supreme always and forever.

In my own life, I have experienced the Father's intercession. He has removed me from situations that could have resulted in my death or maiming. I have known for a long time that what He promises, He will do. When He says that no evil shall come nigh my dwelling, I know it is so. I have experienced His protective hand. It gives me the greatest comfort to know that He is in control.

On the contrary, many people experience sleepless nights because they are overwhelmed by problems and worry and they do not have anyone to turn to. They might go to a doctor or a psychologist, who gives them only Band-Aid solutions. The problem is deep-rooted and stems from a fearful heart. We do not want to spend the time to cultivate a pure and dignified heart. No, we want an instant fix—from human beings and not God. It cannot be done.

We must take time to read enlivening books and the Word of God, for by so doing we will know the plan of God for our lives and will come to know the highest joy. Someone has said that when the heart is pure, the vision will be clear and we will see God. All the dross will be filtered out. A pure heart enables clearer vision. We will indeed see things as they are, objectively and realistically. Again, I must reiterate that the person who is not on the Lord's side is fighting an uphill battle. The odds are stacked against such a person.

One man told me that the only time he has for himself after a busy week is on Sunday. Should He withhold the air that we breathe, we would all be dead in a minute, and yet we are too busy building our own empires and have no place for Him. Shame on us, although *shame* is too gentle a word to use for such neglect. God does not want to be any place in our lives but first place. He created us and has bought us back with His own blood. As for me, He has first place in my life.

He has given His life for me, so the least I can do is to live for Him like young Daniel of the Bible. When Daniel was sent into captivity, he simply resolved in his heart that he would serve the Lord. Well, because of his resolve, his resolute determination, he survived the lions' den. This incident stands as a gigantic monument proclaiming throughout history the power and protection of God to those who would dare to trust Him. When Shadrach, Meshach and Abednego refused to bow down to Nebuchadnezzar and were to be put into the fiery furnace, the king asked, "Who is that God that shall deliver you out of my hands" (Daniel 15:16–18)? They answered by saying that their God whom they served was able, but if He chose not to deliver them, as it was up to Him, they still would not bow to the king. That was the confidence that those young men had, absolute confidence, not wavering for one billionth of a second. If God be for us, then who can be against us? That is the question, my Christian brethren. No one. Our God is absolutely mighty. There is nothing impossible with Him.

Living a life of debauchery and vanity is a waste of time. There is nothing to be gained at the end of the road for all the self-effort. A life without God is senseless. I shiver to think what mine might have been if I had not heeded God's call at age 22. I am almost sure I would be in a grave.

While writing *What's Up?* I lost a cousin in a car accident. The person who was with him, another of my cousins, was just making his way out of intensive care. Not long before the accident, I sat at a table with the surviving cousin and his wife and pleaded with them to give their lives to God and bring up their kids in the church. They didn't give a definitive answer. I am sure that like most other young people, they were busy providing for their kids' physical needs. Thank God my dead cousin gave his life to the Lord, according to his pastor.

The stubbornness of human beings is beyond understanding. The Bible says clearly that we prefer darkness to the light. You might not agree with such a saying initially, but when you analyze and scrutinize the saying, you will come to agree. I once worked at a company where a co-worker was killed while on his way to Nova Scotia on a weekend. Having fallen asleep while driving, he crashed and was thrown out of the car. As I discussed this accident at lunch, another co-worker said he would wear his seat belt from that point forward. It is the law in Canada to wear a seat belt, but more than that the seat belt is a life saver in case of an accident. It is a great safety device, yet many do not use it. We would say, "How foolish that is." Of course, it is foolish to ignore such a law that is in place to save us from harm. God has made a provision to save our souls, but we frivolously ignore it too. Many have no interest in even listening to this claim. Others are not aware of it in the slightest degree, and many outwardly scoff at the idea that there is a God.

This is but one side of the coin. On the other side is the group of people who have accepted God's highest gift and are revelling in the joy it brings. They have the deepest gratitude for the provision made for the redemption of their souls. We are all under the condemnation of death. Here comes One who offers life, and we shun Him. We would rather live in the pigpen and eat the husks with the pigs than revel in the mansion which He promises and in the light of His blessed Son the Lord Jesus Christ. Who would refuse the offer of a bright future? No one should, but yet the majority of the world's people who hear of such an offer reject it. They refuse to believe it absolutely or else they would receive it.

Life is full of choices, and rightly so, because it is through choices that we are greatly served. While that may be so, perhaps we are not better off. Many choices make us a confused people more than a fulfilled people. A North Korean boy entered a U.S. store and was surprised by the many different brands of soaps he could get compared to what was on offer in Korea, where he had no choice at all. I wonder if we North Americans are cleaner because we have so many choices of soap. Perhaps not.

Our Western culture places a high value on what is worthless and throws away as worthless what is of eternal value. We are literally off course and do not know it. We have become distracted totally and are being driven by the pursuit of nonessentials. The gadgets we invented to serve us are the very things that we give our essence to in order to keep up with them. We have become slaves of our inventions.

We are not the first to be so driven. The Israelites made and worshipped a golden calf instead of their living active God, who nurtured and provided for them throughout the wilderness journey. Again I will say, how very foolish we are as human beings and how quickly we forget the blessings of God. From a hand-to-mouth situation, a person will find himself in a very prosperous situation with a job or a business. As soon as he begins to thrive, his mentality changes. He forgets to give thanks to God and many times turn his back on Him completely.

Joshua said to the people, "As for me and my house we will serve the Lord" (Joshua 24:15). That was his resolution, and that is mine today—and also that of countless others like me. We will, under the threat of death, serve the Lord. That is our present position in this world. We are under the condemnation of death without God. Death is our only prospect outside of Christ. We are under the law of sin and death. That is our inheritance from the first Adam.

But that is not the end of the story. There is hope stemming from that penalty of sin and death. There is redemption through faith in the crucified and risen Saviour, the Lord Jesus Christ. Here lies our way out, the escape hatch, if you will. Death shall not triumph over us if we believe. That is the good news. Amen and amen.

chapter 27

NO ESCAPE

Have you ever been cornered with no way out unless you surrender? It is frightful even to have a dream of being cornered in this way. We want to have a way out at all times. To be in a place of pure darkness—with no light—is frightful, to say the least. We strive to keep a way out open at all times. It is logical to have an escape route available. That is the position an intelligent person takes in living his life. Very seldom one does not have a contingency plan in the event the main plan does not materialize. To be cornered is a place we do not want to find ourselves in. All our houses have a back door, not to let in the thieves but to give us a way out—just in case.

In real estate, a buyer may put conditional clauses into a contract–such as a condition on him being able to arrange financing; that the house or property is asbestos-free; and any liens against the property and so forth. These clauses alleviate the buyer's risk of losing his deposit or down payment if all the conditions are not met. It gives the buyer comfort to proceed.

When Pierre Elliott Trudeau was Prime Minister and was travelling to the west coast of Canada, where he was not well received, he took along his son Justin, who was about 6 years old—just in case. My daughter and I were in the kitchen when we heard the announcement on the radio that the Prime Minister would be taking along his son Justin on the trip. I blurted out, "Just in case," which caused my daughter and I to share a big laugh that morning. I have never forgotten that spur-of-the-moment quip. I must add here that I now have my own Justin now. He is my grandson who is studying law at Manchester University in England. Everyone wants a measure of guarantee to alleviate worry.

We cannot live carelessly; we must have strategies by which to live by if we want to amount to anything in this life or even to survive here.

I spoke to a man recently who played church all his life. As a matter of fact, he was brought up in the church yet had not surrendered his life fully to God. He came to his senses when in a dream he faced death, died, and found himself in a dark place. After awaking from his dream, he finally realized that if he had died in reality, he would be in such a place. So you guessed it—he is now a new man, trusting God and delving into His Word as never before.

Rightly so, my friend. Today if we hear His voice, we should not harden our hearts. God is constantly pleading with us and placing the invitation in our path. We would do well to respond in the affirmative, because one day it might be too late, forever too late. Should that day come upon us, it would be tragedy beyond repair. All along life's journey, God is placing people in our paths who will give a word, which we forget. At some time we encounter one of these people and suddenly realize that probably the Lord is speaking to us.

Here in the West we are privileged to hear the good news of salvation through different media every day of our lives if we desire, but to some of us the Gospel has become passé. We have become Gospel-weary. Some preachers have even dumbed down the Gospel to reach the masses. It is not here but elsewhere, in other parts of the world, that the Word is precious. People are hungry for the good news and do relish having a person of God present the Word to them. They have longed for communion with the One for whom they searched for all their lives.

I must reiterate that here in North America, the distractions are too overwhelming and our needs are much too demanding for us to find time to assemble as we ought to in the churches. Our fervency for the worship service is woefully lacking. More and more churches are cancelling their evening services because of dwindling attendance. The question is, where are the Christians and what are they doing on Sunday nights?

Many families come intact to church on a Sunday night. It is surprising that some kids come only to engage in other activities while sitting in the service. I have been in a Sunday night service where a girl sat knitting with her needles, creating a noise that disturbed me to the point that I was compelled to turn to look at her. Only then did she stop. I've already spoken of the disdainful attitude coming from some worshippers.

What Is Brainwashing?

In North Korea, where communism is the form of government people are brainwashed into thinking that their leader is their great god who provides everything for them. Generation after generation will grow and die without the people having the privilege of knowing that there is a Creator and that it is to Him we owe everything, including our allegiance, not a amn. The North Koreans say there is no God. We North Americans say there is a God, but we do not behave any differently from the Koreans. I suppose missing the mark is missing the mark and it does not matter by how much. We all fall short if we do not serve Him in spirit and in truth.

Sir Winston Churchill once stated, "Socialism is the philosophy of failure, the creed of ignorance and the gospel of envy." Socialism keeps people enslaved and blinded to the truths that are the purview of every person. Little gods they are who oppress their people.

What great burden lies on a man or a woman who denies a child the privilege of knowing God? What greater burden lies on those who deny a whole generation and in most cases many generations, that vital part of their existence? No one can envisage the punishment that is in store for such people. God will hold them responsible and will not let them go free. Of course, that also goes for anyone who has the responsibility to lead others to the Saviour and reneges on that responsibility also.

Countries under socialism and communism are regressive compared to their neighbours. *Stagnant* is a mild word to use to describe such places as Cuba under communist rule. A once prosperous and thriving nation came to a standstill under communism. Stubborn people who will not relent until the need becomes stark, dying with the ideology of socialism. O the sinfulness of sin cannot be overestimated.

It was Nikita Khrushchev who said that the Soviet Union would bury the United States, and that they would triumph over such a nation with its ideology. The freedom that the Americans enjoyed would paralyze the nation, he claimed, saying that they would become a nation of addicts. There democracy or freedom does not prevent them from becoming addicts but they also have the freedom to worship publicly.

On the other their ideologies have not alleviate the problem of addicts either, many Russians are listlessly and hopelessly caressing the bottle as their only comfort. They have no hope. It is very sad. "No God," they say. It is the height of brainwashing.

The despotic North Korean leader clings to the ideology of communism and has so brainwashed his people that they think he is a little god. They see him as their eternal saviour or father. That is the influence he has, at least, on the young, whom he is indoctrinating. They magnify him as great, not knowing anything more and having no idea how oppressed they are. It is difficult to live without a choice not knowing that life exists outside of the present state.

There is such a stark contrast between North Korea and South Korea that those visiting from the North are shocked to see how affluent the South is. One girl remarked that in the South everyone has cell phones and other amenities that only the rich have in the North. It is the communistic doctrine that has brought that rottenness upon the land controlled by communists. The doctrine of "no God" will certainly bring out the worst in these people eventually.

We are enraged at the idea that one person is responsible for leading a whole nation into desolation, but here in the free world we see many who are also leading billions into the same plight. Who then is more horrible and deplorable? Some people in the West deny the power of the cross and the efficacy of the blood of Christ as the only means of salvation. They promote themselves above the cause of Christ. Anyone anywhere who does not serve the risen Saviour cannot bring glory and prosperity to their land. They remain as a stagnant pond, neither generating nor supporting life.

For many, there is little hope of lifting themselves out of poverty, but for all, there is no hope outside of Christ. Unless a person embraces Christ, he is poor and destitute and is perishing. Serving our God has as much practical applications as anything else. We hear it often in ads:

"Look no further. We have the very thing you are looking for." Everyone has the same message. Is it true that everyone has the truth? Of course not. Perhaps everyone is lying. Yet in the final analysis, we must make a decision about whatever items we will purchase. Perhaps soon after the purchase, we are made to understand that we made a good purchase and are satisfied. But more often than not, we are duped.

In certain situations, there might by a law that protects us against buying a lemon, but in most cases we have to take our losses. The Latin term *caveat emptor*—"let the buyer beware"— is used in real estate. Before the purchaser signs the sales agreement, he would better be sure to do his due diligence, making certain that what he is signing for is something he is satisfied with. The onus is on the purchaser to check out his prospective purchase before he buys. If it comes without a warranty, then the buyer is out of luck in the event that he does not get what he thought he purchased. (So it is with this book as I checked the editorial corrections or suggestions, I have found a certain gender bias which I had not intended, fortunately I have decided to read every word over so I was able to correct it.)

The same principle applies to your soul, my friend. You alone are responsible to secure your soul's salvation. Do not entrust it to anyone, as no one can secure its redemption for you. It is a fallacy that someone else can intercede on your behalf. The work of salvation has been done by Christ on the cross. All we have to do is go to Him in repentance to secure our pardon. It has to be asked for individually and personally, not on behalf of someone else. We can petition God on behalf of someone else on any matter but if it on salvation that person has to make the move him or herself. There is no getting around that fact.

A famous American wrote a letter to another famous man and asked an even more famous man to deliver it personally. The content was about the soul of the writer. His request was for intercession for his soul when he died. I have heard a preacher say of the man who wrote the letter that he had witnessed to him and he outright dismissed the thought that there is a God. He was a God denier as he worked, lived and prospered, but as death drew near, he sought some help and the closest he could get to God, whom he despised or denied, was through a man who himself was playing god. How very sad, my friend.

For many, It is when everything is waning and all is lost that they feel the need for God. Why would they believe now that there is a God but as they remained healthy and prosperous they denied Him. It is because they can feel the terror of going out into outer darkness alone. Need I say more.

I urge you to be diligent in searching the Scriptures to see if the things that your preacher tells you are supported by the Word of God. Many preachers are giving us their opinions on spiritual matters, and oftentimes their opinions are not worth a grain of salt. We must be diligent in searching for ourselves to be sure what our preachers say is so. We must not trust anybody, period, let alone trust someone with our most valuable possession, our souls. I once witnessed to a co-worker, and he told me that that is what he paid his priest to do for him, claiming that his priest would secure his redemption for him. In other words, that was the priest's job. Those who believe that the role of the priest is to pray for our sins are centuries behind the times. They are too lazy to find out things for themselves.

Too many are trusting in humanity's devices and human wisdom and are neglecting to verify the truth for themselves. I urge you to examine your religion and see whether it can stand the test. See whether it is based on man's wisdom and cunning or whether it is based on the Word of God. Apply the acid test, as is done in certain professions. It has been pointed out clearly that many who come in sheep's clothing are wolves and others who come as angels of light are devils.

In any event, your soul is a valuable commodity on the auction block. The highest bidder will claim it. You will be bought, either by another taskmaster, the cruelest yet, or by one who will set you free. The good news here is that you have a choice in this matter. I spoke of *caveat emptor,* "let the buyer beware." That is, the onus is on the purchaser to choose wisely or suffer the consequences. My friend, in the realm of—or in the light of—eternity, this matter is weightier; in fact, it is the weightiest matter there is. We will not have to do another thing in our lives that is weightier than making sure we are on the right path, that our religion will get us to Heaven.

Whoever you are and if you can leave all, simply drop it and follow Jesus and never look back at any of the things you were engaged, you would not lose one thing.

If this thought hits home with you, then do yourself the biggest favour you will ever do for yourself and investigate the legitimacy of what I have said. Get a Bible and begin to read it. Find out what it has to say about you in your present condition and what you need to do to get out.

There is a way, the Bible says, that seems right unto a person, but the ways thereof are the ways of death. Think on this. Every person is travelling on a path right now; one leads to Hell, and the other leads to Heaven. No euphemistic term will lessen the reality of those two places. You will go to one or the other. You might think, as many have, that you are following holy people of God, people with good intentions, but for some it is already too late. Like the North Korean children who do not see beyond what is taught them, many so-called Christians cannot see that they are on the wrong path, trusting the wrong religion to do the right job. This matter is light years away from material and temporary things, as our decision on eternal matters is final the moment we close our eyes in death. The idea that one can pray your soul out of Hell is a hellish doctrine, originating from the throne of Satan himself. May God open our eyes to see this absurd deception now?

Such teaching is spurious and is designed to shift the burden from self to others. You are responsible for your sins, not your father, your mother, your brother or your sister. You are responsible. No one can exonerate you but God Himself. He sent His Son to die in our place. When we put our faith in the finished work of Calvary, then—and only then—are we forgiven. We are forgiven and at the same time have the burden and guilt of sin removed. Here I must add, if you still have the burden of sin and guilt, then you would do well to go back to Calvary with that burden. It has not yet been removed from your back. You bear it still.

If You Will Allow Us, We Can Help

Have you, fellow Christian, spoken to anyone lately about the load they are carrying and where they can go to have it lifted? Have you given out a tract? Are you living a life that will attract others to the Master? Do your co-workers make you out as a Christian, or do they think that you are one of them since you engage in the things they engage in, share in the same unwholesome jokes and drift along with the crowd? My friend, you know who you are. I beg you, think of your responsibility to your children, your friends, your neighbours and everyone else. We are here to help the suffering, to lend a hand to the blind and show them the way to Calvary, where burdens are lifted. Dr. John Moore has written this song: "Burdens are lifted at Calvary." That is where everyman's burden of sin is lifted, right at the cross of Calvary.

We are now the light of the world and the salt of the earth. The darker the night, the brighter the light shines, so let us trim our wicks and sharpen our knowledge of the Bible so we can counteract some of the spurious gospel that is out there and influence some people. As salt, let us retain our savour and not be useless and trampled underfoot. As light, let us shine always. I know, we Christians sell ourselves short, very short sometimes. We place little or no value on our influence, but when we are taken away from the earth, as we will be someday, the earth will see a deluge of ungodliness such as has never been seen on the earth since creation.

Christians are the restraining influence that keeps sin from engulfing the population. Others scoff at us, but little do they know that we are holding back the judgement of God on their lives. They think that things are harsh now, but God is only giving them a warning, a nudge so to speak, to turn and repent before the big day of the Lord appears.

I personally can hear the rumblings, which are only a foreshadowing of the big event. I plead with those I meet to repent, for the Lord is at hand. In Matthew 24:6–8, Jesus spoke of the days ahead: "And ye shall hear of wars and rumours of wars: see that ye be not troubled: for all these things must come to pass, but the end is not yet. For nation shall rise against nation … and there shall be famines and earthquakes in divers places.

All these things are the beginning of sorrows." As I write this on May 8, 2016, there are numerous earthquakes in Oklahoma, a state in the United States of America. In the past year, there were about three earthquakes. Today the news says that there is an average of two per day. This warning is for the children of God, not for the world, so that we might get our houses in order.

I have a picture framed on my desk of an earlier tornado in that same state. The inscription reads as follows:

Oklahoma, a shattered city, June 3, 2013

Whole blocks of an Oklahoma City suburb were flattened when a three-kilometer-wide tornado tore through the area. Dozens of people, including nine children, were killed.

When I saw the devastation then, I could not believe my eyes. Houses were so totally destroyed that the scene was like an emptied box of matches. Strewn with the debris were many automobiles. I framed that picture and would have missed the news now about the earthquakes in the same city except that I have this picture of the previous disaster. God is trying to get our attention, dear friends. He is shaking us from our slumber and complacency, but will we listen?

As I write these words, in Fort McMurray, Alberta, Canada, there is the worst fire in the country's history. A whole city of 80,000 people had to be evacuated. Houses, automobiles and all manner of property is being consumed by fire. The day before, five men were burned in a house. As I write, the news says the fire has doubled in size. No one knows what will be the end result. As Christians, we have been warned and have heeded the warning. We know that these things are bound to happen because Christ said they would.

Recently at a birthday party, I sat beside a woman who claims to be a Christian but who thinks that things will get better on this earth, not worse as I told her they would. Many Christians do think alike. Our politicians tell us that they are at the cusp of making things better for us and that all they need is time. Well, time is certainly not on their side. As a matter of fact, they are on the wrong side of time. It is only the ungodly who have no clue of the imminent danger who live their lives oblivious to the dangers at their heels. God cannot be mocked. We only deceive ourselves when we ignore His Word.

To the Christian, God is a mighty fortress and a very present help in time of trouble. That is our assurance, and as a result we have confidence in Him. If Christ has shed His blood for our redemption, then there is nothing He will not do hereafter for us. He has said that no good thing will He withhold from His children. We are to live in that expectant mode. We will be fulfilled and satisfied. The Christian is secure in Christ. That is a fact. Forever secure, I might add.

A Harvest with Few Labourers

I pray now that God through the Holy Spirit would awaken every one of us to the realization of a lost and dying world and that He would place upon us a great burden to seek out the lost so that we may tell them the good news. Amen.

No Christian should be spiritually unemployed. We all are planted in a ripe harvest field. Men and women everywhere are feeling the effects of sin in their lives and need to be directed to Calvary. They need to be told about Christ. The response is theirs and not for us to worry about. We must discharge our responsibility to them. Let us see each one as a potential recipient of His mercy. The vilest of sinner will be part of His little flock someday. I used to be a vile sinner.

If we look at things closely, we realize that the only history God looks at is the history of His little flock. In as much as He has revealed what He did in creation, it is us that He is concerned about. The greatest consideration is given in the warning and guiding of His children. He attends to their needs and listens to their cries, and when they go astray, He draws then back again. How the Lord draws us back is as varied as the colours of the rainbow. He deals with each of us differently, some even harshly. Consider how he dealt with Saul of Tarsus, inflicting him with blindness because of his stubbornness and resistance to the truth.

People will bark at the idea of a God even though they live wretchedly outside the camp. They live in a state of fear and uncertainty. Of course, they must dread the unknown out there, as there are too many variables. Fear is a dark spectre that overshadows a vast portion of humanity. I will say it again: the greatest tragedy that this world has known is that the Light has come and we still remain in darkness. That is tragic, but then people prefer darkness rather than light, because their deeds are evil.

Will not they put themselves first? They will go as far as acknowledging that there might be a God. But so what? They will contend that even if there is a God, they will continue to put themselves first. That is how much they think of themselves and how little they think of the Creator. We have turned everything on its head. First becomes last and last becomes first. Bad becomes good, and good is something we push aside as worthless and unworthy of our full attention.

Some are afraid of life; of death; of the Judgement; of losing their jobs, their money, their health, their friends; of growing old; of poverty; and of a host of other things. How can one live like that? They live like that because they are stubborn. They are simply too proud to surrender to the One who gives peace and security. They would rather die failing than surrender to Him. They will not surrender now, but remember we said earlier in *What's Up?* That everyone will bend the knee to Christ upon His return.

I worked in a delicatessen in the evenings after school in New York. A co-worker to whom I witnessed said: "If he saw Jesus now, he would spit in His face." He is going to see Him again. What will he do at that time? He must bow. He will be powerless to even approach Him, let alone to do what he thinks he would do.

The bending of the knee is a condition that all the inhabitants of the universe will meet. It is not optional. I wonder, however, if those kneeling before Christ who have rejected and hated Him will do so out of fright or because they have been convinced that He is alive and want now to acknowledge Him. Whatever the reason they kneel, if they kneel as rejecters, their position will remain the same. The time for repentance will have passed on Judgement Day. Now is the opportune time for us to take hold of things. We can miss that time and in many cases miss it forever. That day will be an opportunity missed forever for the unbeliever.

Matthew 8:12 tells us, "But the children of the kingdom shall be cast out into outer darkness: there shall be weeping and gnashing of teeth." (There are two kingdoms, one of light and the other of darkness).

My friend, from my vantage point, this position seems too horrendous a situation even to contemplate. We would have to have no conscience at all to hear these words and let them slip by without considering their import. God has spoken it.

chapter 28

ARE WE THERE YET?

Weeping and wailing and gnashing of teeth. "Depart from me, ye cursed, into everlasting fire, prepared for the Devil and His angels" (Matthew 25:41). How terrible and loathsome are these words. Who would ever want these words to be directed at them, let alone to experience the things they describe? No one. The time is coming. I see the signs pointing to His imminent return, the time that the born-again person is eagerly awaiting and jubilantly anticipating. It will be an event like no other. The believer knows that every other event hinges on this main event.

It is indeed the main event since creation and the fall of humankind. It is the restoration of fellowship between the Creator and the created. That relationship was severed by sin. As a result, we became enemies of God, which we remain until we come to faith again, at which time are we the sons of God and of the Kingdom of Heaven. Marvellously delicious, I would say.

Things will not remain in limbo; we will not continue to live with sin around us. Redemption draws near. We will be taken from the scene and will be cleaned up and comforted in a comfortable dwelling place. Every other person around us will be a happy and sinless person. No sin, no tears, no hunger, no death; only a blissful existence as it was in the beginning in the Garden of Eden. Lot was grieved living with the sin and immorality of Sodom, but one day God took him out before He destroyed that place. Our day is coming, dear brothers and sisters. The Christians can almost ask now are we there yet? We are beginning to feel the cool breeze, it is like approaching the ocean, and you feel the breeze and then the sight of the glorious water.

The Bible says that Lot's spirit was vexed each day when he witnessed the sin around him. Today every righteous person has the same experience. We see that more and more values are being eroded and biblical principles overridden by governments of every stripe. It is a day to mourn and cover ourselves with sackcloth and ashes. We are undone and saddened by the sinfulness of humankind, and the haughtiness of government to dash to pieces the authority of the Bible. In every walk of life, we find the standards being lowered. Men and women who once represented high moral values are now stooping to embrace the most heinous of sins and getting in the fray to defend their propagation. We must ask, "Is it much farther that we have to go? Are we there yet?" I know redemption draws near, very near.

We know that this situation is about to change for everyone and forever. God is wrapping up this sinful earth. The faithful will be ushered into a place of bliss that is true, and the ungodly will be sent to a place of torment.

Now lets us revisit the words "Depart from me. I never knew you." These words will be spoken to the so-called Christians who, while time lasted, played church. Let me use a well-known expression: they played the fool. They outwardly professed to be Christians but lacked true possession of Christ. They were not careful to walk according to the dictates of God's Word. They were careless. They can be likened to the servant who buried his talent because his whole heart was not in his master's business.

These people never actually had the Spirit of God dwelling in them. They went through the rituals and shifted stealthily through the crowd without detection. Remember the warning: "Be not deceived God is not mocked, for whatsoever a man soweth that shall he also reap" (Galatians 6:7). We can fool only ourselves; we cannot fool God. The law of the harvest is an indisputable one. We see it occurring with our friends and neighbours all the time. How can we not see it? We hide our sins, but the Bible says that our sin will find us out. It will, my friend. The only worthwhile thing to do with sin is to confess it to God, not humankind.

He alone can and will forgive us of our sins. He has promised us this great release, to lift our burden of sin. Remember the refrain "Burdens are lifted at Calvary."

The person whose image is more important to him or her than a contrite heart will remain obdurate. A person such as this purports outwardly to be perfect before God and humankind, but lo and behold, on Judgement Day he or she will be found out. The reward will be to hear, "Depart. I never knew you." There are things we know nothing of and other things that are mysteries. Then there are the things that are made very clear, such as the Word of God. There are no mysteries in the Word of God to those who can read. It is self-explanatory in each instance. There is therefore no excuse for the person who is able to read for not falling in line. Unrepentant reader, will you join the millions who are death-free today? Will you invite grace in and shut out the intrusion of death? Join us today and let the procession begins.

There is no excuse for us not to know thoroughly the things that are made crystal clear to us. The Bible states clearly our position with God at all times. If you go out into the rain, you will get wet, and if you stay in the shelter, you will not get wet. How much clearer can it be made to an intelligent person?

Are there things in your life that are keeping you from riding the surf? Are there things that are weighing you down and keeping you from running the race? Albeit slowly, drop them off one by one, little by little. Please, I beg you, do not allow anything to give way to that pronouncement, "Depart." May God give us sleepless nights until we come clean with Him. He is waiting with outstretched arms to welcome you, dear brother or sister. Tell Him that you are coming home today, that you are tired of playing the hypocrite and you want to be His child absolutely. He will be delighted to hear you say those words.

Let Him know that you have laid everything on the altar and that you are now saying good-bye to this world and are looking forward to the New Jerusalem. Now praise Him with a song, a new song, of course.

Now let us consider for a moment with all seriousness the implications of being a Christian and all the attendant ramifications. Being a Christian is not merely paying lip service. You and I know that there are many who say, "Lord, Lord," and yet do not do according to His commands. There are many who will only sing hymns, or parts thereof, when they are drunk. In ordinary times, they sing other songs, but not to the Lord. Jesus warns that if a person would follow Him, he must take up his cross and deny himself. Following Christ is total commitment, my friend, but hear me, it is well worth it.

Following Christ is done with singleness of heart. We cannot have two masters, not the world and its allures and a little of Christ. No, my friend, we must have all of Christ all the time. We grow closer to Him each day in fellowship, and we see Heaven in a sharper light as the earth recedes in our rear-view mirror. We do not serve Him according to the world's dictates but according to His Word. Is serving God a serious matter? You bet it is. The reward is out of this world, however. Nothing here can compare to it.

Casting off Every Encumbrance

If you were going to run a race, would you not practice to strengthen your muscles and increase your stamina so that when the day comes, you would be confident that you could run that race? I have done two half marathons, one in 2007 and another in 2008. I prepared for those races. I was not going to attempt and fail as I had seen so many do. The Christian life is also a striving. Paul says in Philippians 3:14, "I press toward the mark for the prize of the high calling of God in Christ Jesus."

This statement by Paul does not make the race sound like a casual adventure but like something that exceeds anything he has attempted before. This calling is a resolve that demands his very life. May God help us to see what Paul saw. He calls it the "high calling of God." If Paul's calling was the high calling of God, do you think ours is a lesser calling? The same miracle that was wrought on Paul is the same one that we received. Like Paul, we were dead in trespasses and sin. It took a miracle to resurrect us. Any effort less than the most strenuous one is not enough to gain the prize. Let us then be up and doing, dear brethren.

If we take the time to scrutinize this statement, then we find out that Paul is speaking of a tremendous calling. Every day here on earth, men and women are being called to high positions by their governments. What high honour is bestowed upon them. After the calling, their lives are never the same. Ambassador, high commissioner, governor general and so on—these are positions of high honour bestowed upon citizens of the land. After they are appointed to office, they become honourable citizens.

Our high calling is simply out of this world. Nothing here can be compared to it. We get to sit not with earthly royals or presidents but with the King of Kings and Lord of Lords. That is where we are called to serve, in the court of the living God. Every Christian presses toward that mark of the high calling of God in Christ Jesus. It is a race that every one of us is in to win. We know that we are fit for the race when we know that He is in us and that His Spirit bears witness that we are His. It is when we feel free from the guilt and burden of sin that we know we are ready to enter the race. There are many who are fighting on their own to do work for God or to work in his vineyard, but they have neither His permission nor His blessing because they are not His. What they are doing is falsity and a presumptuous lie. We have seen the indictment that will be pronounced upon such that are not possessors: "Depart. I never knew you."

If after serious consideration one determines that it is the thing to do, then let that person delve in with all his heart, soul and body. Let us all be worthy contenders for the faith; children serving in the kingdom as ambassadors of Heaven. Let us see the Lord in all His holiness and beauty as Isaiah did. Isaiah, a prophet, thought he was fine, but then he declared the following:

In the year that king Uzziah died I saw also the Lord sitting upon a throne, high and lifted up, and His train filled the temple. Above it stood the seraphims: ... and one cried unto another and said, holy, holy, holy is the Lord of Host: the whole earth is full of His glory. ... Then said I, Woe is me! For I am undone; because I am a man of unclean lips, And I dwell in the midst of a people of unclean lips: For mine eyes have seen the King, the Lord of hosts. (Isaiah 6:1–5)

After Isaiah's vision of the Lord and of His majestic splendour and those who worshipped Him, he was greatly humbled; he felt like nothing. His attitude toward the holy God was totally changed. My friend, why is it that we are so careless in our worship of the Lord of Hosts today? We approach Him with such disrespect, it is most appalling. The familiarity with which we address Him is in stark contrast to the behaviour of Moses, Isaiah and other prophets. We show no more reverence to God than we would show to a co-worker or a friend.

That is the picture I have of God. Before Him, we see ourselves as we are, unworthy and undone. We fall on our faces before Him not stare Him in the face if we could.

The boldness that emanates from some people is enough to let you know that they do not have a clue who God really is, let alone have any connection at all with Him. You cannot barge in to speak to a mayor, a president or a prime minister, let alone God. To see any of these dignitaries, you have to go through the secretary and make appointments. The rules, if I may refer to them as such, to speak to God are similar. You must come through Jesus Christ the Son. He has stated it, that no person can come to the Father except through Him.

Surely He is our Father, but, my friend, He is not like our earthly father; there must be reverence and fear shown him. Of course, our father down here deserves our uttermost reverence and respect also. That is a command. His Majesty is the King of Kings, but we think we can enter into His presence with no fear and trembling. I am personally appalled by the little or no reverence that we bring to the Lord's house. The attire of some makes it plain that their respect for God leaves much to be desired. We need to have a vision like that of Isaiah to bring us back to our senses. I do believe many of us have taken leave of our senses. Otherwise, we would seek to do better at worship than we are doing.

Isaiah 29:13 addresses this problem clearly: "Wherefore the Lord said, Forasmuch as this people draw near me with their mouth, and with their lips do honour me, but have removed their heart far from me, and their fear toward me is taught by the precept of men." The Lord is telling us that we ignore His dictates concerning worship for the preference of human beings. Come as you are, in slippers, shorts and whatever else you want to wear—that is not important. How much of that garb would you see in Buckingham Palace when the Queen is sitting? Is our God less important than she? Would Christ be using a whip in His house these days also? I think so, my friend. Personally I feel like using one some days myself.

There are certain denominations that approach their worship service with awe and reverence still. I see in some churches that the atmosphere is quieting and humbling in the presence of God. Need I say more on this matter? I think we are all concerned as deeply committed Christians. The house of God is a serious place for many. I thank God for those men and women who see it that way.

Did we wander off topic a bit? Yes, I think we did. But we will get back now to the main thrust.

Isaiah was shaken up and his bones became as pulp, no doubt. He could not stand for days after his vision of the Lord. We need a vision of the Lord, every one of us, to shake us into our proper places. I believe many of us have fallen out of place and need to be revisited by the Holy Spirit. We make a lot of noise when we worship, making melody unto God in the Highest, but are we in a right relationship with Him? We must all examine ourselves, my friend, to see where we are in the worshipping of His Majesty the King.

These words are meant for self-examination also. We must come clean and not deceive ourselves, because in the final analysis we might find ourselves coming up short, which would be regrettable. It would be more than regrettable; it will be damnable. Damnation is what awaits those of us who, as we say today, play the fool.

My friend, the Bible says in 1 Peter 4:18, "And if the righteous scarcely be saved, where shall the ungodly and the sinner appear?" How very scary is that statement. That question is thrown out there for our preponderance. When a person is righteous in the eyes of God, God's righteousness is imputed to him and that imputed righteousness is just enough to gain him entry into the kingdom, wherein he may ponder the question "Where shall the person who is careless about his or her walk appears?" The righteousness that is imputed to us is tailor-made; there is no excess anywhere. It fits perfectly.

When I ponder this phrase "If the righteous scarcely be saved," I see that this statement is telling us of something that is an impossibility without the direct intervention of God Himself. It is a question worthy of our full attention. In Christ, we are secure. There is no doubt that if we are in Christ, we are forever secure, but the statement is made to show us that there is nothing we can do to help the process. We cannot add to it in any way. Therefore, those who think that their effort can secure their way into Heaven are dead wrong. It is such a narrow way that the entry is made possible only by God's hand.

"He that saith, I know Him, and keepeth not his commandments, is a liar and the truth is not in Him" (1 John 2:4). Like everything else, there is a standard to be observed and kept in the kingdom; there is the uttermost order and rules there. You will live by obeying them or die by disobeying them. There are many who believe that all that is required is a sincere heart. Too many people have been sincere throughout the ages and have been sincerely wrong. They believed something wholeheartedly but were wrong in their beliefs. Perhaps Cain was sincere in bringing his offering, but he was wrong. His offering was not according to God's requirements. We have to play by the book, my friend. Perhaps Cain was trying to elevate himself before God by his own endeavours. It is not a bad thought, but God demands a certain sacrifice, and that we must bring. Cain brought an offering that God did not prescribe. He brought a convenient offering, and that is why his offering was rejected. It is God's way, not our way, that counts.

Some years ago, a young man from Britain visiting the Niagara region thought he was invincible. He jumped into the whirlpool in the Niagara Gorge and did so to his demise. He sincerely thought he was invincible and would come out unscathed, but he was wrong. There is a way that seemeth right unto a person, but the ways are the ways of death. We must listen and follow God's Word for direction in our lives so that we can survive down here, and then move up to higher ground when He calls.

The Antichrist

"Who is a liar but he that denieth that Jesus is the Christ" (1 John 2:22)? Many profess to be serving God when they deny the Son. They have discounted the Son totally but still believe that they have fellowship with the Father. John goes on to say, "Whosoever denieth the Son, the same hath not the Father; [but] he that acknowlegeth the Son hath the Father also" (1 John 2:23).

Many are not willing to follow a manual when doing their repairs. They are flying by the seat of their pants. A mechanic does not have the skills required to repair the sophisticated vehicles we have these days. One has to be a technician of no mean order to be able to repair the gadgetry on the latest automobiles. Just a pair of plyers and a screwdriver will not suffice. Likewise, those still living in the Old Testament era with no awareness of the New Testament and the new covenant are two millennia behind the times.

Such people busy themselves about as though they are relevant when indeed they are passé. What they receive are simply common blessings from God, the same as any other sinner receives. Some think that they have an inside track with the Father and discard the Son altogether.

There is absolutely no substitute for believing the truth of God's Word. There is no chance of a person ever entering His kingdom and not coming by the way of the cross. Christ Jesus who gave Himself for us cried out to humanity with the words "I am the way the truth and the life no one comes to the Father but by me" (John 14:6). Was His statement false? Was He not able to back up His words as we saw Him rising from the dead, after He said He was the resurrection and the life? If we believe in Him, though we were dead, yet shall we live also? There is nothing more that is necessary for me to look to; there is enough proof of His existence to allow me to trust His Word fully.

The sad thing is that even the greatest enemy of the cross, Satan himself, believes in Jesus and trembles, but sinful people needing a Saviour are bold enough to scoff at Him. While Jesus was on the cross, one vile wretch scoffed at Him, although the other next to Him found eternal peace by submitting to His authority. Many beneath the cross watching mocked Him and taunted Him, saying that he should come down if He were the son of God as He claimed. Others bowed in humble submission as they recognized Him as the Son of God.

Christ is always causing division among human beings, some willingly and faithfully following Him when they come to the realization that truly He is the Son of God, and others standing around and mocking, saying:

"He cannot be man and stand in our place bearing our sins." He is indeed the God-Man. He became man to identify with us. He is the sinless Lamb of God slain from the foundation of the world for our redemption. Read on, my friend, and familiarize yourself with the Scripture, for in it are the treasures of life.

Many today make a mockery of things when they behave in a halfhearted manner; they lay claim to God's Word but only partially. For whatever reason, they will not turn all the pages of Scripture and get to the truth. Their knowledge is only superficial. They claim to know the Scriptures and even teach it. I have a prime example from my own experience. I will relate it as follows:

When I studied at Tyndale Seminary, my professor in my Systematic Theology class said he was inviting two of his friends to speak to us, as he had done many times before. One was a professor at the University of Toronto, a Dr. X. The other was a prominent radio host and author whom I had seen on TV and heard of as being a Christian gentleman. Dr. X was an atheist, and the other speaker was a Christian, or so he claimed.

They were to come in at different times, of course. We were warned to be polite, and told to be attentive and ask questions. The first one to visit was Dr. X, who told us of his past Christian heritage and how he had lost his faith as an adult when he began teaching as a faculty member of the religious department at a certain university, where he saw the hypocrisy and deceit of some so-called Christians. I would say he was a fine gentleman and responded graciously to the questions we asked. He went away with his beliefs, and we kept ours. He could not shake the class's faith, I am sure.

The next man, the so-called Christian, had quite a number of his books on display, hoping of course that he would do some business that evening. After the discourse, he walked away without selling a single book. I think he might even have regretted coming to speak to our class. He went away hating one student, I am sure: Trevor Turner.

Here is how it played out. After the visitor speaking about his religion, its relevance to the world today, how it is coping and adapting, what changes or dialogues he thought the church leaders should address in the future and so on, we students had our chance to ask our questions. We were all geared up for him since his religion was a part of our studies also. Earlier on, I said that many fail to turn all the pages of Scripture in order to discover what is written. Mostly they speak about what they think, feeling important enough to pass on their opinions.

I had two questions for this greatly influential author. The first was "Mr. Z, are you saved?"

His reply was: You must have been reading Chuck Colson's books, who introduced this idea about being saved.`` Mr. Z said that this question was crass. He said, "If a man were invited to a party and he was muddy and wet, he would stay on the porch and clean himself up before entering the house." (The only way you can enter the presence of God clean is after you have arrive dirty—just as you are, as a sinner.)

My second question was "Did Mary have more children besides Jesus?" His reply was as follows: "No. No young lady who bore the Lord Jesus Christ would go on to have more children? Certainly not." We see that his answer was pure conjecture. He had no knowledge of what the Scriptures have to say on the matter. It is sad, isn't it, an author with so little knowledge of the most important Book of all time being questionable, especially when he calls himself a Christian?

There is a belief that Mary was a perpetual virgin, but the Bible teaches us otherwise. In the Gospel of Mark 6:3, we read, "Is not this the carpenter, the son of Mary, the brother of James, and Joses, and of Juda, and Simon? And are not his sisters here with us? And they were offended at Him."

In this portion of Scripture, we see that Jesus has four brothers and at least two sisters, so we know that Mary had at least seven children, including Jesus Himself. I can say that Jesus grew up with His brothers and sisters, played with them and helped in His father's carpenter shop. I can picture him and his father finishing up an order for a family two or three miles away and then loading up the donkey cart with the furniture for a three-mile delivery in the sun. He would have been a willing hand, I am sure, not like the other boys, who probably complained when they had to help with errands. (By the way, Jesus was left-handed, so all you lefties are in good company.)

In class the following week, the professor said to me, "Trevor, Mr.

Z was rough on you last week." I said that he was only showing his true colours. After all, his remark was not a condemnation of me. Neither was it a summation of my ignorance. I said that after listening to both men speak, I knew that one claimed to be a nonbeliever and the other a believer, but both men were in the same boat. They were both heading down over the rapids. Some of my fellow students said they agreed with me.

The so-called rebuke I got from Mr. Z is mild compared to what he will be getting from the Master Himself on that great day if he does not repent: "Depart. I never knew you."

Isaiah 8:20 reads, "If they speak not according to this word, it is because there is no light in them." There you have it, folks: if they do not speak according to the Word, it is because there is no light in them. You be the judge and know when a person has the light in them or not. It is imperative that we know the Scriptures so that we will not be blindsided by falsity. There are a lot of people who are running around with little or no knowledge of what is written in the Bible, but they are making a great impact on society as though they have been with Jesus. They claim to be representatives of God but know little to nothing of what God wants done.

The child of God has no light of his own just like the moon has no light of its own (it reflects the light of the sun). We are only reflecting the light of Jesus Christ in our lives. If we have no light at all, then we have no contact with Him.

My first job here in Canada was selling encyclopaedias. We had to memorize verbatim a 45-minute presentation. If we did not know it, we could not leaving to go on the road trip into neighbouring cities to sell the encyclopaedias. Why shouldn't we Christians know what our Book says and teaches? We have the truth, and as such we are happy to present it to the needy world. "The truth, the whole truth and nothing but the truth" is what we are expected to present to the enquiring person.

Proverbs 3:5 tells us, "Trust in the Lord with all thine heart; and lean not unto thine own understanding." Say you work away to finish a job but the job simply is faulty. The boss comes to check and finds that you have a part left out. He disqualifies the job, points out that the manual says this goes there and that goes there, and asks why did not you follow the manual. That is what it is there for, to be your guide. Why must we approach the Lord's work differently? In all decency we are expected to represent our Lord truthfully.

In the summer of the year 2015, I did some evangelistic work in Jamaica at the border of Manchester and St. Elizabeth. I spoke to many people, young and old. There were many who welcomed the Word and many who already knew the Scriptures. It was gratifying to have had such an experience with my own people. Almost all of those whom I spoke to believe in God in one way or another. Some live in very meagre surroundings and amidst almost desperate conditions, but notwithstanding, they thanked God for life itself. That was their attitude; they were always praising God for whatever they had and whatever the condition. God was central in their thoughts.

To a group of young people I met under the shade, I asked the same question I'd asked Mr. Z: "Did you know that Jesus had brothers and sisters?" They did not know. I got one young man to read the same portion in Mark 6:3. After reading it, he was delighted to know that he had learned something new that day. Surely our knowledge of anything that we are not eyewitness to must come through the media or from the history books. Why then do we believe some accounts and not others? Someone is influencing our beliefs. Guess who that is?

Some accounts are plotted with a certain slant, but the Scriptures have been corroborated by so many people over so long a period that we can trust them as being God-driven. It was Chuck Colson, who was involved in Watergate, who declared that the Bible has to be God's Word, saying that if a few of the people involved in the Watergate scandal could not agree on a certain lie for just a few months, how could so many men and women lie over so long a time and keep that lie together? His conclusion was that it would have been impossible to do.

A person does not reject Christ for lack of evidence. Instead, a person rejects Christ because he or she simply won't bother to investigate the evidence. A good lawyer wins a case because he or she investigates every piece of evidence available. A good lawyer does research to unearth any evidence that will help in winning the case. The process is elementary.

The account of Jesus's birth, death, burial and resurrection comes to us from the accounts of eyewitnesses. Like anything else, we believe the account. If you go to Jerusalem in the archives, you can look up the birth of Jesus and see his father's and mother's names. Someone who relegates this account to the status of myth is a reprobate. He dwells outside the camp now and will be forever.

We are not even consistent in our behaviours. We will choose to believe that some historical events took place but not others. Are we so untruthful even to ourselves? If there is a story to be told that is worth telling, let us get the facts straight and not recount some distorted version of it. Some have done little more than imagine the facts. It is one thing to embellish our facts, but it is quite another thing to imagine things and present them as facts. Would not Mr. Z in my class be imagining his facts? Many people are doing little more than imagining their facts. They are false prophets or counterfeits, dispensing half-truths.

The story of the cross is the only story that matters, but still some preachers cannot get it right. It stands above all other tales with its everlasting value. That is its worth, dear friends. Know what you believe. The facts are laid bare from Genesis to Revelation. Get acquainted with those pages as some of us have. Read some Scriptures each day and little by little you will be conversant with the message of the Bible. Before long, you will know a lot about your beliefs. In simple language, know what you believe and know it well.

I drive a school bus. Some of the kids I transport to school, in Grade 5 or 6, are indeed some of the brightest on the planet. Listening to some of them talk, you would think that they were ready for the corporate world. These are very bright children making their way to rule the country or the world. If they are able to know so much about so many things already, why would the Christian who has served the Lord for many years not know more of what is written in the Bible? We know so little because we do not put a high value on the Bible's message.

I must take the time here to congratulate all the parents who send their children who ride my bus to Pleasant Public School in Toronto. I am laying claim to the best-behaved and politest kids in all of Toronto. Some fight to be the last to leave the bus in the mornings to go to class. I know that they enjoy their ride and their bus driver, and the love is reciprocal.

My day is always a pleasant one working with these kids. May the Lord bless them all. I know they will make good citizens and grow up to take their rightful places in this world. I will not forget them there at Pleasant Public School. (Some are purchasing an autographed copy of this book)

On one evening in June 2016, after my bus was loaded up, a teacher said a boy was missing and asked me to wait for him. After waiting for about five minutes, she decided that she would send two boys to see what was happening with this kid. She entered the bus and asked for two volunteers to go and find him. The first volunteer to stand was Dennis Marr, the very boy who was the object of the search. Well, we all laughed. As I drove, I realized that if a boy has a name like Dennis, he has to be mysterious. This kid is very pleasant, always giving me a big smile as he greets me in the mornings and leaves in the afternoons. I hope I will see you someday, Dennis, perhaps at your place of business. May the Lord bless you.

Remember what we said earlier, that the cross is not only the most essential message for humankind but also the only essential message. Look around you at all the books and magazines. You could put them all in the fire and keep only your Bible and still be able to live a successful life. Most of the other books and other reading materials are simply fodder for the fire. They keep us informed about many things, information we can easily live without, but our souls need nourishment, and that nourishment comes from the Word of God. Let us keep growing by nourishing our souls.

chapter 29

THE DEVIL ACKNOWLEDGES CHRIST

As we have said before, even the Devil acknowledges Christ in many ways at different times. The mystery lies not in the acceptance of a Holy God but rather in our dismissive voice against His existence. Surely He not only exists and is known but we are connected, for we were created in His image. We bear the marks of our Creator, and yet we fight hard to distance ourselves from Him. Some would rather identify with a monkey than with God.

At times one would ask to what profit should one fight to distance himself from his maker. Is it only to be popular as the popular voice cries out away with Him? Our cry against God is not new, there have been, great people throughout the ages with brilliant minds who appeared to see far beyond the ordinary view of things still they disallowed for a Creator. Indeed, many prominent figures have not figured in the Kingdom of God. People such as the French philosopher Voltaire faltered in their last days. On his deathbed, Voltaire called for his doctor and offered him half of his wealth if he could add six months to his life. I do not understand why he would want to keep the other half. When a person is on his deathbed reality sets in. If a person has given himself only to worldly affairs, then he will go out as a defeated person because he must now leave all his possessions behind. If all there is before a person is a dark entrance to the other world, then all is lost.

Voltaire and others like him boasted of being brilliant men influencing their world. They promoted themselves to the top of the food chain. They garnered from life what the ordinary person could not dream of. They set themselves up as kings and lived royally, decked in fine clothes, entering famous places and attracting a large following. Certainly, these are the men who boast of having knowledge, and as such they must be listened to and followed. In essence they are going places, for they cannot be fooled. There is a contradiction, a travesty, a miscarriage of justice, however, because how could not they know, why should they not know? Why did they not find what they sought? Even a small measure of peace in their passing from this scene would be worthwhile and comforting. They did not find even that small measure of comfort as they made their exits because they failed to find the *essential password* that would allow them into Heaven.

The great American novelist Ernest Hemingway gave us a sample of what it is like to leave this world without God. He declared on his way out, "Life is just a dirty trick, a short journey from nothingness to nothingness." In addition, he said, "My doubt and torment, my fear, that I had done nothing of lasting worth. My conviction [is] that I must die without adequate assurance."

These are lamentable statements made my popular personalities, legend if you will but defeated foes at the end.

That was the summation of his life, the sum total of his value or worth. Perhaps he thought that life was a problem to be solved and he failed to find the formula. As a result, in disgust with life, he took his own life. We would all declare, "What a waste." Seeing, then, is certainly deceiving. Many looked up to this man not knowing he was only an empty shell. He had absolutely no life within. We can confidently say that he died for lack of life. We can ask, "Is that all there is?"

Hemingway's statement "I must die without adequate assurance" is one that rings true to many people. He must have known of God. Of course he knew, as he lived among a people who knew their God. Surely he was inundated with great sermons, but he blotted them out. He believed but only partially. He reasoned that Christians could be right, yet he failed to indulge. He was sure of one thing, that he needed to have what they possessed, but he was not sure he had a full measure of what he needed to get him through the Pearly Gates. There is that treasure we all can have, the treasure of full assurance. That assurance is laid out clearly in the Bible. Why do we still hesitate to indulge to the fullest?

John Eldredge declared, "Life is not a problem to be solved but an adventure to be lived." How exactly do we face an adventure? Do we face it with doubt and trepidation, or do we face it with hope and optimism? Of course, it is with 100% optimism that we start. We face an adventure with the assured confidence that we shall overcome whatever difficulties that beset us on our journey.

That is the way Hemingway summed up his life, as purposeless, but we see life differently. We see a purpose to all that is happening and an ultimate conclusion to it all. We see a bright light at the end of the tunnel, whereas for the ungodly there is nothing but darkness. Choose, my friend. Choose now. Nothing can be fully understood without reference to God's creation and His divine plan for this world. Creation can be readily seen, but His plan must be discerned with a spiritual eye. Pascal declared, "We never shall be happy if we aspire to no other happiness than what can be enjoyed in this life." Pascal knew of a greater dimension to life than what we presently enjoy. We should not be so engrossed with this life that we neglect the afterlife. That is his message.

For those of us who believe in Jesus Christ, no one can contradict that fact. We have that magnet implanted in our navigational system and we are homeward bound. We have the all-clear signal and are heading home for landing. On the other hand, for those who do not believe in Jesus, no explanation is possible. They will falter and sputter and self-destruct, but they will not take off. There is no lift in their sail.

God has planted eternity in every person. Those without a sense of eternity are those who deliberately push it out. When the great Greek philosopher Socrates was on his deathbed, one man asked him, "Great one, is there life after death?" His reply was "I hope so." My friend, the child of God or the believer does not think there is life after death; he or she knows so. It is clearly taught in the Bible, and we believe it. We believe it implicitly and totally, not partially.

Closer to home is our own Bertrand Russell of the 20th century, called by A. L. Rowse "the Socrates of our time". In a review of Russell's book *An Inquiry into Meaning and Truth*, Rowse endorsed the author in *New*

Statesman as "the most clear-headed of modern Philosophers". Bertrand Russell was a revisionist, seeking to unearth and turn every boulder of truth on its head. Like many others, he was restless, finding no satisfaction or peace in his work and getting none from it. He remained empty and unfulfilled all his days.

Russell wrote, "Truth is the fundamental concept and that knowledge must be defined in terms of 'Truth.'" Here his words are philosophizing, certainly. The profundity of his words is far-reaching and rings true, but what did those words mean to him. Did he live by those tenets? I guess not. Where was his zest for life and truth? He spoke of truth as the basis on which to build life, but he did not practice any of what he knew to be so. A person's philosophy is a person's life, nothing more, nothing less. We are in essence two-faced, saying one thing and doing another.

Here are some of Russell's own words that will substantiate what I have just written. Anticipating his death, he said, "There is darkness without and when I die there will be darkness within. There is no splendour, no vastness anywhere; only triviality for a moment, and then nothing." My friend, if what we have just read from a great mind is all that can be hoped for, then life would not be worth the first breath. How would you like to have a brilliant son like such a man? that would be the biggest disappointment.

Here is a man who died for lack of life, and yet he is lauded as great. The only great that could be attached to his name is a great failure. Russell and people like him are nothing but champions of failure and death. They exhibit nothing call life. So these are our great minds, we say. They are applauded as such by many.

Thank God that today, as in the days of old, wise men still seek Jesus. People came from afar to worship at His birth, and people everywhere still seek to worship Him today. Lives are being transformed daily just by bowing to Him. He will not turn away the seeking heart. He is still dispensing life to whosoever will have it.

One believer wrote of death in this way:

> Death for the Christian is not a prison cell, it is a blessed release. It is an entrance into our Father's wonderful house.

> It is a passing from a world of gloom into a world of glory.
> Going from trouble to triumph,
> It is leaving the cross and receiving that glorious crown.

Death, I might add, is ceasing the struggles and dropping the burdens of life and receiving our rewards, entering into His promised eternal rest. That is the believer's prospect and experience, not a dark, uncertain nothingness. Human beings will refute and antagonize and shred to pieces established truths to make a name for themselves, but when the time comes for them to go out of this world, and go out they must, there is the loneliness that comes to settle in. And then despair and agony follows as they make their exit without God. It is sad indeed.

These people must face eternity alone. They will have no cheerleaders. As a matter of fact, some do experience the Devil and his demons coming to take them. They show their fright and unwillingness to go, but they have no choice but to yield. They have flitted away their chances and now it is over. God is not willing that any should perish but that all should come to repentance. "For God so loved the world that He gave His only begotten son, that whosoever believeth in Him should not perish but have everlasting life" (John 3:16). The sufferings of Christ here on earth and lastly on the cross were not meant as an exercise in futility but have real value and a consequence. If you reject Christ, you have rejected life.

The nations that reject God will labour and will do so under great stress and agony, not having the blessing of the Almighty. Ultimately they will wither and die. The days of their existence are limited, brief. They are likened to the chaff, which the wind blows away. They can roar like a lion at times, but soon, very soon, they will meet their demise, because the Lord has decreed it. Psalm 107:33–34 reads, "He turneth rivers into a wilderness, and the water springs into dry ground; a fruitful land into barreness, for the wickedness of them that dwell therein." God will give a person or a nation its just reward.

I am a Baptist. In certain denominations, Baptists preferred to be called Biblicists, the reason being that too many people call themselves Christians but lack a full understanding of what a Christian is. A Biblicist is a person who adheres to and believes the Word of God. He will not add his own interpretation to what God has said. We Biblicists would rather be thought of as people with a one-track mind who, as they say, follow the Word blindly. There are many, on the other hand, who claim to be of open mind but who indeed show that that openness is nothing but emptiness. The openness is like a sieve in that things pour out easily.

I spoke to a man recently who claimed to know God, but in essence he knows only of God. Another to whom I spoke claims to know God also, but all he is interested in is keeping the Ten Commandments. The first man says he has read the Bible through twice but he does not know that we will be resurrected after death. He asked me, "Why would God raise us up again after we are already dead?" I would not have known that we will be raised up for our reward except that the Bible says so. This is information in the public domain, for anyone who would read it.

In 1 Thessalonians 4:14–18, it is clearly shown what shall become of every person, dead or alive.

> For if we believe that Jesus died and rose again, Even so them also which sleep In Jesus will God bring with Him. For this we say unto you by the word of the Lord, That we which are alive and remain Unto the coming of the Lord shall not Prevent them which are asleep. For the Lord Himself shall descend from heaven with a shout with the voice of the archangel, and with the trump of God; And the dead in Christ shall rise first. Then we which are alive and remain Shall be caught up together with them In the clouds, to meet the Lord in the air: And so shall we ever be with the Lord. Wherefore comfort one another with these words.

> The things that will happen are foretold and they are as though they have already happened, it is only a matter of time. I will make a comparison, here in the earthly affairs of men. Leader do things that they promise and many are not mentioned until after they get in power.

A new President has been elected in the United States of America by the name of Donald Trump. On the campaign trail across America he promised many things: among them were two very significant ones. One is to deport illegal immigrants and the other is to build a wall across the Mexican border. To many, this decision seemed far-fetched but one month into his presidency he has instituted and signed plans to reinforce the promises. We all know now that the promises were not empty. He has hired 10,000 new immigration officers and 5,000 border patrol officers to enforce his policy and the roundup is on right as I type this sentence.

If man would have the courage and the power to make and enforce a promise even against popular opinion and much opposition, how much more will God keep His word? These illegal immigrants have to be rounded up; no one wants to be deported but God has sent out a decree and everyone will appear voluntarily and on his or her steam.

In 11 Corinthians 5:10 there is a proclamation sent out to mankind and it reads. "For we must all appear before the judgement seat of Christ; that everyone may receive the things done in the body, according to that he hath done, whether it be good or bad." There will be no truants.

The Christians do not labour senselessly, as some think. We have a basis for our strength and endurance; we have the comfort of the Living Word of God because we believe what the Lord says. The world is busy building as though everything is going to continue as it is. We see things differently; we see them as only temporary construction that will all come tumbling down like the walls of Jericho at His bidding. As such, we do not glory in bricks and mortar but in God Himself. There is where our hope and security lie.

Neither Socrates nor Voltaire sought a place in the eternal Heaven and as such and could not tell where they were going. Why would such confident men who were so sure of themselves while they lived became so shaky and uncertain when it was time to make their exits from this scene? They fed their souls on the husks of this life, and as a result their souls famished and starved. Death was the ultimate outcome—spiritual death, that is. In contrast to such men, is author and explorer Sir Walter Raleigh, who, the night before he was beheaded, wrote in his Bible, "From this earth, this grave, this dust, my God shall raise me up." That was the confidence he had in God's Word, my friend. And every born-again Christian has the same confidence. We no longer fear death. Instead, we see it as a glorious entryway into the presence of God.

The songwriter Charles Wesley puts it succinctly in these words:
>Rejoice in this glorious and wondrous hope
>Our Lord, the judge shall come
>And take his servants up
>To their eternal home.

Voltaire wanted more time and Socrates when asked about life after death said: ``I hope so.``

To think that such prominent figures on earth should make fodder for the fires of Hell is staggering, but it is so. Pride, my friend; pride has hindered many from bending the knee and humbling the spirit. The Lord Jesus spoke of them as stiff-necked and wicked, not only keeping themselves out of the kingdom but also blocking the entrance for others who want to get in. The influence that these people have on the minds of the young is tremendously debilitating. We continue to reap the results. A person who purports to be wise is shown to be a fool in the end.

Socrates, who lived in the 15th century, was eventually charged with introducing strange gods and corrupting the young. He was sentenced to death. He was a Sophist propagating his fallacious arguments, which are basically immoral arguments. We do not see that immorality corrupts these days or else we would lay charges against many people. I know charges will be laid; as a matter of fact, charges have been laid already in the Higher Courts and sentences have been pronounced. They will be cast into the lake of fire (Revelation 20).

Darwinism has been one of the greatest plunderers of the minds, especially of the young. I wonder, if Darwin was given a chance to come back to earth for one year, what would his mission be? Would he sleep, take a cruise or spend every waking hour trying to undo his error? Outside of Christ, we spend our lives as a tale told, empty and absurd.

Recently when I picked up my copy of the *MacLean's* magazine, I saw this headline: "The thrilling account of our extraordinary history—from insignificant apes to rulers of the world." The author of the article speaks eloquently of a thrilling account of our extraordinary history. I have just shown you how so-called brilliant minds have faltered and spluttered when they reached their end without God. God's Word says that He created us and gave us dominion over the animals, birds and so forth, which includes the apes from which this writer purports that we came. People like this are subterranean dwellers whose minds are filled with deceits and lies, surfacing to "enlighten" us who live in the light. Just what can they tell us of their experiences that we care to hear? Nothing.

As a human being, I know that I am a special creation made by the mighty hand of the Lord God Almighty. I will have no part with the writer of such articles and his apelike brain. These so-called great people love to throw out lofty statements in an effort to promote themselves and even to lift themselves to great heights where they are esteemed as brilliant minds, but the reverse is true. Without God, they are like the chaff that the wind blows away. Useless. That's what they are, useless in the eyes of God.

Our history shows us clearly that humankind has been on the descent, and not on the ascent as some would have us think. The evidence is stacked against those so-called brilliant minds who try to tell us otherwise.

If we scrutinize the statement made by that headline, we see right away its nonsensical import. Let us ask the question, Where are your ancestors today? Where are your grandparents, your great-grandparents and your great-great-grandparents? Are they hanging around your home, or do you visit their graves? To imply that we exist alongside our ancestors is bordering on the ridiculous. The caterpillar does not coexist with the butterfly. One has to give way to the other.

The argument that we came from monkeys is not even a logical one. It would seem a more plausible argument if there were no monkeys around.

If monkeys were extinct, then a person with half a mind could grasp the argument that they are our genetic ancestors. The grain that is planted must die for a new plant to sprout; the two do not exist together. This is my argument. If we evolved from the monkey, the monkey would be extinct. It could not exist side by side with us.

It seems strange that evolutionists claim that we descend from monkeys. Some time back, one member of the British Parliament asked another member which side was more sacred to him, the monkey side or the human side. The latter was offended. How easily people will sell their souls to make money. And then we are suckered in by the vain eloquence of these people. There is an apt description for such crowds: "the blind leading the blind."

chapter 30

CONNECTING WITH GOD

Connecting with God is not us ascending to God but God coming down to meet with us. It is like a meteor hurtling toward earth, rather than a rocket bursting through the atmosphere. Of ourselves, we are impotent to reach out to God. We are natural enemies of God and seek to do that which is contrary to His will. The value is not what we do for God but what He has done for us in His Son the Lord Jesus Christ. The Bible says in Isaiah 53:6, "All we like sheep have gone astray; we have turned everyone to his own way." We have a natural bent to go our own way. We have a propensity to go it alone, and more so now, especially since we have developed tools that make our existence easier. As such we even think we have arrived.

We have become more industrious and busier than the bees. We hasten to build more highways to accommodate a greater flow of traffic. Back and forth we roam, up and down, in and out. We harass ourselves to build that which we all will soon leave for the next generation to worry about and we make no plans for the journey ahead after this life.

Purpose is in short supply. There is no real purpose in living. That is why for some, entertainment is important during every waking moment. Is there a connection between a lack of purpose and the rash of suicide we see among our youths? There certainly is.

It is stated, "Many a scientist have an encyclopedic knowledge of the world, many a philosopher can survey vast systems of thought, many a theologians can unpack the profundities of religion, but all that is theory, and without a sense of personal purpose, vanity." Why would a person give his time and energy to things that have no substance? Vanity. Humankind is inherently vain.

The distraction has become so pronounced that it is bordering on immorality. The manufacturers throw out their products backed by bizarre ads, and we follow blindly, almost as hoarders, to gobble up their merchandise. In the final analysis, these things have taken the place of God. They have become our idols, and we literally worship them. When we fail to see that the final purpose of life is not within this life but beyond it, we live in vain. We sell ourselves short, eternally short.

Our actions are summed up in Psalm 2:1–4: "Why do the heathen rage? And the people imagine a vain thing? The Kings of the earth set themselves, And the rulers take council against the Lord, And against His anointed, saying, Let us break their bands asunder, And cast away their cords from us. He that sitteth in the heavens shall laugh: The lord shall have them in derision."

In our day, more than ever, the rulers of the nations seek to do just that. They want to bring in their own council and push out anything that pertains to God and godliness. They are turning things on their heads. They give the people whatever they want, passing laws that favour the few who are the instigators upsetting the moral fibre of the nations. Every day we hear of human rights being trampled on and it is because the bad and ugly want to force their ideologies and sometimes their immorality upon us. This is what is upsetting the equilibrium.

The lawmakers are ungodly men and women turning upon any laws that pertain to the honour of our God. They overturn these laws established by godly people in order to get some votes and to increase their popularity among people. In so doing, they diminish their standing before a holy God. They shall pay big time. The records are being kept and the results will not be good.

The rulers want prosperity for their population, that is true. Many are genuinely sincere in seeking and striving for the good of their nations, and yet they avoid seeking the face of Him who prospereth the nations. How sincerely wrong can they be? Their plight shall come upon them like a whirlwind. We are witnessing the plight of nations before our very eyes.

The Lord will hold them in derision. The Lord said He will mock and laugh at such a nation that thinks it can have other gods before Him.

We are seeing the plights of civilizations running on empty. A greater harvest is elusive, because they have to expend more and more energy to get the same harvest. It is a joke that whereas ten horsepower could get us where we wanted to go, now we need twenty times that to accomplish the same goal. We are literally witnessing Wordsworth's phrase "The still sad music of humanity." We are still kicking up our heels even though the music has stopped playing. We are lost and do not know it. There is a dereliction upon the land that is shunting us off into eternal darkness. Will we heed the warning and change our direction?

The Living Dead

Living. Many of us have stopped living. We are dead and do not know it. We have dug our graves and are already occupying them, some at their jobs and others at home. The entertainment industry is a prime example. There are many who have already crossed the threshold of no return. They planned and plotted and cheated and strove to become what they sought, and once they achieved the success they sought after, they experience that the air at the top stings. They can no longer breathe and are suffocating. They cannot stand without the puffer, which could be alcohol or other drugs. They have lost the art of living. Many are crying out for a good night's sleep, but it is too late, as they have already sold their souls to the Devil.

These people have been caught in a vise of an empty dream from which they cannot extricate themselves. They long to be the simple person they once were. Without the guidance of the Word of God, people do not know when they have reached their resting place. I do think that there is a level at which we are comfortable in life; once we reach it, our lives becomes manageable and exciting. If we do not know when we have attained that plateau, then we laboriously strive in vain.

Jonathan Swift wrote, "May you live all the days of your life." How very kind of Mr. Swift to wish us such a wonderful thing. That is a wish that I am wishing for you, reader, here and at this moment as you read these pages. We are all allotted a certain time, but some of us fail to grasp the import of it. Through our behaviours and actions, we have shortened and diminished the quality of our lives. We have done despicable things to our lives and to our Maker. We have sailed away from the safe haven of rest and have not caught the wind of His blessings ever since. We are adrift as a ship without a rudder.

The psalmist reminds us in Psalm 90:9, 12, "For all our days are passed away in thy wrath: we spend our years as a tale that is told. ... So teach us to number our days, that we may apply our hearts unto wisdom." Numbering our days—well, what a sobering thought. When we open our eyes in the morning after some sleep, we recognize that this day could be our last on this side of eternity. How very careful we should be with each moment of each day. Ben Franklin once said, "Be careful with your time for it is what life is made of."

Let us quieten our hearts before God each moment of each hour and remain in a state of constant communion with God every day, let us pray for power to walk and not faint. That is the power we have been promised, the power to soar above the vicissitudes of life and live lightly. I say live lightly, meaning, let us as Christians let loose of the many worldly goods that we crave and cling to. We must maintain an even keel, an equilibrium that eludes the world. We can be an example to them of how life can be lived successfully.

Learn to Control Yourself

We all have instinctive needs. One at the top of the list is the need for control. We love to control, perhaps even those around us. One thing you can learn to control is yourself. If you can do that, then you are well on your way to bettering your life. However, to master this life totally, you have to spend time with the Master. You have to find time to spend in his Word daily. By so doing, you will grow to be an overcomer.

My friend, as Christians, we must and can go through life feeling confident that we know the outcome. Yes, there is a predictable outcome, and it is only the Christian who has that knowledge. A Christian trusts the written Word of God where it is revealed. Any other prediction is only speculation. Life is a great ocean to navigate. I personally find that it has become a far less burdensome and worrisome affair since I have entrusted myself to the Saviour.

As I look back, I wonder how else would I be able to raise eight children unless God was at the centre of my life, supporting and guiding my actions all the time. That is some peace to have, my friend. Many say of us Christians that we are haughty. Far from it. We are sure but not timid, and confident but not proud.

Even in these last days when we expect a deluge of persecution, we will have to rely more and more on His power to see us through. By ourselves, we would shudder and give in, even deny our faith to save our lives and property, but those things are nothing compared to the reward for those who endure. Even as I write this, in the United States the Christian faith is under attack. Christians are losing their livelihoods on account of the backlash for their standing firm upon the Word of God and refuting government regulations in favour of God's Word.

The *Epoch Times* of May 12–18, 2016 reported: "Former CIA director laments all-consuming focus of War on Terror." How easily and quickly we forget. One of the founding fathers predicted that if the American people would not hold dear to the principles on which the country was founded, the United States would not survive.

Is the United States floundering today? Sure it is. It is smouldering under the pressures of racism, secularism, immorality and many other ailments. The war on terrorism, of which the former CIA director General Michael Hayden (Ret.) laments, has distracted the United States from addressing the rise of China and rampant industrial espionage.

I liken this distraction to Churchill's experience during the Second World War when he was greatly hampered in the House of Commons. Before he became Prime Minister of Great Britain, his perceptions of things were not always accepted by others. He likened his experience to "Hunting the tiger with a swarm of angry wasps about your head". The turmoil that pervades the U.S. government today is like that swarm of angry wasps. There is confusion and a great disunity, even among members of the same party. There is no longer a strong consensus of right and wrong among government leaders.

The assertion that the former CIA director made is only a distraction from the real war at home. A surmounting evil influence has taken hold of the nation, and the men and women of God are literally fighting for their lives and their freedom. Their freedoms are being eroded every day, bit by bit. The onslaught is on and it is not letting up. It will get worse until God intervenes. He is already showing His hand, but no one in the ungodly crowd is listening or watching.

We Are All Philosophers

We are all philosophers seeking meaning and truth in life. If we miss these two quests, then we will fail, whether or not we have a degree in philosophy; our lives will have been lived in vain. According to the "Canadian Oxford Dictionary" a philosopher is a person who, among other things: "Uses reason and argument in seeking truth and knowledge of reality.'

A philosopher then ought to be a great and exceptional person, one who has found a good path to tread in life and one who can show others how to walk surely and securely. Did many great philosophers miss the meaning of the Word? I believe they did.

In light of the two so called great philosophers, Socrates and Bertrand Russell that we have discussed, either the dictionary has defined them wrongly or they did not learn much in class, given that they were such dismal failures. It seems to me then that neither Socrates nor Bertrand Russell had a good grip on life and no hold whatsoever on eternity. They both went out of this life in darkness, disillusioned and miserable.

In our times, we have a philosopher of a different stripe who knows the meaning of life. The Czech philosopher Václav Havel speaks of the Gospel as a constellation of truths. He said, "The tragedy of modern man is not that he knows less and less about the meaning of his own life but that it bothers him less and less." We know more about our universe today than any other nation in history, peering into outer space with its magnificent and glorious constellations and yet, we are not in awe of its Great Creator.

We have created a culture of distraction where it is fashion vs. God and popularity vs. morality.

To miss the meaning of life and the reality of our existence is indeed the most dismal of failures and, in summation, is to miss life itself. If I might advise you, my philosophy is in seeking and finding knowledge and truth, which is present in the words of the Bible. The Bible serves as a guide to wisdom and nobility of character; it builds a person's confidence and stature. Follow the Bible, my friend. Get to love it and know its Author. Don't sit around "sipping whiskey and singing Hallelujah."

In walking through life, we may take clear paths to arrive at a predicted destination. There is a Guide who has been before us and knows the way. We must know Him and follow Him. He has a plan for each of our lives. Life becomes sweet when we connect with Him and His plan for us. I am not here advocating that all we do in life pertains merely to spiritual matters. We have things to do and we do them, but we do them in a certain light. We must never forget or neglect the spiritual dimension. To remind you, that is the most essential dimension of our existence. We continue to do our duties, excelling at our professions and in our jobs, but when we partner with Him, things are more meaningful.

Many are crying out for help. They are exhausted and frustrated because they have no guidance. If your passion is to climb Mount Everest, then I say drop everything and climb it. Climb it, providing you can do so without defrauding anyone, be it your family (if you have one) or anyone else. Gather up the loose ends, and plan and prepare for the climb.

If you try but do not reach its summit, at least you have tried. You will go out knowing you have tried. You will be relieved of the burden of not trying. Not exerting the effort to satisfy a longing can be regrettable later in life. One person has said, "We do not grow old until we begin to wish we had done something we wanted to do." We must try to satisfy the urge if it is not a sinful one.

However, if any of the things you set out to do, do not satisfy or has become a burden, then drop the pursuit. Do not let anything hang like a millstone around your neck. Live free. Freedom is something we must all seek to obtain. Freedom and not possession is our right, but in modern times we have enslaved ourselves. The vast majority of people in Western societies are enslaved by material possessions. It is indeed a culture of exuberance. Think of the promotion of "Toy Mountain" at Christmas time here in Toronto. The idea is obnoxious when there are millions who do not have a good meal at Christmastime.

We must not let the things that should embellish and strengthen our lives diminish and strangle them instead. Many of us can say truthfully that many things that we craved for and that should be satisfying and bring pleasure to us are now strangling us. We have to know at what point it makes no sense to keep certain things and then be willing to let go. Letting go might mean a monetary loss or even a severance of ties, but we must do what will give us the greatest comfort and happiness. When we lie in bed, we want to sleep, not to think of strategies to survive. So many have well passed survival mode and are now struggling to reach another level. That is where the problem lies: we do not know when we have arrived.

As a philosopher, I can only give advice. You will have to do the spade work. As your philosopher, however, I have another piece of advice. There is a Chinese proverb that goes like this: "If you do not push out you will lose both mule and horse and if you push too hard you will also lose both." The wisdom here is to achieve a balance. After reaching and acquiring horse and mule, be careful with them. Wanting more and more horses and mules might lead to the eventuality of losing all. Having a good balance is the prudent thing to do.

Benjamin Franklin once said, "There are two ways of being happy, we may diminish our wants or augment [make better] our means. Either will do, the result is the same." In today's society, we see that many are dashing to implement the latter part of this formula. They would rather be miserable with much than be happy with little. It is no longer acceptable to us to have what our neighbours have; we must have twice as much. There are many happy and free men and women among us still, however. I have encountered some personally. I will give you just two examples here.

In the year 2015, needing two more rims to mount two snow tyres on my Jetta, I went to a junkyard to get them. I followed the man attending to me out to the back of the building, where he found a Jetta. He jacked it up and retrieved my two rims. Conditions were not ideal, as it was in the fall and it was damp and muddy out there. He carried one tyre and I the other. After I paid the owner for the wheels, the attendant and I carried them to my car out front. Once I had stacked them in the trunk, I handed him a ten-dollar bill as a tip, and wouldn't you know it, he dismissed me graciously. He simply would not take the money.

The other experience I had was with a panhandler, a woman whom I had seen seated on a downtown sidewalk when I passed to see my ophthalmologist every six months. I often gave her some change when I passed her. Once I asked if she wanted something to eat or drink. She said she would like a chocolate milk. I bought one for her when I was returning from my appointment to catch the subway train.

One morning as I was getting dressed, I thought to myself, *Why don't I give this woman a twenty dollar bill?* As I proceeded to dress, a thought came to me. *Instead of giving her the twenty, why don't I make her an offer?* I would give her a choice. In my wallet I had a five, a ten and some twenties. When I approached her after the normal greeting, I said, "I have here a five, a ten and a twenty. Which would you like?" She replied, "If I refused the twenty, I would be a fool, but then again I do not want to be greedy, so I will take the five." What would a hundred people do in that situation? How many out of a hundred would do as these two people did? Not everyone is sucked in by the lure of money. Not everyone, dear sir or madam.

When my wife Estel and I operated a bed and breakfast in Toronto, a German gentleman and his son stayed with us there. When he returned to Germany, he sent me a note and a ten-euro bill. How very unexpected and pleasant that gesture was. One more kind gesture comes to mind. The same property that I retrofitted for the B&B used to be run as a rooming house. There is an extra lot at the back where neighbours would rent parking spots from me. One gentleman rented a spot and gave me a series of cheques in advance. He vacated the spot, with me holding about three uncashed cheques. He told me when he was leaving that if I wanted to keep the cheques, I could cash them. I could not believe what I heard. I told him thanks and cashed one cheque, only to test the genuineness of the offer. It was genuine.

My dentist is a Christian man. When I visit him, he tells his secretary not to charge me the normal rate for the work. The last time I visited, she told me that my bill was $160, but the doctor said she was to bill me for only $100. Thank you, Doctor; you made my day.

I have told these anecdotes to show that everyone is not out to get you; there is kindness still in this world. Without these experiences, I would think that I am the only honest and kind person I have ever known. Now I know the truth. There is the law of sowing and reaping demonstrated in the anecdotes I have shared. In Proverbs 11:25 it is stated, "A generous person will prosper, those who refreshes others, themselves will be refreshed." How wonderful are these words, my friend. Do not be a tightwad. Be generous instead, it will afford you more freedom.

Take stock now of where you are, where you want to go and what vehicle you will need to make the journey. You might need a better one than you have now. You might even be near or at your destination and require no more gas in your vehicle. Know what you are after and be not confused by friends' and neighbours' activities. I am advising you from my own life experiences.

chapter 31

THE PROFUNDITY OF SIMPLICITY

I can remember my uncle fixing his car with only plyers and a screwdriver. It seems those were the only two tools he needed to repair his engine. When I started owning cars, I was able to do some work on engines myself. I knew when a spark plug wire was off because I could see it—and all the other wires in the car for that matter. If the problem was not in the engine block, I could diagnose the problem and find a solution quickly. All of the electrical components were visible to the eyes.

Nowadays, I cannot see the spark plugs, let alone to get at them. This is a prime example of moving from simplicity to complexity. What worked before and worked well enough is simply not good enough today. There are changes for the sake of changing. You hear of things being new and improved, which is a misnomer—as if the previous models were partly new. A man was building a house and a passerby said to him, "John, I see you are building a new house." The reply was "That is all I build, new ones."

Of course we are prone to believing anything these days. Deep into the era of conspicuous consumption, we will hand over our cash for anything and everything. Just change an item's colour or turn a light upside down this year and you have a market. Who needs or buys for functionality? We need style and change and we are happy to dole out exorbitant sums for the items.

The complexity of life is what intrigues us; we must follow inquisitively. The rapacious heads of companies are enticing us each day with their new gadgets and wares, and we are running after them breathlessly. They advertise them as must-have and we cannot resist the temptation. We enrich those who are already rich and simultaneously diminish our health and wealth, thinking that we are living meaningfully.

It is springtime now here in Toronto. The leaves and blossoms are blooming. The red crab apple trees with their purplish foliage are especially appealing to mine eyes. As I drive about, I enjoy every moment of my day. I am able to see these things, freed from all encumbrances that would otherwise block my vision. I wonder, as I see people rushing to and fro, how many others are enjoying the scenery.

I am not there yet, but I am close. I am learning to live free. Life is worth living when it becomes and remains remarkably fresh and fascinating. It is a mode we have to get into. No one but you can create that atmosphere. Remain eternally optimistic and dream big, because the future belongs to those who believe in their dreams. Create your own world and do not allow many intruders. Live with a generous heart; be free with your time and money. Do not live miserly like Mr. Scrooge. Live with a smile on your face, which a generous heart can give you. Be the Scrooge after his change of heart.

Learn to simplify things in your life. It is often in the simplifying of life that the most satisfaction is found. We need to relax more. Craving and longing for bigger and better things is too costly to our health and wellbeing. These desires must be supressed. Shut them out as an evil visitation. Acquisition of flashy stuff will not necessarily bring the happiness you are hoping for. So what if you are driving an economy car, a car that is paid for and cannot start anymore? Thank God that you still have a set of wheels.

Anticipation vs. Reality

Quite often the novelty of the new acquisition purchased at an unaffordable price wears off too soon and we are back to square one, unfulfilled and bored. That is the world for you. With all its allurements, it cannot satisfy. We will not be satisfied until we drink at the Fountainhead, which is Jesus

Christ. The water He gives will spring up into everlasting life, and with it we will be eternally satisfied.

The irony of life is that we search and search, but when we come face to face with the truth, we still reject or hesitate to embrace it. A certain man who was witnessed to by a pastor rejected the witness. Later on his deathbed, he sent for the same pastor. The pastor wondered what he might want this time, since he would not have anything new to tell him.

They talked. The dying man suggested to the pastor that he knew that Heaven was too good a place for him and Hell too horrible a place, but since he was not fit for either, there must be a place that he could go to. That man would rather be told a lie. Tell him of a place other than the places God says we will be going and he will readily believe it. Half the world is believing the same thing. This idea is a money-maker. Others are using simony to cash in.

The Gospel, the most important message in all the world and all of history, runs throughout the Bible. It is what history is made of; it is the history of humankind and their God. It is the only essential message in all of history. The Gospel is God calling human beings to return to Him. He speaks in the wind, the fire, the storm, the earthquake and the thunder, but human beings are plugging their ears with all manner of gadgets to drown out His voice. They are listening to the call of the world. *El mundo parace pequeño* (The opinion of the world is small). Do not listen.

If we would be quiet for a while, we would hear His voice. The path of trouble, says one man, is sometimes the path home. God can bring us to our knees whenever He wants to, but why would we be so stubborn as to wait until He does such a things? Would we rather not heed the warning and come freely to get the blessings now?

How often do I get the reply, "I have not the time to go to church?" There are so many that do not have the time to go to church until they are brought to one in a hearse, and then it is of no value to them. Even on their deathbed, people resist the call of God. They ask for more time. I often wondered why a person who lives to be 70 and gets sick will do everything possible to get another six months of life. I have also wondered what exactly such a person would do with those extra six months.

I urge you, dear friend, do not wait. Get right with God and you will not want any more time, because you will be roaring to leave this sin-sick world. I say "sin-sick world" because that is what it is. Have you seen any of the videos of motorcyclists wandering around on the highway upsetting traffic and endangering their own lives? Why do they do this? Because they are purposeless.

The old adage rings true today more than any other time, at least to me: "All that glitters is not gold." When we look on, say, Ontario's roads these days and observe the abundance of cars and see the high-end cars, we wonder if all of those people own oil wells. Just how can so many people afford such expensive cars and expensive houses? Just what is happening? Is all this wealth real, or is it illusionary?

A bumper sticker reads, "He who thinks having a lot of toys brings fulfilment is already dead." The Bible distinctly states, "For where your treasure is, there will your heart be also" (Matthew 6:21). People are changing their world by consciously and deliberately storing up treasures down here. That is where their hearts are, of course. They are putting down roots because they have no idea that the storm is looming. O the sad song of humanity.

> Not what we have but what we use,
> Not what we see but what we choose—
> These are the things that mar or bless
> The sum of human happiness.
>
> —Anonymous

The operative word here in this poem is *choose*. We must choose wisely or else we will find ourselves giving all our substance to things that could drag us down the drain. If we seek after the wrong things, those choices could be our undoing. A life of enslavement could be built around such desires. Covetousness cannot be satisfied by things or money, or else the Ponzi schemers would know when to stop and not get caught. Greed becomes like a magnet that grabs and connects tenaciously. It will not let go until it sucks one in like quicksand.

Jesus warns of covetousness in Luke 12:15: "Take heed and beware of covetousness: for a man's life consisteth not in the abundance of the things which he possesseth." Today's world sees things differently and looks at things in the opposite light. Every person wants to be the richest in the graveyard. We have become too vain in our journey through this life. A kinder, gentler approach would do us a lot more good than a greedy one. This rapacious nature is literally strangling our happiness.

We would do well to learn another language, perhaps the new language of kindness. Everyone can understand it. Even the blind can see it and the dumb can speak it. Some of us have far too much of what we need to live anyway. Most people would agree with me when I say that our lives are being hampered by things getting in the way. We do not need a lot of cash in the bank. Give some to some poor souls living in abject poverty. Be generous, the most generous person you can be. Start now. Leave yourself with the bare minimum and live free.

chapter 32

A BINDING DECISION

If you have not yet made up your mind about Christ and you are wondering about your position without Him, I beg you to read Romans 8:1: "There is therefore now no condemnation to them which are in Christ Jesus, who walk not after the flesh but after the spirit." From this passage it is clear that there are two types of people roaming this earth: those under the condemnation of death and those who have been set free. Some would dare to say I am wrong, but there you have it, my friend, in black and white.

A number of us drivers were in the TTC lunchroom one afternoon when one of the drivers said he had been paid an incorrect amount. I said to him, "Let me see your pay stub." I quickly worked out his pay and found that it was correct. One of the other two drivers said to him, "There you have it. What else do you want?" We have the Word of God, which states that we have been set free, exonerated. Our debt of sin has been paid, and that is all we want. Whom the Lord sets free is free indeed. There you have it, Christians. Now why are some of you still doubting? I say this because I have talked to men who claim to be Christians but have not the assurance that they are in. Remember, it is not what we feel, it is what we believe. If the Word says we have been set free, then we have been set free. Believe it. Do not linger with a doubt.

An old Christian woman on her deathbed was asked whether she was confident that she was going to Heaven. Her reply was "God cannot go back on His Word." Why would not God's Word suffice to satisfy our doubts? Why should we doubt His Word if He is wholly trustworthy? We must not.

Paul scolded some Christians, saying that they had again put themselves under bondage after they had been set free. That is such a common thing in our lives. We are afraid to live as we ought to: free. We tend to live below our level. We do not have full enjoyment of our trip, which has been paid for.

The story is told of two buddies travelling from Britain to the USA in the old days on a ship. After they paid their passage, they got together to devise a plan to save some money during the voyage. They got some cheese and crackers to eat on the way so they wouldn't have to spend too much money on meals. After travelling for some time, eating their rations, they came by the cafeteria, smelled the food and asked someone what the cost of a meal was. Well, the person was astonished. He said, "You mean that you have been travelling for so many days and have not had a meal? It is included in the price of the ticket." Need I say more? Some Christians are travelling as second-class citizens in their Father's world. Wake up, my friend. Smell the roses and enjoy the coffee.

Salvation. Anyone can have it for nothing; no one can have it any other way. It is surprising that we are surrounded by such clouds of witnesses and a vast sea of evidence that God exists and yet we are stuck in the mire. These people are busy building their own domains as a child would a sand castle on a beach. Soon the tide overflows it and washes it out to sea. All is gone.

chapter 33

SUBTERRANEAN DWELLERS

There is a way and a way and a way,
The high soul climbs the highway,
The low soul gropes the slopes
And in between on the misty flats,
The others drift to and fro.

—Anonymous

This poem sets forth the theme of this chapter, which I hope to put forth in a practical way. As Kenny Rogers says in his song "The Gambler," "Every hand is a winner." That is not just words thrown out there; it is a fact. Every hand is a winner, and conversely, every hand is also a loser. It depends on how you play the game. We are all dealt a hand at birth, some a glorious hand, some a short hand and we must learn to live with whatever hand we have.

We look around us and we see handicapped people, those without all the faculties or limbs others of us have. We call them handicapped and rightly so. However, many of these people have learned to live independently with their handicaps. They are not dependent beings as some of us with all the functioning parts are. Independence is all in the mind and how we imagine ourselves.

My uncle Wilbert was a musician and nothing else. He had a band, but his mother and father provided his food until they died. He had great plans, but he could not get up to execute any of them. Riches did not yield to his wishes whatsoever. He remained poor all the days of his life. If plans were horses, he would be riding high.

That brings me to the earthly dwellers. There are some of us who are destined to dwell as worms on or under the ground. We like darkness and rottenness. We are comfortable in dark and dank places. We love to dwell where no one else comes. Others of us are like the pigs, who like the mud. You have seen these people live. You always make sure you are full before you enter their homes, so you can say that you have just eaten and do not need any food at present. You could not keep down any food you managed to eat at their filthy houses anyhow.

Oftentimes I see people scratching their lotto tickets anxiously and I wonder, *If that person should win the grand prize, how would he or she improve his or her life?* I think that if the individual is currently living in a pigpen, then maybe he or she will get a bigger pigpen. These people are living like pigs and loving it, so that is what they are. These are those of whom the poet speaks: "The low soul gropes the slopes." These are the earth dwellers literally.

How can I spot a subterranean dweller? You will not be able to tell him by the clothes he wears, by the car he drives, or by the house he lives in. Listen to the words he speaks. On second thought, you do not want to listen to the words, as they will pierce your sensibility. You will spot the subterranean dweller right away. After that, you will hate to shake hands with him. He will have offended you so grossly that to keep company with him will be a chore. His language is disgusting and repulsive. His is the language of the sewer.

We move up the ladder one rung and find another set of people who have also reached a comfort level. These people are the rolling stones that gather no moss. A person like this will not live in a dump or in a mansion. He roams like the wind, neither giving nor taking, just roaming. He is not careful to help and not careful to build. He upsets everything in his path, at times becoming something more than wind: the tornado that destroys. We see these people roving the land continuously, wreaking havoc upon it. They are destructive forces personified.

We approach the high soul last. This is the man or woman who is in command of his or her life. Such a person has a good and pleasant life.

His or her company is such that it attracts people as a flower attracts a bee. People like to be around this person because he emits an aroma that is sweet. Is this person's life easier to maintain than the others'? I do not think so. It is placing things in their proper places that counts with these people. As the old adage goes, "Everything in its place is best." That is the motto they live by. As a result, they manage on the minimum of energy. They are the high souls.

chapter 34

THE SUMMATION WITH TWO KNOCKS

There is finality or a summation to all things. If that is so, then the end will come certainly and eventfully, just as I see the end of this book coming. God has promised that He will bring all things to a halt. His promises are as good as done. He does not promise and forget about it as people forget things. He is the Architect whose blueprint is already made. Each of us is playing out our individual part, just as the different tradespeople do their part in the construction of a building. None of them knows what goes on at the other side of the building, nor are they concerned. Each looks upon the blueprint that pertains to him. If he is the electrician, he gets that particular blueprint and works from it. When every tradesperson has done his or her work and then come the painters and the locksmiths to complete the building.

Each of us is doing our part in bringing this world to its final end. Those of us who are working in the Lord's vineyard have certain people to reach with the Gospel. Those working outside likewise have their work to do. The ungodly must fill up their cups with degradation and sin before the Lord will destroy the system. The Lord has a timetable. We would do well to recognize this fact.

Rudyard Kipling wrote the following:

> All are Architects of fate building in these walls of time;
> Some with massive deeds and great;
> Some with ornaments of rhyme
> Nothing useless is or low, each thing in its place is best;

And what seems but idle show;
Strengthens and supports the rest.
Build today then strong and firm with a sure and ample base;
And ascending and secure, shall tomorrow finds its place.

It is true, then, that we are all crew members on Spaceship Earth. There are no idle hands. We are all engaged in one thing or another, be it good or evil. But we are all pulling.

After our work is done, there will be the first knock. "Trevor! I have come to get you." When death has knocked, there is nothing I can do about it. It is either the heavenly angels who have come to bear me away or it is the demons that have come to get me.

In Exodus 12:13, which describes the night of the Passover when the Israelites left Egypt, the blood of animals was placed over doorposts. When the Angel of Death came and saw the blood on a particular house, the firstborn would be spared. The Angel simply could not enter such a house. "And the blood shall be to you for a token upon the houses where ye are: and when I see the blood, I will pass over you, and the plague shall not be upon you to destroy you, when I smite the land of Egypt."

This is an historical event. All Jews know of that event. What God promised, He will fulfill. Those who did not believe what was commanded suffered the loss of their firstborn like all the Egyptians. Similarly, no home with blood sprinkled on the doorpost, be it Jew or Gentile, was visited by Death. For people living in our time, 1 John 1:7 tells us, "When I see the blood I will pass over you." We see here the correlation between the two accounts. Both show the power that is in the blood. The blood of animals on the doorposts was only a symbol of greater things to come. And if that was effective to stave off the Angel of Death, how much more effective is the blood of Jesus Christ in washing away our sins?

Is there a correlation between the two events? Yes, of course. When the Devil's demons come to our door and see the blood, they cannot enter, as they are repelled. They cannot force their way in, either. There is power in that blood. There is wonder-working power in the blood of Jesus Christ, my friend. There is only one set of angels that can take us home as Christians, and those are the angels of God. There will be no mistake there. The person whom you serve has your name written in his book, and when it is time, He will dispatch His angels to come and get you. "Knock! Knock!" You will know the knock. You will respond with fear and terror or with a warm, welcoming voice, saying, "I have been waiting for you." People will believe the event of the Israelites' Passover and acknowledge the power in the blood demonstrated that night but will discount the power that exists now in Jesus's blood. Strange, I'd say. How blinded we have made ourselves. We cannot see because we do not want to see.

A booklet that I used last year on my mission trip to Jamaica has the most terrifying account of a man who was dying in a hospital. He was strapped down on a bed. The account is as follows: "Shaking with violent jerks, sweat begins to pour off his forehead, and his breathing becomes shallow and rapid. All at once his eyes open wide and a fear of terror crawls across his face. With a bloodcurdling scream that is heard clearly down at the nurses' station, he cries out, 'They're coming after me! Don't let them take me!'" The story continues. The doctor could not inject a dose of morphine into the man's body as he continued to convulse and scream. His body became tense and hard, so the needle would not penetrate.

The booklet, titled *Five Minutes in Hell*, was written by Allen Jackson. Many other cases have been documented of people crossing over, that are fearful to the point that they are crying out for help. For them it was too late, with God's mercy gone. Take heed now, dear reader. Take heed now. The opportune time to act is *now*.

I gave this booklet to a very intelligent man I met at the gym. We speak often of world affairs and spiritual matters. Clearly he is not a believer. When I gave him a tract and this booklet, he promised me that he would read them. After missing each other for some time, we met recently and spoke of the booklet, among other things. He said he had read some of it and found it to be an example of fearmongering.

I told him that it describes a real event, not a made-up story. It is a fact just as the sun melts the butter and hardens the brick. I am not done with him yet, as he promised to buy a copy of *What's Up?* As a matter fact, he said he cannot wait to read my book.

There will be another knock, my friend. Even if we are dead, we will hear another knock. We are coming back to life just as Lazarus was brought back to life. There is a difference this time, though. Whereas Lazarus was brought back to demonstrate the power of Christ and prove that He (Jesus) is "the Resurrection and the Life," we will be brought back from the dead to collect our rewards. Have you considered what kind of a reward you will receive?

chapter 35

PREPARE TO MEET THY GOD

"Prepare to meet thy God" is a saying you will find all over the world on road signs warning you not to speed. You might see a sign that reads, "Do not speed," and farther down the road you will see the another that reads: "Prepare to meet thy God." This second sign is telling you that you will crash your vehicle and die if you keep on speeding. And of course when you die, it is Judgement Day for you. Judgement Day is the end of the line for all of us, when our wound-up clock runs out.

That sign appears on roadways, but in the Guidance Book, or the Bible, the exhortation is mentioned many times. Every sane household should be aware of this saying. Parents should teach their children when they are young to observe that sign which reads. `Prepare to meet thy God.`` You might say you do not use the word *death* with your kids or tell them about death, but you do. If you have boys, you tell them from an early age to be careful or else they will kill themselves.

In normal times and throughout our lifetime, we must prepare to meet God. Either we are going or He is coming, but there is an appointed meeting. Since death is part of life, or the other side of the coin, we need not be afraid of it. We are afraid when we cannot face it. We cannot face it if we think it is coming upon us too soon or that it may come unexpectedly. Too soon, yes, but unexpectedly, no. How can that be when we are, or should be, expecting it? From the first breath we take, death is on its way. Thank God that for many of us, we do not die until 70 or 80 years hence. That is a long time to prepare to meet our God.

Amos 4:12 tells us, "Therefore thus will I do unto thee, O Israel: and because I will do this unto thee, prepare to meet thy God, O Israel." How very wonderful that we have a God who, before taking action, will send a prophet to warn us of the steps He is going to take. Will an enemy planning to attack us send an emissary to warn us? Hardly will he do that. God does not destroy us; literally we destroy ourselves if we ignore His warnings. If we do not flee the fire or the flood when warned and when it comes, we have no one but ourselves to blame. Our God is a conciliatory God, one who is willing to put in as much time as possible to negotiate with us. But will we sit and reason?

Those who set upon Him as a dictator and tyrant are people of deplorable standing who deserve the wrath of God. They will be more than deserving His wrath; it is earning His wrath. As human beings, we know that our wrath would be poured out long before His. Of course, with God being all-powerful (omnipotent), there is no appointed time that He must strike. His time is anytime. He has also appointed that time; the date is already fixed when His judgement will fall.

We can meet Him in due time and as a friend. He is everywhere reaching out to us. People today are pointing their telescopes into outer space hoping to encounter life. If they ever do, they will claim to know just where the human race came from. Actually, these people today are more sophisticated than their predecessors who searched in African jungles to find their ancestors. They can do their research without getting mud on their boots or scratches on their faces. What a change in beliefs. We can sit back in our armchairs and have the evidences come to us.

In essence, we must prepare to meet our God as a Friend and Father. When we have that relationship with the Great Creator, all will be well when He comes. The trumpet we hear will have a soothing sound and not a frightening one. For all our Christian lives, we have been expecting that sound. It will be our day of triumph when that trumpet sounds.

When the Lord comes to take us home, that will be the greatest of home-goings the world will ever see or witness. Nothing on this earth can ever compare to it or even come close to what that day will be. Are you anticipating that day dear Christian friend?

I can remember the excitement that gripped me when I was a small boy and my dad was building a new house. We lived in a small place loaned to us by my mother's dad. It was cramped, to say the least. The new place was large in comparison, situated on a 4.5-acre piece of property, which grew to 8 acres as more land was bought around the home. Eventually my parents owned 14 acres not to include their inheritances from their parents.. We did not feel as if we were poor anymore.

Our home was abuzz with the activities of eleven children. To cook and feed the children and workmen in the field, it was, as we say, something else. My mother used to say she did not have time to scratch her head sometimes. My dad never gossiped because he said that he did not have time to mind his own business, let alone to interfere in someone else's.

My mom ran a business from home. Women would come to the house every Sunday morning with braids to make hats, which they plaited from sisal. My mother bought these braids and sent them off to Kingston, the capital city, where another person would distribute them. During the week, our mom would mind the grocery store while my dad was in the field with the workers.

We children grew up and left home and the island, one by one, sometimes two by two, until finally all but two remained, a sister and a brother. Some went to England, Canada, the USA and the Bahamas. The day I left for Canada, a younger sister left for the Bahamas. Some of my siblings have settled back home now. Many of us are still abroad, while some are off into eternity. Our parents did their uttermost to lift us out of poverty. Will our heavenly Father do less? No! No Christian is poor anymore.

Here I am again, wearing this old home thin and roaring to see my new home and settle in it. From what I hear, it is going to be a mansion, a doozy. The streets there are paved with gold. There will not be any streetlights because the glory of the Lord will brighten that place more than any sun could. Work—well, that word is not used there. There will be no tears either. We will be totally satisfied with our lot. We will be praising our God for all eternity. It will be a day of rejoicing indeed.

I believe too, for those of us who like to travel, that there will be places to see, lots of places: Mars, Jupiter, Venus and so on. We can go planet hopping for as long as we feel like, whenever we want to. What a life, my friend. What a life that will be.

Every man, woman or child who has read *What's Up?* to this point has the opportunity to be in the lineup awaiting the Lord's return. I hope you will be there.

"Now the God of hope fill you with all joy and peace in believing, that ye may abound in hope, through the power of the Holy Ghost" (Romans 15:13). Amen.

.